Haiti Rising

Haiti Rising

Haitian History, Culture, and the Earthquake of 2010

Edited by

MARTIN MUNRO

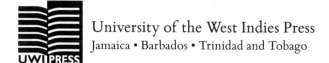

University of the West Indies Press
Jamaica • Barbados • Trinidad and Tobago

First published 2010 by
University of the West Indies Press
7A Gibraltar Hall Road
Mona, Kingston 7
Jamaica, West Indies
www.uwipress.com

A catalogue record of this book is available from the National Library of Jamaica

ISBN 978-976-640-248-8

Typeset in Calluna by Koinonia, Manchester
Printed and bound in the UK by Bell & Bain Ltd, Glasgow

Contents

Part III: History

Part IV: Haiti and Me

Introduction:
Fall and Rise

Martin Munro

The word disaster has its roots in the Old Italian *disastro*, which means "ill-starred," or ill-fated. This original meaning reminds us that in human history the causes of terrible events have often been attributed to the stars, the fates, or the gods. When the earthquake struck Haiti at 4:53 p.m. on January 12, 2010, one might have been forgiven for thinking that the fates had conspired in this case with unprecedented malice, and that Haiti itself is inevitably a star-crossed nation. A country whose intermittent appearances in the global awareness are often preceded by disasters of some kind – hurricanes, floods, uprisings, and now earthquakes – was thrown into an almost inconceivable state of devastation and suffering that made all previous disasters there seem insignificant in comparison. It is not however accurate or helpful to attribute Haiti's suffering completely to non-human forces, to the fates or the gods. Nothing could have prevented the earthquake itself, but human, historical, and social forces were to a large extent responsible for the terrible scale of destruction and the great loss of life. It is all too easy to couple Haiti with disaster, to view its misfortunes as the result of a social and historical fatalism that would resign the nation and its people to an unending tragic destiny. The only emotional response that this fatalism provokes is pity, and Haiti neither needs nor asks for pity. What it needs, what it has needed for more than two hundred years, is genuine and lasting support, understanding, and respect; and it is in this spirit that the essays in this book have been assembled.

The earthquake has cast Haiti into the consciousness of the world as never before. The terrible events there have piqued public interest in this remarkable country and its history and culture. There is now an unprecedented empathy for and interest in Haiti, and a related need for information and insights into Haitian reality, beyond the clichés often associated with the nation. In particular, there is a special interest in the earthquake and the questions of Haiti's future development. This book responds to this public interest and has three fundamental aims: to raise awareness of Haiti, its people, culture, and history; to allow some of those who were in Haiti during the earthquake a chance to testify to their experiences; and to raise funds for Haitian artists, who have been very badly hit by the disaster.

All author royalties from the book will be donated to the Haitian Art Relief Fund, which works to assist Haitian artists through commissioning works and selling them internationally, and to restore damaged art works. For more information, see http://www.haitianartrelieffund.org.

The book is a collection of over 20 essays from a range of well-known public figures, artists, filmmakers, scholars, and writers, each with strong personal connections to Haiti. The book is divided into four parts. The first part is dedicated to survivor testimonies – short essays by Haitian, American, and French authors, scholars, and filmmakers who were in Haiti at the time of (and shortly after) the earthquake. These essays provide compelling and moving accounts of on-the-ground experiences during and after the event, and reflect on the future of the nation, its people and culture. The author Yanick Lahens writes of her initial shock, the patience and solidarity of the people, their communal singing, and considers the ways in which Haiti has long been at the center of "accidents of fortune" that have given it a unique and prominent place in the modern world. Marlène Rigaud Apollon tells of her personal grief and loss, and of her frustration (shared by many authors in this volume) at the errors and misconceptions perpetuated by foreign reporters. But she also expresses her pride at the resilience of the people and the ways in which the earthquake brought together people of all social classes. Laura Wagner, a graduate student in anthropology doing fieldwork in Port-au-Prince at the time of the earthquake, provides a remarkable testimony of her experience of being rescued from under the rubble. Haitian people, she asserts, are not "epic victims," born to suffer. Importantly, too, Wagner insists that life in Haiti before the event was quite normal, that amid the poverty and everyday difficulties, people went about their lives in an unremarkable fashion. She thus provides a vision of Haitian life that challenges the clichéd, exaggerated images that are often filtered through the media. Jason Herbeck had only been in Haiti for about an hour when the earthquake struck. His account tells of how by chance he had decided to leave his hotel building to send an e-mail at the moment the tremor occurred. His abiding memory of his first visit to Haiti is the shrill, repeated call of a woman crying out at the loss of her home. Herbeck had been in Haiti to attend the Etonnants Voyageurs literary festival, organized by Michel Le Bris, who provides his own account of the earthquake and its effect on the festival organizers and the Haitian authors who were to be celebrated during the event. Le Bris also writes of his experiences on returning to France, the difficulty of relating to people who had not been in Haiti, and of the importance of culture, notably literature, in rebuilding Haiti. Thomas C. Spear writes of his many and conflicting emotions in the wake of the disaster. His feelings of anger, principally against the U.S. and its longstanding neglect of Haiti, are tempered by his laughter at times spent in Haiti and with Haitians, and the overriding love for Haiti, its history, its painters, musicians, authors, and everyday people. The filmmaker Raoul Peck arrived in Port-au-Prince several days after the earthquake. His account paints a picture of the disorganized aid efforts of the Haitian government and the international aid agencies, which contrasts with the determined pragmatism of the people most directly affected by the disaster. He also reflects wryly on the presence of international journalists and their motivations for being in Haiti, before striking a defiant, hopeful note and asserting that Haiti will overcome and rise again. A similarly sobering analysis is offered by Nadève Ménard, who writes of the post-earthquake difficulties and paradoxes in Haiti: a plentiful supply of foreign food and a continuing lack of consultation with local groups in the reconstruction process. A nation, Ménard argues, cannot be saved by NGOs; the impetus must come from within, and must recognize the intrinsic value of each and every Haitian. Evelyne Trouillot's essay echoes those of Peck and Ménard in its skepticism about the ability of the earthquake to disrupt the longstanding social inequalities in Haiti and the chances of the substantial sums of money raised in Haiti's name reaching those who need it most.

The second part of the book contains essays on key themes related to aspects of Haitian culture, society, and politics. These essays explain the various themes and explore the ways in which the earthquake might reconfigure longstanding social and cultural structures. As J. Michael Dash comments, Haiti was in ruins at the time of its independence in 1804, and if its subsequent history has not yet realized the egalitarian promise of the revolution this, Dash says, is largely due to the stark economic, social, and cultural differences between the nation's elite and the impoverished masses. Post-earthquake reconstruction, in Dash's view, must involve and develop the many grassroots organizations that emerged in the post-Duvalier period and that still today offer the best hope for establishing a more equitable and just society. As Leslie G. Desmangles and Elizabeth McAlister show in their chapter, the three main religious groups in Haiti – Vodou, Catholic, and Protestant – reacted in differing ways to the disaster. Whereas Protestant evangelicals perpetuated the idea that Vodou and Haiti's "pact with the devil" were the causes of the country's malaise, the Catholic and Vodou faiths, which have historically been intertwined to a large extent, were more nuanced and less condemnatory in their pronouncements. In a highly religious country such as Haiti, the various faiths will have important roles in the process of reconstruction. Régine Michelle Jean-Charles focuses on gender issues, and the particular ways in which the earthquake has affected women. Reflecting on the deaths of important women's rights campaigners, Jean-Charles argues for the continuation of their work in the post-earthquake period to ensure the centrality of gender issues to the reconstruction process. LeGrace Benson writes on visual art and the great losses inflicted on this important aspect of Haitian patrimony. Benson also considers the ways in which the earthquake has pushed Haitian visual art into international public awareness as never before; networks of collaboration between Haitian artists and their international counterparts have served as sources of support in the aftermath of the tragedy. Elizabeth McAlister is similarly interested in the ways in which artists – in this case, musicians – from across the world have reacted to the earthquake. McAlister finds that music has been a key means of maintaining a sense of solidarity among the survivors, and also a means of making sense, through religious music, of the earthquake. Widening the scope, McAlister also considers the reactions of global musicians to the earthquake, notably in the *Hope for Haiti Now* telethon, on which the author focuses to consider some of the ambiguities and contradictions of such events. The final essay in this section, by Deborah Jenson, looks at the historical perception of Haiti as a nation founded on and shaped by disasters. As Jenson shows, the emergence of a free black state in the Americas was roundly viewed in the international sphere as a catastrophe. Discourses of disaster – ecological, humanitarian, social, economic – continue to proliferate around Haiti but as Jenson finally argues, the association of catastrophe with Haiti is not inevitable, and the nation is not in itself a synonym for disaster.

The third part of the book presents essays on some of the major historical shifts since colonial times, and seeks to help readers understand the development of certain key social and political structures in Haiti. The first essay, by John Garrigus, deals exclusively with pre-revolution colonial society, and suggests some of the ways in which the social, economic, and cultural features of contemporary Haiti are rooted in the colonial period. In particular, Garrigus focuses on militarism in Haitian society, environmental problems, work and economic patterns, popular culture, and the stark division between the cities and the hinterland, and thus demonstrates the very real ways in which colonial structures shaped post-revolution Haitian society. The second essay, by Jean Casimir and Laurent Dubois, considers the period from the revolution to the mid-twentieth century, paying particular attention to the relationship between state and society that emerged from the revolution, and which continues to characterize contemporary Haiti. The third and final essay in this section is by Patrick Bellegarde-Smith and investigates the political and social changes in Haiti since 1957, including the rise and fall of the Duvaliers, Jean-Bertrand Aristide, the bicentenary of independence, and the immediate political context at the time of the earthquake.

The final section contains more general, personal essays by authors with longstanding or recent connections to Haiti, who write of their interest in the country, the ways in which it has influenced their lives and work, and their thoughts on the earthquake and its possible consequences. These essays complement the more focused, thematic pieces in the other sections and provide insights into the ways in which Haiti has shaped the careers of these diverse artists, authors, and activists. Maryse Condé writes of her first encounters with Haitian history and culture in the 1950s, and notes that in her native Guadeloupe, she had never heard of the revolution or of its great leaders. Through regular subsequent visits to Haiti, Condé has deepened her understanding of Haiti, its culture, and its people, and was particularly saddened to hear of the destruction of the city of Jacmel, the city famous for its architecture, arts, and Carnival. It is Haitian culture, Condé says, that has longed served as an antidote to the everyday struggles and hardships of the people. Beverly Bell also has a long attachment to Haiti, particularly in the domain of democracy and human rights. Her chapter relates her thoughts and reactions in the two weeks that followed the earthquake, and tells of her sadness and frustration, and also of her hope that Haiti's reconstruction will be driven by the long-held aspirations for equity and justice. Madison Smartt Bell's chapter recounts his interest in Haitian art and reflects on the differences between fine art and craft, *artisanat*. These distinctions lead in turn to insights into Haitian notions of collective identity, and the motivations of both Haitian artists and their developed-world public. This latter theme is pursued in an ironic and provocative vein by Bill Drummond, who writes of his experiences during the Ghetto Biennale at the end of 2009 and in particular his interactions with Haitian artists, which led Drummond to reflect on the incongruities and ironies of the relationships between Third- and First-World artists. While these exchanges are for Drummond fraught with contradictions, he does say that the staging of his performance The17 in Haiti was the most personally rewarding for him to date, and thus seems to suggest that not all north-south cultural contacts are inevitably beset by contradiction and misunderstanding. The organizer of the Ghetto Biennale, Leah Gordon writes on her twenty-year association with Haiti and the ways in which it continues to inspire her, most notably as a uniquely visual nation, and one in which history is never far from the surface. Citing Michel Rolph Trouillot, she questions the idea that Haiti is unexceptional, and suggests some of the ways in which it stands apart from its Caribbean neighbors. Matthew Smith's concluding essay is a eulogy to Port-au-Prince, the city that became the colonial capital of Saint-Domingue in 1770, the year of a devastating earthquake. Smith's story of the city's re-emergence as one of the Caribbean's major cultural and economic centers spans nearly two and a half centuries of history and serves as a reminder that Port-au-Prince is no stranger to upheaval, and that its spirit has been bruised many times, but never crushed.

As such, it is a fitting way to close the book, which stands as a written document of this cataclysmic event in Haitian history and as an expression of solidarity with Haiti and its people. We therefore finally join with the sentiments of the artist Edouard Duval Carrié, whose cover illustration proclaims: *Ayiti Kanpe Djanm* – Haiti, Hold Strong.

PART I
Survivor Testimonies

I

Haiti,
or the Health of Misery

Yanick Lahens

At 4:53 p.m. on Tuesday, January 12, 2010, Haiti plunged into horror. The earthquake lasted less than a minute. When you are standing in a doorway, with the walls wanting to give way all around you, the ground shifting under your feet, less than a minute seems like a very long time. In the seconds that followed, the clamor of thousands of loud screams of terror and cries of pain rose as if from a single stomach from both the surrounding shantytown and the most stately buildings around the square and seized me by the throat, asphyxiating me. I then opened the gates to the house as the horror was beginning. Right there, at the end of my street. Bodies littering the ground, dusty faces, walls demolished. I knew that further down in the city it would be terrifying. We immediately brought relief to the victims, but we could not help but weep.

And in this tropical twilight that is always so quickly swallowed by the night I could not help but ask this question that has plagued me since: Why the Haitians? Us again, always us? As if we were in the world to measure human limitations in the face of poverty and pain, to hold on to our salutary creativity through an extraordinary ability to resist, and to create vital energy from our many trials. I found my initial responses in the fervor of the songs that rose up without fail each night. As if these rising voices were turning their backs on misery and despair. The next morning I traveled across a chaotic city, littered with corpses, some already covered with a white cloth or a simple cardboard box, children's bodies, young people stacked in front of schools, flies already dancing around other corpses, injured people, haggard older people, destroyed buildings and houses. All that was missing were the trumpets of the Angel of the Apocalypse to announce the end of the world, if our collective courage, solidarity, and immense patience had not kept us tenuously attached to the essential. That is, to the principle of humanity and solidarity that should never be lost and that the poor know so well. This is to speak of the power of life, of those so fiercely alive in a dead city. Patient in the extreme. The

9

acts of the few inevitable looters systematically relayed by the international media were greatly outweighed by such a clamor for life and dignity.

And later I learned a lesson by thinking about one of Camus's notes sent by a writer friend: "We now are familiar with the worst. This helps us to fight some more." This determination seemed to me not to be the result of some kind of fatalism (let us leave that to those who still wish through laziness or evasion to evoke the cliché of an evil Haiti), but of certain accidents of fortune that have propelled us to the heart of all that is important in the modern world. Our role is to teach and learn new lessons in humanity. Time and again....

The geological accident that placed us in the infernal path of earthquakes, the geographical accident that situated us in the passage of hurricanes, calling on us and the world at each of these disasters to rethink the profound causes of poverty. The historical accident that led us to realize the "unthinkable" at the beginning of the nineteenth century, a revolution to free ourselves from the grip of slavery and the colonial system. Our revolution came to show to the two others that preceded it, the American and the French, their contradictions and limits, which are those of the modernity that they had outlined, the difficulty in humanizing the Black and in making their lands territories of their own.

We responded to the excesses of the oppressive system with the excesses of a revolution. To exist. To exist, at the cost, among other things, of a debt to pay to France, and of becoming a pariah among the nations of the world. This did not deter us from our duty to stand in solidarity alongside those like Bolívar in South America who were fighting for their freedom at the beginning of the nineteenth century. And since we opened the land of Haiti to all of these freedom fighters, we have a head start in this kind of knowledge. A knowledge that is highly relevant at this time when, around the disaster that is hitting Haiti, there should be reciprocity, and why not the redefinition or the overhaul of the principles of solidarity on a global scale? The exceptional momentum of this time may provide the opportunity to do so.

The American Revolution and the French Revolution, unlike ours, advanced the issue of citizenship. We have not been able to exercise either the consistency or the moderation necessary for the construction of a citizenship that should have protected the men and women of this land from subhuman living conditions. Because excess has its limits, as has the sterile glorification of the past as a refuge. Let us remember that in Aimé Césaire's play *La Tragédie du Roi Christophe*, the wife of the king asks that the misfortunes of the son not be judged by the excesses of the father.

In spite of these failings, in spite of its poverty, its political upheavals, its lack of resources, Haiti is not a peripheral place. Its history has made it a center. I have always lived it as such, as a metaphor for all the challenges humanity faces today and to which modernity has not kept its promises. Its history puts it on an equal footing in its dialogue with the rest of the world. This disaster in Haiti once again poses essential questions on north-south relations, on the equally important south-south relations, and demands concrete responses to the most pressing emergencies. It also calls on the ruling elites of Haiti to radically change the paradigm of governance. Some events by their nature require us to reach a certain height. All of the already weak symbols of state have collapsed, people are desperate and the city devastated. From this tabula rasa the state will have to rise finally reconciled (if even partially so) with its population.

But Haiti has another dimension that is just as essential: its creativity. For we have forged our resistance to the worst, by constantly transforming pain into the light of creation, in what Rene Char called "the health of misery." I have no doubt that we writers will try once more to give to the world our own particular flavor.

January 2010

Translated by Martin Munro

2

Manman, Pa kite yo koupe janm mwen!
Mommy, don't let them cut my leg!

Marlène Rigaud Apollon

My husband's son, my son, died during the first hours of the earthquake that devastated Port-au-Prince and other cities of Haiti on January 12, 2010. I don't have the strength to talk about the nightmare we have lived day after day since we learned the news. As I said at the commemorative mass for him on Saturday, January 30, his death was like an earthquake in our hearts, leaving us emptied, in shock, crushed, amputated of him. It will take time for us to recover. However, considering the immensity of the suffering of the tens of thousands of people of all nationalities who were mourning their loved ones or did not know whether they had survived and continued to hope against all reason, how could I not share their tears of sorrow and anguish? So many feelings, so much emotion rushed through me!

I cried with joy each time a happy survivor was rescued from under the wreckages. I felt frustrated when a young woman who was asked what had happened to the corpse of her baby answered "Yo jeté Li," (They threw it away), and the reporter, no doubt in good faith, translated her words as "*I* threw it away." A faulty translation that spread across the planet, giving to the whole world a bad impression of that poor mother. And I was annoyed by the error of the well-known journalist who reported that a young wounded boy would not stop asking "Why, why?" not knowing, obviously, that our "Way" of pain sounds the same but has nothing to do with the English "why?"

In my soul, I howled with terror along with those who howled with fear because their limbs were being amputated while fully conscious, often without fully understanding what was happening to them, or because they hurt badly, or because they were afraid. I was horrified and I howled for them.

But of all the horrors in this maze of horrors the TV was constantly assailing us with, the one that I found the most intolerable was the sharp, raw, and palpable distress of the mother who was asked to make the quick

12

and terrifying "choice" between authorizing the doctors to immediately amputate her son's leg, and refusing her permission and condemning him to certain death. I am still shaken by the violent leap of her whole body saying NO with all its strength. I am still shaken by the piercing screams of her little boy begging, begging, begging her, again and again with all his strength: "Manman, Pa kite yo koupe janm mwen! Manman, Pa kite yo koupe janm mwen! Manman, Pa kite yo koupe janm mwen!" (Mommy, don't let them cut my leg!). "How have you managed to bear all this atrocious suffering that we've been seeing in Haiti these last few days?" an Internet friend asked me. What could I answer?

I was comforted by President Obama's rapid mobilization of the United States' vast resources; by the outpouring of aid from all over the world; by the generosity of individuals and organizations, and by the love, the compassion, and the solidarity that people have expressed toward Haiti. I was proud of the Haitian physicians of the diaspora, those of the AMHE (Association of Haitian Physicians Abroad) and all the others, among them my sister Michèle, who, along with other Haitian professionals, immediately flew to Haiti to put their expertise, their cultural and linguistic affinity, and their knowledge of the country to the service of their compatriots. Proud also of the Haitians in Haiti who helped each other, without regard to social class, freeing survivors from the rubble, often with their bare hands, or sharing water, food, or other necessities with each other, and who demonstrated patience, resilience, faith, and the determination to move forward. But, more than everything else, I could not help feeling a surge of hope at the glorious reaction of that little guy, seconds after being pulled out of the rubble, having survived longer than anyone could have hoped for, throwing his arms open in a V of Victory, eyes sparkling and a radiant smile on his dusty face. He will remain for me the symbol of this catastrophe.

I thought of him when a friend of my sister Marie Jose, who lives in France, wrote to her that a few days after the earthquake, she had re-read my first poetry book, *Cris de colère, Chants d'espoir* (Shouts of Anger, Songs of Hope). And among all the poems that had struck her and whose pages she had noted, the one she had recopied was "Resurrection," which, she found, had "much significance for us." It says simply:

> Spring follows Winter
> Calm, the storm
> And dawn follows dusk.

Love follows hatred
Hope, despair
And life will follow death.

"Such are our wishes for our dear Haiti," she had concluded. Such are mine also.

February 5, 2010

3
Salvaging

Laura Wagner

"If this is the best of all possible worlds, what are the others like then?"
– Voltaire, *Candide*

Time passes, and the earthquake is turning into a narrative. It is already shifting from a lived event to a written-about one, leaving the realm of experience and entering the realm of reconstituted imagination. The earthquake was unthinkable in the moment it occurred, but now it seems unthinkable that life existed before it, that we ever went through life without hindsight. With each telling it becomes scripted, and the earthquake begins to seem like an inevitability. The memory is becoming glossy and smooth from overuse.

The first thing that I want to tell you, so that you know but also so I don't forget, is that before the earthquake, things in Haiti were normal. Outside Haiti, people only hear the worst – some of it real but selected, some of it exaggerated, some of it lies. I need you to understand that amid poverty and oppression and injustice, there was banality. There was always banality. Haitian people are not epic victims, however cursed the country may seem. They are people with complex, sometimes contradictory internal lives, like the rest of us. In Port-au-Prince there were teenaged girls who sang along with the love ballads of Marco Antonio Solís in hilarious theatrical fashion, despite not speaking Spanish. There were men who searched in vain for odd jobs by day and told never-ending stories about simpleminded, trusting Bouki and cunning Ti Malis as the sun went down and rain began to fall on the banana leaves. There were young women who painted their toenails rose pink for church every Sunday and stern middle-aged women who wouldn't let me leave the house without admonishing me to iron my skirt and comb my hair. There were young students who washed their uniforms and white socks every evening by hand, rhythmically working the detergent into a noisy foam. There were great water trucks that passed through the streets several times a day, inexplicably playing a squealing, mechanical version of the theme from *Titanic*, which we all learned to ignore the same way we tuned out the overzealous and confused roosters that crowed at 3 a.m. There were families who finished each day no further ahead than they had begun it and then, at night, sat on the floor and intently followed the scandals and intricacies of Mexican *telenovelas* dubbed into French. Their eyes trained on fantastic visions of alternate worlds in which roles become reversed and the righteous are rewarded, dreaming ahead into a future that might, against all odds, hold promise.

On the afternoon of January 12, I was sitting on my bed, catching up on ethnographic fieldnotes and re-reading bits and pieces of *Candide*. (The last part is a detail that is so implausible that it must be true.) When the house began to shake, I knew what it was. I thought: "Oh. One of these." Then the shaking grew stronger, and it no longer resembled the semi-regular seismic events I had experienced as a child in the San Francisco area. This was different. I had never known such a loss of control, not merely over my own body but of reality, as though the existing world that contained me were being crumpled.

I braced myself in a doorway between the hallway and the kitchen, trying to hold on to the frame, and then a cloud of darkness and cement dust swallowed everything as the house collapsed. I was surprised to die in this way, but not afraid, and then I was surprised not to be dead after all. I was trapped, neither lying down nor sitting but strangely twisted, with my left arm crushed between the planks of the shattered doorway and my legs pinned under the collapsed roof. A slab of cement lay across my left hip. With each aftershock, the rubble descended, settled and grew heavier on me. Somewhere, outside, I heard people screaming, praying, and singing, which reassured me because it meant the world hadn't ended. I heard "Mèsi Jezi! Mèsi Jezi!" (Thank you, Jesus! Thank you, Jesus!) – the insistent, unpleading, fierce gratitude of those who survived.

I think I was under the rubble for about two hours. Buried somewhere in what had been the kitchen, a mobile phone had been left to charge, and now, surreally, it rang over and over. The ringtone was sentimental, the chorus of a pop love song in French, sung by a woman in plaintive, seductive tones. Above the city, I could hear helicopters flapping. There was something sticky and warm on my shirt, at first a little bit and then more and more, seeping through. I thought it was *sòs pwa*, a Haitian bean soup eaten over rice, which we'd had for lunch. I thought it was funny, that *sòs pwa* was leaking out of the overturned refrigerator and all over me. I thought, "When I get out, I will have to tell Melise about this." Melise was the woman who lived and worked in the house. I spent a large part of every day with her and her family – gossiping and joking, polishing the furniture with vegetable oil, cooking over charcoal and eating pounded breadfruit with our hands. She said my hands were soft. Her palms were so hard and calloused from a lifetime of household work that she could lift a hot pot with her bare hands. She called me her third daughter, and had given me incredible insight into the struggles and ambitions of people staying and working in other people's homes. I thought Melise would laugh to see me drenched in her *sòs pwa* from the bottom hem of my shirt up through my bra. It took me some time to figure out that what I thought was *sòs pwa* was actually my blood. I wrung it out of my shirt with my free right hand, and it pooled on the ground. I couldn't tell where it was coming from.

Melise did not make it out of the house. She died, we assume, at the moment of collapse. My landlady heard her cry out, "Letènel, oh letènel!" and that was all. She had been folding laundry on the second floor – the floor that crumbled onto the first floor, where I was pinned, thinking absurdly of *sòs pwa* and trying to turn back time with the force of my will. Melise worked and lived in that house for fifteen years. She had come to Port-au-Prince from Jérémie thirty-five years before, as a twelve-year-old unpaid child servant who eventually became a paid servant. She dreamed of one day having her own home and being free. She talked about it all the time. She died in the wreckage of a place that she did not consider her home.

*   *   *

As a young American woman not affiliated with any of the large organiza-tions that dominate the Haitian landscape, I was overwhelmed every day by the fierce generosity of nearly all Haitians I met. People who had little were eager to share their food, their homes, their time, their lives. Now I've cobbled together this narrative – these nonconsecutive remembrances – in surreal and far-removed settings: first a hospital bed in South Miami, then a Cinnabon-scented airport terminal, and finally a large public university during basketball season. I can't do enough for those same people who gave of themselves so naturally and unflinchingly. My friends, who for months insisted on sharing whatever food they had made, even if I had already eaten, promising me "just a little rice" but invariably giving more. My friends, who walked me to the *taptap* stop nearly every day. I feel I can't do anything except to write these words and encourage whoever reads this to do whatever they can, to keep screaming about it, now, after the first excited journalistic glow has faded and the images have disappeared from cable news.

The only thing I witnessed after the earthquake was people looking for, or looking for information about, their loved ones, looking to build connections, trying to be together. In a totally transformed landscape, when everyone had lost so much, finding each other was the only thing to do. This meant extraordinary acts of heroism by ordinary people, including the men who risked their own lives to save mine. The idea that a society will fall into atavism in the absence of the iron hand of a strong governing state presumes that there is a functioning state to begin with. This is not the case in Haiti; it never has been. Haitians know this. Irrespective of class or politics, they largely concur that the government isn't helping anybody. Their lives have always been their own responsibility. This has produced a grim resourcefulness. So after the quake, no one waited for the police or the UN or imported search and rescue teams to save them or their friends and neighbors. People climbed into the wreckage almost immediately, with their bare hands and inadequate tools, and set about the necessary business of salvaging whoever they could.

But inevitably, these innumerable acts of humanity and sacrifice by ordinary Haitians are erased. The news that emerged in the first few days after the earthquake salivated over "looters" and "criminals" set loose on a post-apocalyptic wasteland. This is the same story that has always been told about Haiti, for more than two hundred years, since the slaves had the temerity to not want to be slaves anymore. This is the same trope of savagery that has been used to strip Haiti and Haitians of legitimacy since the revolution. These are the set of assumptions that led a local news reporter in Raleigh to ask me, "Weren't you afraid, after the earthquake?" I responded, with unconcealed impatience and confusion, "Well, *yes*. Of course I was afraid. We were all afraid." And she said, "No, not of after-shocks or anything. Of *people*."

I want you to know that at the moment of the quake, even as the city collapsed and, for all we knew, the government and all existing institutional authority with it, Haitian society did not fall into Hobbesian anarchy. This stands in contradiction both of what is being shown on the news right now, and everything we assume about societies in moments of breakdown.

In the immediate aftermath, there was great personal kindness, sacrifice, and grace in the midst of natural and institutional chaos and rupture. In Haiti there have always been such actions. Why do we assume that disorder necessarily produces cruelty? Amid the injustice of everyday life, and amid extraordinary upheaval, acts of decency and nobility are a way of controlling what one can, of salvaging and reaffirming one's humanity in "inhuman" circumstances.

I owe my life to the perseverance and selflessness of two men, my friends John and Frenel. These men had spent years trying without success to get ahead in life. John – or, as we sometimes called him, in the Haitian fashion, with reference to his background in construction work, Bòs John – lived in the so-called *bidonville* behind my landlady's house, in a small roofless house that had begun, months before, to break apart and slide down the hill. Unable to find steady work, he did occasional jobs for my landlady and, though generally good-humored and voluble, sometimes lamented his inability to provide for his family in the way he wanted. Frenel was a *jeran lakou* in my landlady's household, who did yardwork and repairs and mopped the floor. He is quiet and diffident by nature, and my landlady would sometimes accuse him of insolence.

John was a father figure to me when I was in Haiti. He used to tell me folktales in his deep voice, and I'd go to him whenever I needed a Creole term explained, because he knew all the terms from the countryside – funny words like *aloufa* (which means a person who eats everything). When, two days before the quake, Melise's daughter Monica lent me a leopard-print dress to accompany her to church, John laughed and pronounced, "*Wi, pitit mwen!* Yes, my child! Now you look like a grown woman!" John used to tell me, "Laura, we love you because you come and sit and eat with us and tell jokes and talk." By "us" he meant my landlady's workers. This made me uncomfortable and depressed, and instead of being flattered I got political. "I don't deserve to be loved for that. I'm normal. Sitting and talking with people is normal. You just don't think it's normal because your society is sick." This would just make everyone laugh and say, "*Laura, ou pale twòp laverite!* Laura, you tell the truth too much!" And sometimes they'd point out, "That can get you killed."

I know now that the reason I was trapped as long as I was is that John ran from Bourdon to Delmas 32, as night fell on a suddenly unrecognizable and barely navigable terrain, to find a hammer and the flashlight. I heard John outside, and it sounded like him but unlike him – his low warm voice was filled with a panic I had never heard in it before. Frenel, though, sounded collected. He created a passage through the still-falling debris using only that small hammer – the kind you would use to nail a picture to a wall. Completely trapped, the nerves in my left arm damaged, I could not help him save me. He told me, in a measured voice, "Pray, Lolo, you must pray," and I, though no believer, did. He broke up the cement both under and on top of me, and pulled it out, piece by piece. Once I was out, he gave me the blue and white rubber sandals off his own feet. (I still have them). Frenel guided me to the UNDP compound, holding my hand

and steadying me as we hiked through the darkness over a once-familiar, paved street transformed into an uneven jumble of concrete, barbed wire coils, and overturned cars. "Melise is dead, isn't she," I told him blankly. "I don't know," he said, still calm. "It seems that way. We didn't hear her voice. But maybe she is unconscious. We'll go back tomorrow and look for her." When we got to the UNDP building, he pounded on the metal gate and told the security guard that he had to let me enter. "When will I see you again?" I asked Frenel. "Tomorrow," he reassured me. He must have known that this wasn't true, and if I had been thinking clearly I would have known it, too.

At the UNDP compound everyone sat together on the cracked asphalt of the parking lot, bleeding and dazed, huddled and praying as the after-shocks came. I thought that nearly everyone I knew had to be dead. A young woman in a pink dress on an adjacent blanket reached over with a sad smile and took my hand wordlessly as we both cried. "What's your name?" I asked. "Esther," she said. "I'm Laura," I told her. That's all we said. An eleven-year-old boy who had arrived alone trembled on my lap. The back of his head was bleeding and bandaged. "Do you want to sleep?" I asked him. He shook his head. "Do you want to talk?" He said yes. I couldn't think of anything to talk about, so I stroked his hair and told him Creole riddles half the night instead.

"*De mòn kontre, yon zwazo vole.* Two mountains come together, and a bird flies between them."

The boy looked up at me. "A fart," he said quietly. He knew that one already.

Another family huddled under the same gold metallic emergency blanket with us. Their youngest child looked at me, warily – a foreigner, bloodied and dusted white with cement powder. His grandmother told him, "*Ou mèt chita. Li malad, menm jan avèk nou.* You can sit. She's hurt, too, just like us." A middle-aged Haitian woman who worked for UNDP staggered across the parking lot, crying over and over "*Mon mari est parti! Mon mari est parti! Mon mari est parti!*" Aftershocks came in waves all night, each time setting off a new wave of screams, and making the little boy in my lap shudder anew. I looked up at the motionless starry sky. It seemed strange that the stars could remain fixed above us while the world moved.

As the sun began to rise at the end of that dark night, cries rose from the surrounding neighborhoods, I suppose either as people became fully aware of the magnitude of the devastation and death around them, or as those who were still trapped regained hope for their rescue in the morning light. It felt like the end of days. At dawn, the city filled with cries of *woy, woy, woy* – a lamentation, a sound of pain and grief that transcends words.

*   *   *

Five days after the earthquake, by then in Miami, I received word that my best friend, Marlène, was alive. Her survival is a small mercy that keeps everything from becoming unbearable. She is a beam of light from Cité Soleil, that most vilified and misunderstood of Haitian shantytowns. Marlène is somehow both a realist and an optimist – she makes optimism seem like a viable option. She is one of the most comfortable people I know. When a mutual friend went to Cité Soleil on January 13 to see if she was alive, she immediately sent him to the house where I lived to see if I had survived. I learned, too, that another friend, a woman who works as a housekeeper in a wealthy home, spent three days putting announcements on the radio searching for me. And – astoundingly – I have learned that John unearthed and saved my laptop computer and fieldnotes from that fallen house. He is keeping them for me until I return.

I had worried that I'd never be able to reconstruct those notes – those imperfect records of life in Port-au-Prince before this unthinkable event – without them being mediated by my own hindsight. That journal of mundane interactions, normal things before they became soaked with nostalgia and meaning, remembrances of how life was before – because as time passes I am afraid that people will become fossilized, that their lives and identities will begin to be knowable only through the facts of their deaths. Now those notes are an artifact, a record of a lost time, stories about people when they were just people – living, ordinary people who told off-color jokes, talked one-on-one to God, compared whose butt looked better in blue jeans, and made their way through a life that was grinding but not without joy or humor, or normality. I don't want my friends to be canonized.

Now we talk on the phone, and friends in Haiti say, "Laura, *chouchou*, you were saved! We are so glad you were saved!" and it's not totally clear what they mean. They are concerned that while my life was saved, my soul was not – to them it is unthinkable that I could emerge from this situation without converting to evangelical Christianity. They say: "God has a plan for you!" and "Everything happens for a reason!" I don't believe it. They tell me I should thank God. I tell them if God exists, I'm furious. But I remain in the world, excavated. And then there is the matter of the salvaged field-notes. They have transformed from imperfect methodological tools into something like relics.

*   *   *

Social scientists who study catastrophes say there is no such thing as a natural disaster. In every calamity, it is inevitably the poor who suffer more, die more, and will continue to suffer and die after the cameras turn their gaze elsewhere. Do not be deceived by early claims that everyone was affected equally – fault lines are social as well as geological. After all, I sit writing this, with my white skin and my U.S. citizenship, listening to birds outside the window as the gray-brown North Carolina winter gives way to crocuses. The people who welcomed me into their lives are still in Port-au-Prince, within the wreckage, living under bedsheets, having hastily buried their dead.

On January 14, as I sat at the peacekeeping logistics base about to be evacuated, trying to convince myself that in Haiti I was just another injured person using up scant food and resources, a non-Haitian man whom I presumed worked for the UN approached me. "Can you do me a favor?" he asked me. "Could you write something down?" I nodded, and he handed me a pen and two pieces of paper. "Tear the paper in half, and on the first half write UNIDENTIFIED LOCAL FEMALE in block letters. Then on the second piece of paper write the same thing." I looked up. They were loading bodies into the back of a pickup truck. The woman's floral print dress was showing and her feet were hanging out. There were not enough sheets and blankets for the living patients, never mind enough to adequately wrap the dead. The UN guy looked at me and sort of smiled under his moustache as I numbly tore the paper and wrote. "After all, you need something to do. All the bars are closed." I stared at the bodies on the truck and I hated him. I did not know which, if any, of my friends had survived. I imagined the people I loved – Marlène, or Damilove, the mother of my goddaughter Alissa – wrapped up in some scrap of cloth with their feet hanging out and some asshole tagging them with a half-piece of paper saying UNIDENTIFIED LOCAL FEMALE. UNIDENTIFIED, meaning unnamed and without history or background, and LOCAL, meaning Haitian – two classifications that are supposed to make this life not matter.

I am saying two things that seem contradictory: that people in Haiti are suffering horribly, and that Haitians are not sufferers in some preordained, cosmic way. Do not presume that suffering is an organic, intrinsic aspect of Haitian existence, just because the only times we in the U.S. hear about Haiti is when some unfathomable horror happens. Do not naturalize it and do not get used to it. The dead were not always dead, and the agonized victims you see in newspapers were something before they were victims. Haitians do not deserve this and they are not accustomed to it, just because people outside the country are used to seeing them that way.

In Haiti I was treated with incredible warmth and generosity by people who have been criminalized, condemned, dehumanized, and abstractly pitied. They helped me in everyday ways the whole time I was there, and in extraordinary ways in the hours after the quake. Now I feel I can do so little for them, except to employ the only strategy that was available to us all when we were buried in collapsed houses, listening to the frantic stirrings of life above ground: to shout and shout until someone responds. The initial moment of rupture is over, but this disaster has no foreseeable end. In a matter of seconds, Port-au-Prince was destroyed, turning from a living city to a modern ruin. Its surviving inhabitants are not merely homeless but unmoored in an unrecognizable world.

In the first moments after the quake, as I lay unable to move and each aftershock seemed about to crush me, I was fully convinced I could reverse everything if I just concentrated hard enough. The earthquake had taken place only a couple of minutes before. It seemed impossible that time could not be coaxed into running backward, that something so cataclysmic could happen in so few seconds. The relationship between time elapsed and chaos resulting was incommensurate and therefore fixable. I could not conceive of powerlessness. Like a child or a god, I felt sure I could control the universe.

Writers, documenters, observers, narrators – we recreate the world every day. I can attempt to bring things to light, to unearth them from the ongoing disaster of lazy reporting and salivating sensationalism, trying now to say something about Haiti and its people that isn't being said elsewhere. I could write Melise back to life. I could write the city of Port-au-Prince, however flawed it was, back to life. I could recreate a little world within the pages of a book, and dream these ghosts back to life.

In the end, no one can do enough. We cannot force time to run backward, we cannot lift up and change the universe we occupy, we cannot control this. I understand at last why everyone told me, for months, "Only God can save Haiti." There is no individual, no agency, no state, no organization that can fix what has been lost. Yet we persist in the face of sweeping impossibility, enacting inadequate institutional measures and committing small, human feats of salvaging.

March 2010

* An earlier version of this story first appeared on Salon.com on February 1, 2010, titled "Haiti: A Survivor's Story."

4

When There Is No Echo

Jason Herbeck

"Kay la tonbe. Kay la tonbe. Kay la tonbe."

Two months later, the voice still rings clearly in my ears. At once haunting and now strangely familiar, it is that of an older woman whose shrill, raspy cry carried into the deep blue sky over Port-au-Prince during the days following the earthquake. Although I heard it from a small courtyard surrounded by cement walls, the piercing refrain reached me swiftly and without echo. As if in addition to cutting through the clear dry air, it had been empowered with the ability to penetrate stone and earth, the voice bore down on me in its interminable intervals: the same three words, the same painfully melodious measure, drawn out each time on the final strained syllable. Repeated endlessly, the utterance nonetheless struck me as new each time I heard it – as inconceivable and unexpected as the earthquake itself. The house has collapsed, the woman cried out. The house has collapsed.

In many respects, it seemed like all of Port-au-Prince and much of the surrounding area collapsed on January 12, 2010. Having just arrived at the Karibé Hotel, near Pétion-Ville, half an hour before the earthquake, I had decided to write my wife an email from the hotel patio because the Wi-Fi in my room wasn't working. Three lines into my message, everything began to shake violently: the trees above me, the entire hotel and its twin stairs spiraling up to the second floor, the ground itself as my wrought-iron chair and table lurched back and forth on the stone patio. Unfamiliar with my surroundings, I jumped up and immediately found myself trying to gauge what I hoped to be the optimal distance between the four-story hotel façade in which large fissures were ripping across the red ochre surface, and the stone steps leading down the hillside to the pool area on the terrace below. I feared either might give way at any second and thus ran hunched over to a tree a few yards away and knelt down. When I looked back at the stone steps and wall separating me from the level below, huge waves were surging up over the side of the pool and pounding down onto the pavement. In front of me, the Karibé Hotel was shuddering and moaning as concrete and glass crashed to the ground. I don't remember anyone screaming or yelling during the initial earthquake; perhaps it was because everyone was so taken by surprise, perhaps it was because of the deafening sound of so many buildings being torn asunder in unison.

One of two three-story apartment buildings only 40 yards from where I was kneeling crashed to the ground without my knowing it. The next day, as I walked around the hotel grounds trying to get my bearings, all that remained of the apartment was a twisted metal staircase protruding up into the air. Through its gnarled body, I could see across a small valley to the adjacent hillside where the extent of the damage amidst the concrete-block homes was simply unfathomable. For the first time I thought to take a picture of something other than the fissured façade of the Karibé; the image of the lone staircase and the silent homes in the distance were a first attempt at comprehending the magnitude of what had just happened and the extent of the damage to people and buildings.

Reaching into my bag for my camera (one of the few items I had taken with me to the patio the day before), I noticed two teenagers attempting to console a hysterical young woman supported between them. They were slowly making their way up the small hotel pathway, having surely come from somewhere down the hill. The woman was shouting a man or boy's name – a brother, perhaps a son – amid uncontrollable tears and soon let herself fall onto the park bench to which the two boys were trying to carry her. As she sat there on the bench with the two boys looking on in silence unsure as to what to do, the camera returned to my bag. It was a gesture I repeated often over the course of the next three days. Pictures – I thought – would somehow help me come to grips with what I was experiencing, help me explain to others what I was going through. And yet when others who were suffering far more than I came into my frame, I quickly stored my camera away. What I feared they wouldn't understand was that as selfish as it might be, I was trying to find a way to express what was so painful to witness – to capture *my* pain, not theirs. As little as I knew initially about the extent of the damage immediately following the earthquake, and before learning much more in the days to come – ironically, first on CNN while still in Haiti, and then with my own eyes as the four-wheel drive vehicle I was traveling in took me and others through parts of the devastated city – I knew that I had been very fortunate. And yet that didn't make the earthquake or the destruction it had caused any easier to comprehend.

I think that even after 9/11 it is difficult to fully grasp the horrific significance of a collapsed building. The awe of seeing a structure meant to
withstand time and seemingly all else reduced to a pile of broken concrete
is shocking to the say the least. The Hotel Montana, which had been clearly
visible across the small valley from the Karibé, had completely disappeared. I had never actually seen the hotel, and now people were pointing
out to me in disbelief the scarred hillside where it had once stood. It was
impossible not to be amazed and to try and imagine what the destruction of such a large building – a hotel no less – might suggest in terms of
human loss, but I admittedly could not come close to comprehending the
gravity of such devastation. To suspect there may be people buried in the
debris, or to have such suspicions confirmed, presents part of the horror.
But it is the voices of those who have lived their lives with the individuals
now lost beneath the rubble – the words of the searching and the suffering
– that surely render such events almost unbearable. Survivors' cries transformed the event, for me, into a harshly more tangible tragedy. Such was
it that despite having been part of the earthquake and witnessing much
fear and destruction, I struggled to accept what had happened, what was
happening.

Miraculously, two fading bars of a remote, unlocked, *syslink* Wi-Fi
connection allowed me to inform my wife that I was okay only a half hour
after the earthquake. As a stranger to Haiti, I knew almost no one. I had
met several others at the airport or at the Karibé who were also there to
attend the Étonnants Voyageurs literature and film festival; they, fortu-
nately, were fine. As for the woman I knew prior to traveling to Haiti, I was
only able to contact her upon returning to the States. She and her family
survived, thank goodness.

Given the sheer scope of a disaster my pain could not fathom, it was the
voices of those I didn't know that gave me a greater sense of the loss around
me. For many, vital communication proved far more difficult. I watched in
helpless dismay as survivors attempted to reach loved ones – both physically amid the ruins and by weak or inconsistent cell phone connections.
How do you tell a woman that three people are incapable of lifting the
collapsed floor of an apartment to find her husband and children? What
do you say when someone says, "They aren't answering"? It's so easy to
become part of the dreaded silence. The first night, as I lay on the Karibé's
tennis court with other hotel guests and people from the surrounding
neighborhood, occasional eruptions of cell phone chimes would indicate
that a connection had somehow been established somewhere. However,
people eagerly checking their phones would just as soon report that the

signal had been lost. The most reliable form of communication proved to be the small transistor radios that crackled on and off through the night in French, Creole, and English. Alas, it was one-way. I did not hear a siren until 5 a.m. the next morning, nearly 12 hours after the earthquake.

Starting around midnight on that first night, a crowd of women and children could be heard singing in the dark, farther down the hill. I assume that they feared returning to their homes, or what remained of them; consequently, they had gathered in the safest place possible – the streets through which they were now on the march singing songs of prayer. The hotel generator having not yet been turned on, their high-pitched voices rose evenly up through the darkness, at once frightened and determined. When a huge aftershock rocked the city, the singing broke abruptly into frantic screams and shouts. But just as soon as the violent trembling stopped, the voices came together again, materializing out of the darkness – more frightened now, and yet with renewed defiance and urgency as they called out for their prayers to be answered.

In the days following the earthquake, I traveled through various areas of the city by four-wheel drive vehicle. My first trip was to leave the tennis court of the Hotel Karibé to go with two employees of a USAID contractor to the company's headquarters. It was there – and each time we returned – that I heard the woman's voice.

When it became clear that plans for a flight out of Toussaint Louverture Airport would not be possible at that point in time, we drove up into the hills to Montagne Noire, a neighborhood above the city, to a rented home that was deemed safe to sleep in. I later struck up a conversation with the guard with weary eyes who had opened the front gate for us. After some time talking together about the earthquake and speculating on the extent of the damage, I was shocked to learn that he had been at his post since the morning of the earthquake nearly 36 hours earlier and had no immediate plans to leave. When I inquired hesitantly about how his family was, he shook his head slowly and said only that he hoped to go in search for them once he was relinquished of his duty. The command unit, he added, had mentioned that they might find a replacement for him later in the evening.

As night fell on Port-au-Prince, the city of millions slipped into complete darkness with the exception of sparse lights powered by remote generators. Lying ten feet from the door in the house in Montagne Noire, I realized that barking dogs were signaling each aftershock moments before it hit; the larger ones sent me running out into the darkness. I had only to grab my backpack as I hurried out with my heart pounding since I had not dared to take off my shoes (I was to wear them over 50 hours straight).

When I got up the next morning to leave again for the airport, the guard was still at his post. He shook my hand and wished me luck as I did him. It was only later that day when we returned to the house for a second night that I discovered he was gone. I hope that his search for family members ended well.

I never saw the woman whose voice I heard on January 13, 14, and 15, while I was waiting to be evacuated to the Dominican Republic. Given the clarity and loudness of her voice, she was certainly somewhere close by. But having left the courtyard on several occasions to travel to other locations where the structures were deemed safer, or to be taken to the airport, I was unable to catch a glimpse of her. It is hard not to imagine what she might look like, but in the end it is the deep blue sky over Port-au-Prince that I see when I hear her voice. A clear sky of unobstructed voices full of agony and hope calling out for answers – many of which I fear are far from imminent.

March 2010

5
Finding the Words

Michel Le Bris

"What can literature do?" asks François Busnel, at the conclusion of the *Grande Librairie* show that he eagerly put together on the TV channel France 5.[1] Since we returned from Haiti, we have worked tirelessly to help him. Alas, the Haitian authors Lyonel Trouillot and Emmelie Prophète were not there, as they were stuck in Guadeloupe due to the whims of a military aircraft. What can literature do, in this moment of such misfortune? They could have replied in my place: it can bring people upright, even in the midst of ruins.

I hated the journalists in the first few days after my return. The weight of the words, the shock of the photos! There was blood on the front pages, of course, and there were headlines in the press, as soon as we arrived in Guadeloupe, still shaken by what we had experienced. "Looting," "Violence," followed by the obligatory "damned island," "the inevitability of misfortune." One of our companions crumpled up his newspaper, crying, "Vultures!" The female journalist from the newspaper France-Antilles trying to gather impressions, eyewitness accounts, passed from one to the other, somewhat distraught, as we replied ,"No ... not now ... not here ... later ... forgive us." Everyone avoided her, appearing absent. What words can you find when you return from among the dead? And those looks that everyone gives you, which you just want to run away from....

A few meters from us, in the Pierres et Vacances holiday resort where we were lodged for the night, apparently normal human beings frolicked around in a picture-postcard swimming pool – the first images of a world into which we would have to reintegrate. There was a slight panic in our little group at Roissy airport, then at Rennes, when the radio and television

---

1 Program broadcast on January 28 and 29, 2010, shown on the channels RFO and TV5MONDE. The participants were Philippe Bernard, Serge Bramly, Louis-Philippe Dalembert, Eddy Harris, Alexandre Jardin, Dany Laferrière, Michel Le Bris, Jean-René Lemoine, Alain Mabanckou, Mimi Barthélemy, Erik Orsenna, Atiq Rahimi, and Yves Simon.

journalists called out to us on the station platform, ready to grab a few images. The easiest thing for us was to give them a false arrival time. There was a sudden desire to hide, to return to the place from where we had not really returned, and to find once again the only ones with whom we could share what we were feeling.

We have not really returned: images turn over in front of me of bodies lined up on the sidewalks as we left our shelter; people armed with hammers and chisels facing the maddening chaos of the concrete blocks; the child saved from the rubble, opposite our hotel, after hours of struggle; and those other kids who played among us as if it was nothing – and then those interminable seconds during which everything collapsed around me in my bedroom in the Hotel Karibé, the voice of my daughter, safe.... Back in France, I scan messages from friends still there, news bulletins, rumors run wild, a new aftershock, stronger it would seem, causing great damage, I try to contact Lyonel, Evelyne, Emmelie, in vain, explore the armful of newspapers accumulated in my absence. The Haiti that the journalists describe is a fantasy, the mirror of their fears, or their prejudices. Will not one of them say what we have seen and experienced, what any of us on that plane taking us back to France had seen in different parts of the city, the courage of the people, their dignity, their solidarity in misfortune? Not one to say how this nation was broken in the nineteenth century, put to its knees, bled dry, because it had dared to revolt? Thankfully, there are some: in my car I hear a journalist from France Info in the midst of the Haitian people describing their daily life in the popular district of Canapé Vert – so different from the clichés of the moment that her irritated interviewer at her desk in Paris seems to prefer. And these are not Haitians that I see in the Hollywood disaster movie presented by the TV channels. It is instead the spectacle that we present to ourselves of the aid we bring to a mass of ignorant characters, incapable of organizing themselves, governed by sudden impulses, panic, disorder, and looting. ...

Stop the tide, go on radio and television shows, bear witness, make another voice heard, protest, remind people of history, speak of the extraordinary creativity of this nation, transform the Etonnants Voyageurs literary festival site into an information portal with eyewitness accounts and texts – I hear the voice of Dany Laferrière, on the radio: "What can writers do? Do what they know: write!" An email from Roody Edmé in Port-au-Prince: "Life is restarting with an incredible energy, in the midst of the ruins." What he knew about the supposed "looting" enrages him: nobody denies that there might be acts of looting or stealing here and there, as would happen anywhere in this kind of situation, but what is that

compared to the extraordinary spirit of the people? "There is no gener-
alized looting: just groups of the young and the most desperate people,
especially in the poorest parts of the city, who go looking in shops that are
already destroyed." Then the voice of Lyonel Trouillot, finally:

> There have been a few rapes. Some cases of looting. Carrefour, Pétion-
> Ville, on the boulevard Jean-Jacques Dessalines. ... One thing seems certain,
> neither the police nor the people will spare the criminals. In many areas,
> the young have formed committees. The security of their district is one of
> their priorities. It would not be very wise for anyone to get caught commit-
> ting a criminal act. The people need shelters, drinking water, and food.
> They will have neither the time nor the will to play the democrat with
> thieves, rapists, and murderers.

Communications are being re-established, intermittently. Writing, bearing
witness. Helping François Busnel hastily put together his program on
Haiti, giving to the media the contact details of the writers who are still
in Port-au-Prince – it is perhaps the only way for all of us to recover and
return from those days. Alongside those, over there, who continue to speak
of the situation.

"The year of Haiti!" There were ten international awards in a few
months for the writers of Haiti (or is it 11? You lose count, the way that
Dany is piling up the prizes in Canada). The recognition of the incredible
creativity of this nation of musicians, painters, and writers is nothing less
than spectacular, and is coming from France, Canada, the United States,
Germany, and the Caribbean. A few hours before the earthquake the
Etonnants Voyageurs team, assembled at the Hotel Karibé, said it again:
Dany was coming back from a recording, followed by a Canadian crew that
was specially dispatched for the event. Lyonel did not know where to look,
with all the articles, interviews, and broadcasts. We all had to get ourselves
to the studio of Radio Kiskeya for 6 p.m. Emmelie Prophète, novelist and
director of the Haitian government's literature initiative, a short while
before had rubbed her hands saying: "It is really starting now!" All around,
there was a real sense of anticipation. The following day 40 writers and
journalists were due to arrive for four days of events in ten towns across
the country. The title for this second edition of the festival was: "Haïti, au
miroir du monde, le monde au miroir d'Haïti" (Haiti, in the mirror of the
world, the world in the mirror of Haiti).

The year of Haiti: it will still be so, in quite another way. As we said
goodbye outside the Hotel Karibé, Lyonel Trouillot, Dany Laferrière, and I
promised ourselves to hold at all costs in Saint-Malo in the springtime this

edition of the Etonnants Voyageurs festival that we had to cancel – before holding it again as soon as possible in Port-au-Prince. Fifteen days later, on the set of the TV show *Grande Librairie*, I realized that this cancelled Etonnants Voyageurs was being held in the newspaper columns, on the radio, on television, and right there in the studio where I met again Dany Laferrière, Louis-Philippe Dalembert, and Alain Mabanckou: day after day the wave grew, texts of mobilized writers were challenging received ideas, containing and submerging the journalists' words, making them change their tone and the way they look at things. What can literature do? I replied to François Busnel that it can do precisely this: offer evidence of a creative power that the journalists had up to that point denied or ignored – that power from which something could be rebuilt in Haiti.

They have a treasure to share, which the world needs, which we need: not only the astonishingly powerful works, but the idea of artistic creation that underpins them and that has universal dimensions. This nation that people call so poor also has a richness that confounds the poverty. "A tiny, semi-illiterate country that is packed with painters, sculptors, writers, and poets," says Philippe Bernard, one of the leading specialists on Haitian literature.

> Here different kinds of magic come together, fantasies flow, rhythms exult, dreams proliferate, colors cry out, songs burst forward. In Kreyòl, in French, words rub together, phrases interlock and the language gives birth each day to new expressions that enrich, complete each other, clash with each other, and offer a beautiful demonstration of life. A play is being shown at the theater? As soon as the audience leaves, they recite to each other entire passages. ... You hear a poem on the radio or at a meeting? There it goes on a long journey from mouth to mouth. ... It is a frenetic oral culture captured by the poets, relayed by the musicians, illustrated by the painters.

As we leave the studio, a woman close by me sighs – in some circumstances literature seems quite derisory, when you're faced with urgent needs. ... If only she could have seen these people, in the chaos of Port-au-Prince, coming to thank Dany Laferrière for his novel, which "honored the people!" And how he almost apologized; they, on the other hand were going to need literature more than ever. Because they all know, through having felt it through a thousand trials that books, songs, and poems say obstinately, against all reason, that there is something in humankind that is stronger than time, stronger than misfortune. She shakes her head, pensively. I insist: if a poem born in another time and another culture touches me today, speaks to me still in the present, is this not because there is in it something that vanquishes time, and transcends the contexts in which it was written? And if that is true, is there not in man a real creative power: a transcendent dimension? Poetry would therefore be that which leads us back to this force in each one of us that everything else, in the normal run of things, tries to make us forget. That thing that we forget so easily, trading it for a mundane, reassuring vision of art, you could say that all Haitians know it, that they cherish their artists and venerate them like living treasures. But what else did they have to keep them together in the unending *Nuit et brouillard* of slavery until they broke their chains, other than the force of their religion, their songs, and their dances? To understand this we need to give up our false impressions of Vodou, and to think of it as a kind of metaphysics of the creative imagination, as an attempt to *fictionalize* the world, in order to inhabit it. "A response, of a mystical nature, to the Atlantic Slave Trade and the other great misfortunes of slavery and colonialism," writes René Depestre. "A psychodrama, a theater, an opera, a school of dance, an erotically charged generator of the Haitian magical real in all its existential forms."

The land and the sky as the two carbons of an electric arc that, at a good distance, bring forth light, all the telluric powers that rise inside you, move through you, lifting you up while the drums roll, and then the mystical rush to the doors of another world: that is Haitian magical realism. The most powerful expression of this is found in the work of the brilliant Frankétienne, who emerged alive with Marie-Andrée from their half-collapsed house, and who had just delivered to his publisher the text of a play that places two men alone in a house in the middle of ... an earthquake.

Reading him, listening to him, he seems like a torrent, a cyclone, a volcano, a galaxy in unlimited expansion, the giant drum of a *houmfort* (a Vodou altar-room) that seems to capture the whole world. But for the first time the voice of my friend Frank (Philippe Bernard makes me listen closely to Frank's voice), trembles slightly, as if the collapse of the house built with his own hands has opened up an internal fissure. A month after the earthquake, he speaks for the first time of his worry: fear, it seems to him, is invading the city, as if the earthquake had led to a weakening in the soul of the country, while all over the streets, profiting from the destruction of Catholic churches, the "preachers of the militant hordes of American churches," are calling for people to reject Vodou, which is to them the cause of all the nation's woes. At the moment he speaks there are in the streets close by, he says, "shouts, cries, a real cacophony to the glory of a new Babel, mystic Christians, sectarian Protestants, Pentecostals, who knows what. ... " Nothing would be worse than losing at this time when it seems that everything is uncertain, that which has given this people their particular power: their imaginative world. This would be the kind of guardianship that some are calling for, and which that imbecile Régis Debray seems to be militating for! But already the old lion Frankétienne is shaking himself, roaring: if need be, he would fight to the last! In any case, such are the stakes in Haiti just now, as Frank sees things.

He is right: reconstruction will not be solely a question of money, technical means, and aid, but will happen first of all through the reconstruction of the self, the collective being, and the common imaginative memory of the disaster. Finding the new words in the chaos of the world to make it inhabitable – never in Haiti has the responsibility been so great for artists, poets, painters, and musicians.

It is first and foremost dreams that keep mankind upright.

* * *

When we left, Lyonel Trouillot, Dany Laferrière, and myself made an oath that, even if fate had prevented this festival from taking place in Port-au-Prince, we would reinstate it in St Malo next spring. And this was made true: despite great difficulties, all the writers invited in Port-au-Prince attended the Etonnants Voyageurs festival in St Malo, from May 22–24, 2010. And from that point, we decided to meet again next year – in Port-au-Prince. And we will do our very best to hold to our word.

February 2010

Translated by Martin Munro

6
Point of View

Thomas C. Spear

Ô mon Pays je t'aime comme un être de chair
et je sais ta souffrance et je vois ta misère
et me demande la rage au cœur
quelle main a tracé sur le registre des nations
une petite étoile à côté de ton nom

Oh my Country I love you like a body of flesh
and know your suffering and I see your misery
and with rage in my heart I wonder
what hand drew on the roster of nations
a little star next to your name

– Anthony Phelps, *Mon pays que voici*

At one point in my teaching career, Kurosawa's classic 1950 film *Rashômon* was used as a tool in the campus's introductory humanities seminar to develop critical perspectives from different points of view. Four perspectives of an event – a crime in the film – lead to four different stories.

Reading Lionel-Édouard Martin's *Le Tremblement* and Dany Laferrière's *Tout bouge autour de moi*, the first books published about the event, I thought of the divergent perspectives of *Rashômon* as I discovered a character, played by myself, in these earthquake narratives of January 12, 2010, alternatively preoccupied with distributing cigarettes and dreaming of rum, or risking his (my) life for a beer. While I might want to correct some detail – for example, that I do not smoke Marlboros – something of the insignificant truth inevitably transpires from these two voices; the tennis court of the Karibe Hotel in Port-au-Prince becomes a curious echo chamber of the life and death stories of a disaster of epic proportions.

But there are millions of perspectives of what was seen and felt, as with those of September 11, 2001. I would likely have been near the World Trade

Center for a planned errand on that fateful day had a friend not called me after the first plane hit the north tower. The fall of the twin towers and other damage downtown (to the Verizon building, for example), with the added traffic to overloaded circuits, wreaked havoc on our local telephone service for days, making it impossible to get news from friends. Meanwhile, the rest of the world wanted news, much of which, in New York, we knew only as much as those watching television and gleaning information online. It was even harder to read the larger story when the local version included more urgently preoccupying concerns for friends, transportation, and the ensuing months of smoke, anthrax alerts, and local and national ramifications of the new "Homeland Security."

The earthquake in Haiti also took place on a beautifully sunny Tuesday, but the havoc it wrought to telephone service lasted much longer. By the time Wednesday morning's reality sunk in, there were shortages of gasoline, water, food, electricity, and of course telephones and the internet, with the world *en dehors* – outside – begging for news and play-by-play, from the French, British, Canadian, and U.S. news agencies, and from every Tom, Dick, and Harry who wanted the latest tweet about the world's hottest news item. Up close, we had little idea of the extent of the disaster, or that it was being viewed – likely more clearly – on television screens from Tokyo to Tel Aviv.

It was not worth responding to the pesky requests that managed to get through. We were more preoccupied with contacting the living from whom we had no news, much as they were but a few kilometers away. Once I returned to the U.S., I took an overdose of news, until the newscasters drove me nuts with their ridiculous points of view, especially when most had clearly never been to Haiti.

It was a time to exchange news – *zen* – with dyaspora, with those who could understand, *Ayti toujou kanpe*, dammit; "bloodied, shaken and beloved," wrote Edwidge Danticat in the *Miami Herald*. Through *teledjòl*, Internet, and cell phone highways: shared anger, laughter, and love.

Sometimes, I explode with anger.

Anger knowing U.S. agricultural policy that favors farmers of, say, Arkansas, so their rice can be dumped cheaply on the Haitian market, following a decades-old policy of breaking up peasant farmer organizations. Globalization. "Free trade." Anger knowing the real "price of sugar," as in Bill Haney's documentary of that name, illustrating the virtual slavery of Haitian cane workers in the Dominican Republic, whose sugar still arrives with preferential trade tariffs to the U.S.

Old anger, forgotten, as history repeats itself like a tragically tyrannical King Henry Christophe: Thomas Jefferson's embargo lasted some sixty years; the meddling "big stick" of Uncle Sam murdered the likes of Charlemagne Péralte a century ago; the UN embargo of George Bush *père* lasted only four years, during which the U.S.-sponsored and aptly named FRAPH thugs (*frapper*: to hit or strike) killed off what remained of export industries in Haiti (remember the baseball factories?), killed so many innocent people (the Raboteau massacre a bloody example), and served a trope of U.S. diplomacy: forever killing democracy in the name of democracy.

Anger remembering the story of my friend pulled off a train in Switzerland en route to Italy from France: *no matter that you are well-dressed, Madame, your passport is Haitian and you do not have the requisite papers for transit through our country.*

After the earthquake, anger toward many journalists begins on the tarmac of Toussaint Louverture International airport, when I am airlifted out of Haiti by the U.S. Air Force in the wee hours of Saturday. As the passengers board, a microphone is shoved in my face, the whitest among our disparate and principally Kreyòl-speaking group of U.S.-passport-bearing dyaspora. "I'm Geraldo," I hear, as though I would speak to the fresh face of a Fox News reporter, safely within the confines of the airport bunker of the most recent and urgent of U.S. occupations, far from the actual needs and realities of downtown Port-au-Prince. Who pays the journalist from NPR to enjoy food on this island where others are still dying, when she mentions that the NGO officer supervising food distribution speaks to the natives "in French and in local languages." What planet is she on? A friend offers her multilingual services to journalists, and accompanies a CNN reporter to a hospital, only to be asked where are "the looters," a far sexier story for the evening news.

Anger, knowing that it is not true that *Tout moun se moun*, when the Guadeloupean, located under the rubble of the Montana hotel, knew that his rescue depended on his best use of European French when answering the third question: 1.) Are you all right? 2.) Do you need water? 3.) What's your nationality? *Blessed are the meek, for they shall inherit the earth.* Haitians first? Yeah, right. A month after the earthquake, a French television documentary on "The New Crusaders of Apocalypse" features American evangelicals in Port-au-Prince distributing food and proselytizing God, driving their gas-guzzling vehicles out of the locked gates of their walled compounds. Nothing new under the sun.

God Bless America. In 1995, Frankétienne published (with Claude Dambreville) the novel *Gun Blesse America* (*blesser*: to hurt or wound). *Amen.*

Anger at the American heartland, the American "Homeland."

Anger with the hypocrisy of U.S. foreign relations. Cold War legacies still assure green cards for Cubans and a forcible return for any Haitian, no matter the risk (if not housed, until Uncle Sam needed to make room for other "guests," at Guantánamo). After the earthquake, however, we were led to believe in an outpouring of solidarity by the American people. Then why do three Haitian writers invited to New York for a March event have to spend six weeks with paperwork complications to get a visa to the U.S.? Would the U.S. ask citizens of any other country to travel to another (the Dominican Republic) to get their visas from the U.S. Embassy there, when there was no structural damage to the U.S. Embassy in Port-au-Prince, and the many employees had finished with emergency evacuations? Anger with this attitude towards Haitians, who are told not "welcome," but rather "fuck you."

Homeland.

Security.

Monroe Doctrine.

Banana Republic? Haiti never produced many bananas for Uncle Sam, who preferred the Haitian American Sugar Company, which folded soon after the fall of the Duvalier dictatorship. Today, HASCO is spelled b-a-t-a-y.

"Homeland Security" has such a nice ring to it. *Vaterland*. Lock those doors. *Sicherheit*. In thy name, security, George Bush *fils* offers a leap-year gift to honor democracy and the Haitian bicentennial: thousands of M16s to the paramilitary thugs who cross over from the Dominican Republic to overthrow Haiti's President Aristide. A piece of cake. Again.

Sweet cake with sweet sugar icing, as in Michelange Quay's film, *Eat, for this is my body*.

Merci. Merci. Merci.

Anger seeing the aid monies from the United States, destined for assistance to the Haitian people after the earthquake, distributed not to Haiti or its people or government, but 40 cents of the dollar going to the U.S. military, and much of the rest to private American contractors hiring U.S. security guards, military "mission support," and personnel to "monitor food security." And prices of commodities and rents in Haiti go up with the huge influx of such well-paid foreign nationals.

Mesi. Mesi. Mesi.

Anger when stopping at a check-cashing office in my Manhattan neighborhood with a Haitian friend who, when sending a post-quake money transfer to his family, is accused of paying with a fake 20-dollar bill (fresh from a bank's ATM). Insulted, my friend asks to cancel the transaction, and the Dominican teller calls Western Union to make sure they know that it is "another Haitian counterfeiter."

Tired anger, hearing over and over the superlative adjective, "poorest," applied to Haiti, as though there is nothing rich about the country, its history, its culture, and its people. When I visit the suburban Midwest and see overweight youth, fed on corn syrup (from genetically modified grains), (hormone-filled) meat, and (commercial) television, who speak only one language they can hardly write and know little of any country other than the United States (their own national history, little known and of little interest), I feel perhaps not anger but rather desperation with what can often be seen as a truly impoverished nation, the United States.

At other times, I buckle with laughter.

Haitian laughter – le rire haïtien as Georges Anglade titled his volume of lodyans – a unique Haitian laughter as a response to the frustrations and complications of the everyday. A laughter of impossibility, of fate.

A laughter that cures.

After the "disaster," Léna's pudgy little mouth is ever ready for her regular feedings, between aftershocks; the eyes of this two-month-old Scorpio are indifferent to the traumas of the grownups, while the earth continues to shake like a giant rattle. Léna's face is too small to know yet if she will inherit the oblique, marassa smiles of maman Pascale (whose post-seismic creations range from bright to very dark) and her namesake grandmother: smiles of irony, cynical and creative laughter. Grandma Léna and I make fun of her practical difficulties (with the American, not Haitian, authorities) for leaving the country, knowing we will more likely meet again in this fucked-up land we love than in any god-forsaken New York or Lausanne.

At the moment of the quake, Léna's papa James, the poet and père Noël, was heading out to meet me for a drink. His junker itself brings a smile: only in Haiti can you bring such a car in for engine servicing and leave the mechanic with the motor working but, in exchange, discover the passenger door handle missing.

A few years ago, the joke was why the well-off Haitians had three bank accounts: a checking account, a savings account, and a kidnapping account.

Dated from Paris on January 15, 2010, Jean-Claude Duvalier's letter is one of the best earthquake jokes. Eight million dollars? Offered to the American Red Cross! From which Swiss bank account of dearly departed mother Simone Ovide Duvalier? Even the Haitians circulating copies find the letter too funny to believe its authenticity.

Barbancourt rum is easily associated with laughter; over ice, straight-up, served by handsome white-sleeved waiters, accompanied with poetry, cigarettes, song, fine dresses, perfume, shoes shining on a five-star evening without traces of the dusty streets of Port-au-Prince.

Barbancourt in Manhattan, shared with Jean-Claude Charles (no chaser for Harlem's Haitian Chester Himes). Shared in Paris and Montréal with the melodious laughter of Émile Ollivier.

Barbancourt, a national institution borne with chauvinistic pride. As with Algerian oil and gas pipelines, the geysers of golden brew never slow down at the Barbancourt factory, no matter the political upheaval. In March 2010, however, the company's CEO told the *New York Times*, "We never expected an earthquake." Four million dollars worth of rum down the fault-line drain is no laughing matter.

Four months after the earthquake, I can joke when the eternally irregular and unreliable phone service allows me to get through on one of a friend's cell phones (when was the last time anyone had a working "land" line?), but not when there is another gasoline shortage, now, as was the case immediately after the earthquake, as in January 2009, as during the 1991–94 embargo....

Laughter of the eternally frustrated.

Laughter at the *blan* (me) who has a silly habit of fastening a seat belt. Why bother? This is Haiti. Laughter of the surprised cabdriver after screaming at a car heading toward us in downtown Port-au-Prince. *He's going the wrong way on a one-way street!* How would anyone ever know, I ask, in the absence of any sign indicating the name of a street or its direction.

Hysterical laughter. That of the deranged man, the big-busted naked woman running down the street. Laughter of the crazed, laughter at the crazy.

Tears of laughter. Laughter's relief.

Most often, I am filled with love.

My point of view has three lenses – of anger, laughter, and love – a trilogy overtly inspired by Marie Chauvet, whose masterpiece of twentieth-century letters, *Love, Anger, Madness*, features a cast from the corrupt and racist oligarchy in plots where love, in the context of a dictatorship, is not necessarily that which one expects.

Edwidge Danticat turns anger to love, the anger with U.S. Homeland Security officers in Florida in whose hands her beloved uncle Joseph died. The deaths and lives of this uncle and of the author's father are the central focus of *Brother, I'm Dying*, a book of love for these two men. In her creative and political writing, she often expresses love and support of her homeland, its artists and culture. Hers is a serene love, unquestionably sound, certain beyond death.

It is a love of history, the explosive and unique history of Haiti, which overthrew slavery, defeated Napoleon, and stood firm against a world determined to maintain or reinstate chattel slavery.

The amazement before the immensity of this triumph, as so tragically and majestically seen in the Citadelle, the fortress built for King Henry Christophe, delightfully and obsessively coveted by Trujillo in René Philoctète's novel *Le Peuple des terres mêlées* (*Massacre River*). The cannons of the Citadelle are pointed in perpetuity to the foreign crowns from which they were taken as war booty. Hundreds of metal cannonballs, stacked up behind the massive Citadelle on the Bonnet à l'Évêque mountaintop, are colorful, eternal reminders of the invincible Haitian epic.

It is a love of painting, whose fierce beauty is tinged with joy or tragedy, color and forms that are only Haitian, as with that of Louisiane Saint-Fleurant, Jean-René Jérôme, and, among the more recently departed, Tiga. Falling into the deep black eyes of Tiga's burned faces, mesmerized by the detailed narrative of a Frantz Zéphirin painting, yes, a pictorial love can be spelled in Haitian, as with the ironically human-like roosters of Fritzner Lamour. A point of view indicates subjectivity, but how can one objectively explain the explosive power of Haitian painting and artists, the envy of the Caribbean, if not the world? Streets are filled with hand-painted advertisements, walls are tagged with political graffiti, and taptaps scream out in multiple languages and wild colors with saints, Jesuses, deities, kung-fu masters, flags, biblical verses and Creole proverbs, advertisements, sexy ladies, and testosterone. In metal, Gabriel Bien-Aimé plays devilishly with androgynous and sexy fusions of human, animal, and plant forms. The Vodou pantheon brings a simple beauty to iron shaped by sculptors of the Grand Rue and in the workshops of Croix-des-Bouquets; a profusion of bosmetal gives life to lamps and courtyards.

A love of music. Claudette and Ti Pierre. Manno Charlemagne and Beethova Obas. Not just names, but friends of song: Lody Auguste, Erol Josué.... *Ayiti twoubadouuuuuuuuuuuu.* Gyrating to RAM on the old wood-planked floors of the Oloffson hotel.

Toto Bissainthe.

And especially a love of literature, of the art of words. Classics such as Chauvet and Philoctète. Dynamic contemporaries, from the diaspora – René Depestre, Dany Laferrière, Marie-Célie Agnant, Edwidge Danticat – and from the homeland: Gary Victor, Kettly Mars, Paulette Poujol-Oriol,

Lyonel Trouillot.... Even without mentioning writers of poetry, the list of talent is long. Some day more Haitian literature will be read in translation; after all, it took a half-century for the English-speaking world to discover Jacques-Stephen Alexis.

Rare are the countries where poetry and proverbs are such an important presence in the day-to-day. Afternoons and evenings of shared poetry and text, accompanied by food, drink, and music.

I have never met a single American who could recite from memory as much as every educated Haitian, whose repertoire spans the Bible, classical French and Haitian poetry, and works by contemporary francophone and especially Haitian poets.

A love of the spoken word.

"I feel the earth move under my feet...." When I first regained my senses after "the" earthquake hit, words of Carole King came "tumbling" out of my mouth.

Dany Laferrière noted how some of his acquaintances expressed regret for not having been in Haiti on January 12, 2010, as though they somehow missed out on a defining moment in Haitian history. Silly, no? Had they been there, would they not have missed out on the larger picture?

My point of view is like that of the non-initiated at a Vodou ceremony: an outsider looking in, crying out in a manner different from that of the diversely excited and involved participants.

Ayibobo!

Ayibobo, an expression of joy, of praise, of exclamation to the *lwa*.

Nothing will ever be the same. Much will be the same.

Anger, laughter and love: microscopic echoes of a creative passion.

May 2010

7

Dead-end in Port-au-Prince

Raoul Peck

These words should be titled "ticket to a world with no return," or, closer to the truth, "macabre chronicle of a country that no longer exists." I meet survivor friends who cannot understand how and why they have survived. I listen incredulous to the stories of those who did not survive. Sitting face to face in the same office, one was to survive, the other not. A telephone call allowed one to leave a room, but not the other. The one who left the room disappeared under a concrete screed, then by a swing of the pendulum a last shudder threw him onto the roof, unharmed and without a scratch. Two girlfriends leave five minutes before office closing time. The one in front exits, the other, a split second behind is caught under the mass of concrete and iron. All the possible combinations of events repeat themselves infinitely in these ways. The streets and the soccer fields have been transformed into a multitude of refugee camps. A new life organizes itself. It is wrong to think that this is temporary. Knowing the shortcomings of my country and expecting no constancy in the thinking of the international community (Haiti will not be the first place to be abandoned by the media and the humanitarian agencies), this provisional state of affairs is transforming itself already before our very eyes (in spite of the denials of Haitian and foreign leaders) into something definitive.

At first sight: there is hope.

Once more the Haitian population overall – poor and rich, local elected officials, doctors, everyday citizens – has taken it upon itself to get organized and to respond to urgent needs. Of course there are exceptions. Less scrupulous citizens profit from the distress of others (it takes $6,000 to get a body from the rubble; a little local industry has developed). Of course, there are pillagers, professionals, and opportunists. But, in the end, we are dealing with a mature population preparing itself for the hard times to come. On the flight to Haiti organized by the French Foreign Ministry the conversations around me seem bizarre. It's like listening in utero to benevolent strangers. They have drawn up plans for headquarters, and pore over satellite photos. They pronounce names of places, of districts that are familiar to me, linked to my most intimate memories. For them, these places are the HQs, sites of intervention, impact zones. From time to time, I intervene in a friendly way to correct misunderstandings that could be fatal.

At second sight: catastrophic.

Several days later, one still cannot feel the grip of the state, and one cannot be sure that it will impose itself in the weeks to come. On my arrival, I pass by the government's refuge, a former police station close to the airport. Without judging anyone, I do not "feel" any urgency. Only the simulation of urgency. The gestures, the looks, the sound of the voices do not correspond at all to the urgency I feel in my gut. I feel uneasiness. Worse, a certainty: it's not going to happen. I wonder if all of that is not deliberate.

The original error of the international aid effort was that it had not thought (or wanted?) to put in place as a priority the physical and logistical means so that the surviving administration could react, communicate, and direct. When I see the speed with which CNN installed its office, antennae, secretariat (and emergency bar?) on the tarmac of the airport, I say to myself they could have done better. Whatever the weaknesses of the Haitian administration, it should have had straight away a headquarters, means, logistical support, and expert help. This was not done. Everyone instead got overexcited about occupying the largest intervention space possible, which was the worst thing for practical help, and the best thing for diplomatic vanity.

The demands for trusteeship, direct or implied, can no longer be ignored. In an interview in Paris, before leaving, a journalist asked me if trusteeship might not finally be the best thing for Haiti. This is to misunderstand the Haitian people. Napoleon found out all about that. "Trusteeship" seems on the surface to be an ideal solution for more efficiency, but nowhere in the world has the international community shown itself to be capable of managing crises in a sustainable way. Sticking plasters in an emergency, yes. But long-term nation-building for the benefit of the population? No.

I made a first tour of Port-au-Prince. We came across convoys of international officials (or sometimes of journalists), accompanied by armed men. I really wanted to say to them that they were not reassuring the population. Their appearances, looking so "highly protected" lead people to believe there is a danger that does not really exist. People move around without being overly worried. Port-au-Prince is not Iraq, nor even Rio. Is there a need then to justify such a deployment? To make those in the metropole believe how dangerously we live in Haiti? It is true that prisoners have escaped and that certain stricken areas have still not had any aid, while the cases of water bottles heat up at the airport. I wonder if all that is not deliberate.

On the main road, below the unrecognizable city, a landscape that looks like Beirut at the end of the war. Nothing, or almost nothing, is left standing. I dream of hundreds of bulldozers, the only credible machines faced with these mountains of debris, goods, and bodies.

My friend Maxime shows me two burnt bodies on the sidewalk. It is also the district of small, low-cost hotels. A couple burned in its last coitus. Maxime even knows the story behind it. It was the husband who discovered that his wife was not where she was supposed to be. Further down the same long street, some pillagers. The big skinny guy who was dragging a mattress behind him sees me and runs away. Behind him another does not even dare to look at me. For now, it is a little game (that sometimes doesn't end well). The pillagers test the police; the police are on the lookout for them. We come across some police officers further down the street. We tell them the real pillagers are up the street. They thank us and pretend to do something. But just behind them there is a truck being loaded. I realize that these policemen are making up for a difficult pay period.

I finally found Solène, who has worked with me for more than twenty years. She takes me to the soccer field where she sleeps every night. Everyone has set out their own little place with sheets and posts. In the stands a pastor shouts out a sermon. Some voices respond with a conviction that continues to astonish me. For it must be said for once and for all that the gods, whoever they are, have not done very well in this event. Hell has won out. I wonder if all that is not deliberate.

While re-reading these notes, I just learned that Solène was severely beaten up last night by a gang and everything she owned was stolen.

A woman tells of how a wealthy family paid a group of toughs to find its daughter. They move across the rubble and hear someone crying out. "What is your name?" "Yvonne," the voice calls. "We are looking for Edith." They move on. Three times she was ignored in this way. It was Yvonne, finally saved, who told the story.

Journalists are everywhere, and of every variety, from those with little digital cameras to those in studios with big satellite aerials, protected by ten armed men. You get all kinds: the stars like Geraldo Rivera whom I pass on the tarmac and who throws me a friendly "Hi" (he doesn't know me, but wants to be cool with the natives). "Hi Geraldo," I say back. He is happy that someone recognizes him. Then there are adventurers, often blonds (don't ask me why), with a five-day-old beard, red or blue bandana on the head, straddled across a local motorbike, speeding through the crowds in the poor districts. These guys have no fears; at least they do everything to appear fearless. Two or three cameras strapped across their shoulders, they shoot quicker than their shadows. I go to visit the staff at the hotel Villa Créole. They have survived, but the hotel is half destroyed. The orphan journalists of the ruined Hotel Montana (you know this kind of hotel secured on the roof, from where the journalists like to dispatch their articles between whiskeys on the rocks) wander about as if they have lost their bearings. So, at the Villa Créole, the sides of the pool serve as a dormitory. There too, I feel as if I am in a camp of hirsute legionnaires. Even the thinnest among them seem muscle-bound, so much do they thrust their chests out with importance and superiority. I look around and see no faces that I recognize. I slip away.

There are the journalists who are "close to the people." They often go on foot, searching out the most obscure places, the most unusual people, the most poignant situations. Their articles often begin in this way: "Mèsidieu lives in one of the poorest parts of Port-au-Prince. ... " Earlier, on my arrival, some very nice special envoys tell me they have one or two days to find orphanages, which will be the theme of a forthcoming article. Go figure why abandoned children, and the question of adoption, are the most urgent subjects to deal with in these first chaotic days.

All those compassionate and frustrated journalists! Those who know that the world does not function in the right ways, those who rage against the destructive machine. And instead of smashing the system: their newspaper looking for copy, their editor in chief obtuse, their colleagues jealous, their wives who don't understand why they have to go – again! – and lose themselves in the lands of the savages.... I know, I am exaggerating. I also have my clichés. But all the same. ...

There are a lot of bizarre things involved in all of this. Each time that I hear talk of my country, the notion of complexity seems left out. Four hundred years of history, incomprehensible even for us Haitians, summarized in a single truncated, superficial, alarmist, compassionate image. ... I do however know quite a few journalists. Often, they have deep knowledge of Haiti and its society, and work for the biggest newspapers. They know the country well, but when I read their articles I no longer recognize them. Is this a problem with the editor in chief? Is this down to the need to sell papers and to have the most dramatic and scandalous headlines? An angry female friend says, "More than anything, they want us to conform to the image they have of us." She is reacting to the CNN images showing helicopters dropping supplies to the people, an anarchic distribution that will of course end up in a fight even if it were on Fifth Avenue in New York. The craziest thing is that it is CNN who are filming and broadcasting, live. What does that prove? That Haitians are dogs? That people who are hungry and feel abandoned behave like animals? The worst thing is not the showing of these images, it is the imbalance, the fact that it leaves no room for other images that are perhaps more coherent.

I understand what an Afghan or an Iraqi feels when faced with this excess of testosterone, technological superiority, and media violence. A Humvee full of American marines cuts its way through the crowd, without a word, barely looking at anyone. I am sure that everyone wants to do some good, but there are oceans of history, mountains of misunderstandings, storms of prejudices that separate us. They pass by; we do not understand each other.

At the General Hospital: the very center of the war. It's there that you get a sense of the carnage, the numbers of the injured and dead, the types of injuries (fractures, amputations), the madness and despair. The hospital is guarded by the marines. There are Israeli doctors, Americans, French, and many other nationalities. Everyone has a little section of this great court of miracles; real miracles in this instance.

Death. Even in death, inequalities exist. There are those (like my uncle Fritz Michel and my cousin Hervé Roche) who in the early days were able to be buried in their gardens. There are those who were able to find a place in the cemetery. In Haiti, baptism, marriage, and burials remain unshake-able foundations of society. Then there are all the rest, the vast majority of bodies, which ended up in the communal graves, without being identified or photographed – fallen into anonymity and forever without a face.

A doctor friend returns to our little city of tents, angry. "They are completely mad!" The head of an NGO has asked for each family to have its photo taken (for their files) before releasing food aid. "While these people still have loved ones buried under the rubble, you want me to go and ask them to have their photos taken?" The doctor very nearly took the official's head off. The vast majority of the bodies end up in the communal graves, without being identified, without being photographed (the state of the bodies no longer allows this).

I said to Solène that I would come and spend the night with them, in their "refugee camp." She has added two posts and two sheets to enlarge her perimeter. It's as simple as that. What scares me every day is the natural way in which people adapt to (I don't say "accept") adversity, the failings of their leaders, history, the ingratitude of the world. (Yes, that is not too strong. This country has given a lot to this world. Revise your history.)

One day, the country will have to rise. A country does not die. That day, for sure, everything will be simpler. Deliberate.

26 January 2010

Translated by Martin Munro

8

Helping Haiti – Helping Ourselves

Nadève Ménard

Haitians are used to upheaval and catastrophe. They punctuate our every season. Yet, when the earth shook on January 12, 2010, it stunned us all. Once we began to emerge from our collective stupor to realize the enormity of what had happened, we immediately began to help ourselves. In any way and all the ways we knew how. From pulling neighbors from beneath houses and buildings to driving strangers to hospitals, we helped each other. And when others learned what had happened, they were immediately moved to help us, too. So this essay is about help.

Disaster Capitalism

Each Haitian disaster benefits someone, benefits many. Each one of our hurricanes and tropical storms and coup d'états and general strikes has benefited various groups. Non-governmental organizations and national politicians. Religious fanatics and economic tycoons. Multinational corporations and nations with imperialistic tendencies. The earthquake was no different.

Today, it is hard to look at the Haitian landscape and not think of the rise of Disaster Capitalism. Among those eager to help Haiti, there are those who want to simultaneously help themselves. For example, the Artibonite valley is the heart of Haitian rice land. Yet, in addition to the food aid which includes sacks of imported rice, food-for-work programs have been instituted in which workers are paid with sacks of rice imported from the U.S. Is this practice really helping Haiti? Helping Haitian farmers? Or is it helping the U.S. farm industry and its farmers? The fact that several NGOs have recently stated that they will start buying rice and other goods from local farmers points to the answer.

Paradoxically, the earthquake has created many job opportunities. But most of the jobs that pay decent salaries and do not require manual labor go to foreigners. Speaking English is often a requirement. Countless Haitians lost their sole means of supporting their families when their places of work collapsed. However, they are not the ones being offered jobs with the NGOs or participating in the reconstruction. In fact, many Haitians already working for NGOs are being driven out to make room for foreign experts. Many foreigners here, NGO workers for the most part, seem almost giddy when I see them at the supermarket, at the gas station, or buying art at the side of the road. A Jamaican friend describes them as disaster tourists. And while there is no doubt that they are helping in various ways every day, there is nothing to suggest that hundreds of Haitians could not be providing that same assistance while simultaneously helping themselves and their economy recover.

Thousands of Haitian university students are currently idle. Their schools collapsed and they are waiting for classes to resume. Surely these students have skills that could be put to use in this time of crisis. Many of them began volunteering immediately after the earthquake: those studying medicine, social work, and psychology, for example. Those with training in engineering signed on to help evaluate houses. Why not employ them in the reconstruction effort? Why not offer them jobs with NGOs and contractors?

In fact, as has been the case throughout the world in times of crisis, a great part of the billions of dollars dedicated to reconstruction efforts is being spent on the NGOs themselves. There are the exorbitant salaries and relocation fees, the buying and leasing of shiny new SUVs. An important percentage of the "aid" will not even arrive in Haiti as it has already been spent on contracts and goods in the countries of origin. A large number of UN employees are currently housed on a cruise ship outside of Cité Soleil. How is this helping Haiti? How can these people be drafting plans to help Haiti when they have no contact with Haitian life or even Haitians? Couldn't the money used to house them in a foreign-owned cruise ship be better spent in ways that would actually bolster the Haitian economy?

Projects like Coca Cola's Haiti Hope are unfortunately rare. Coca Cola Company and partners have developed a mango-based juice, which will involve 25,000 Haitian mango farmers. The project extends over several years, will double the income of the farmers involved, and create a new industry in the region.

I recently read Naomi Klein's The Shock Doctrine, and its implications for Haiti are terrifying. The cycle of shocks – be they disasters, coups d'état, or foreign invasions – and subsequent market liberalization she describes read like a blueprint for Haiti's current situation. How many nations and global institutions really want to see a developed Haiti that can fend for itself? Many experts would find themselves without a raison d'être and more importantly, without a source of income. It is countries like Haiti that keep the World Bank and the International Monetary Fund in business. The number of NGOs operating in Haiti has exploded exponentially since the earthquake, many of them operating completely under the radar, recognized neither by the Haitian government nor their own.

Inept Leadership

The government is basing its reconstruction plans on the P.D.N.A., Post-Disaster Needs Assessment – a controversial document. Why is its title in English? If the government is not strong enough, forceful enough to insist upon using its own languages in the reconstruction process, how can we as a population trust them to lead us forward? At press conferences after the earthquake, the president and several government ministers spoke in English, giving interviews and answering questions in that language. Local Haitians as well as those abroad were put off by this. Such a practice not only puts Haitian officials at a marked disadvantage, but also clearly signifies that they are not speaking to the local population, that what they have to say is for foreign ears, that the local population's opinion is of little import to them.

Similarly, there is great controversy surrounding the commission to oversee Haitian reconstruction projects for the next 18 months. Comprising Haitians and foreigners, it is headed by former U.S. President Bill Clinton and the current Haitian Prime Minister Jean-Max Bellerive. Apparently foreigners are included in this commission because Haitians are deemed incapable of deciding which projects we need and implementing them for ourselves.

Of course, the influence of foreigners on Haitian affairs is not just the consequence of decisions made by foreign countries, their firms and NGOs. Many Haitians, at all levels of society are complicit in this development. Those taking advantage of Haiti's hardship are not just foreign.

It is at times of crisis like this that the absence of certain structures becomes glaring. Were the political parties not so weak and/or corrupt, they would have been a valid venue for bringing the population's demands to the fore. Had our national institutions been stronger and firmly dedicated to the well being of Haitian citizens, it would have been more difficult to suggest skirting them to rebuild.

When, three months after the earthquake, free food is plentiful, but jobs are scarce, is that really helping Haiti? Will the world always be willing to give us free food? Shouldn't we be starting now to learn or remember how to earn it? While the government has been calling for an end to foreign aid for a while, it unfortunately has done little to increase or foster national production, in spite of all the lip service paid to the idea. Elections should be held soon. Isn't any government doomed in advance if it cannot continue the practice of free food, free medical attention, and free housing? It is almost as if those in power – on both the national and international levels – want to keep us in a state of constant crisis.

Haitians came together after the earthquake. Many who live abroad came home to offer medical expertise, money, clothing, food supplies, and comfort. Those who live here also donated what they had. They welcomed relatives and relative strangers into their homes. They translated, formed committees, wrote articles, told our stories. And it is all useful, it all helps Haiti to move forward from this tragedy.

But what is most needed at this juncture is a massive coordinated effort. Who will reform the education system, for example? Individuals, even concerned groups cannot do it. Who will ensure that buildings being constructed now conform to standards for earthquake zones? Individual engineers or foreign experts cannot do it. Why hasn't a new building code been established so that we can begin building better? While there are steps that individuals can take to improve the situation, while various groups can certainly exert pressure – political and economic – on those in power as well as those foreign entities that have so much say in how things work here, at the end of the day, for us to really be able to help ourselves, our leaders have to be willing to listen to what we have to say. They have to look beyond their own interests and see those of a nation. And if they refuse, the nation must force them to see. Populations in underdeveloped countries are often praised for peaceful elections when they take place. But sometimes noisy demonstrations are just as important. Sometimes they are the most effective way of making our voices heard.

From the very first days after the earthquake, there were feelings of utter helplessness among the population as we faced the lack of coordination in the relief effort. The government was glaringly absent and slow to respond to local offers of help. The result was many capable, willing people feeling useless and ashamed to be useless. Among them were professionals in several fields: engineering, demographics, psychology, education. They are not participating in the so-called reconstruction of Haiti. Not because they don't want to, but because they've been squeezed out or are not called upon. And the plan is for this situation to continue. The jobs the P.D.N.A. aims to create are all labor-intensive jobs. The idea seems to be to turn

Haiti into a vast pool of unskilled labor, which will of course benefit the disaster capitalists.

While the prime minister decries the fact that dozens of young professionals left the country after the earthquake, he doesn't make use of the ones that are still here. I should know. I am one of them. Would it have been so difficult to ascertain which government employees were available after the earthquake, what their capabilities were, what they were willing to do? Such potential was and continues to be wasted.

Building Tomorrow

Terrible as it was, the earthquake created a moment of opportunity. Not an opportunity in the sense used by disaster capitalists, but rather an opportunity for the Haitian state to do more and better for its people. Reform the school system, live up to the word of the Constitution and provide general access to free education. Make health care available to all Haitian citizens, regardless of class or location. The earthquake brought all of Haiti's problems to the fore. They could no longer be denied or ignored. But if those in political and economic power had no interest in solving those problems before the earthquake, they weren't any more interested in its wake. So the earthquake is slowly becoming an opportunity lost.

It is all too easy to fall back into old patterns, old routines once the sense of urgency has passed. And while routine can be a good thing, there must be lasting changes in the way we live with each other. The Haitian landscape is forever altered; Haitian society must follow. Most of us are conscious of this and would like to make strides in that direction. Unfortunately, our leaders are not leading. For example, schools recently reopened in the areas affected by the earthquake. Instead of seizing the chance to create a truly egalitarian public school system, the government opted for a return to the status quo in which the vast majority of schools are private, thus ensuring that inequalities will persist and become even more blatant than before.

Various programs are available to provide local and foreign NGOs with financial and technical assistance. What of Haitian businesses? Who will help them get back on their feet? Several schools and hospitals have announced that they are closing, unable to secure funds to rebuild or to compete with free medical care. Is Haiti to forever remain a nation dependent upon NGOs to fulfill the population's basic needs? And who will fulfill those needs when the NGOs leave to help victims of the world's next disaster?

If Haiti is to rise again, the movement can only come from within. Everyone would do well to realize that – Haitians and foreigners alike. We need to help ourselves. A nation cannot be saved or run by NGOs. Nor is the answer to flee the sinking ship, as it were.

The university system is a case in point. Several foreign universities have offered scholarships to Haitian students. Two students from the Faculté des Sciences of the Université d'État d'Haïti will be going to Purdue University to study seismology. However, the vast majority of Haitian students will remain here. How can we help them? How can we ensure that the next generation of Haitians will not be devoid of professionals? Although some private universities have resumed courses, the state university where I teach has yet to reopen. How can we rebuild the nation without the university community?

There has been a mad drive to adopt Haitian children, with some in the U.S. Congress expressing displeasure that the adoption process has not been expedited in light of the circumstances. They would like to make thousands of Haitian children available for immediate adoption. While adoption can be a wonderful experience for many families, is Haiti to become a baby mill? Some have forgone adoption and tried to help themselves to Haitian children with no regard for local laws. Why not improve conditions for children in Haiti as opposed to whisking them away? Without its children, Haiti has no future.

In spite of inept local leadership and the disaster capitalists ready to exploit our tragedy for profit, those of us who choose Haiti for better or for worse look towards the future with hope. We recognize the need to help each other build a better tomorrow. That can only be done once we acknowledge the intrinsic value of each Haitian and work together to improve Haiti for each and every one of us. Haiti is our home.

April 2010

9

Eternity Lasted Less than Sixty Seconds …

Evelyne Trouillot

On Tuesday, January 12, 2010, eternity lasted less than sixty seconds. Less than sixty seconds of eternity to erase hundreds of thousands of lives, demolish thousands of homes and buildings, leave thousands of children orphaned, obliterate the educational infrastructure of the capital and of many provincial cities, and forever alter the landscape of a city, a country, and our memory.

It took less than sixty seconds to place us face to face with our weaknesses, our ugliness, to force us to bring forth an unbelievable amount of courage, to bring out our acts of solidarity. Less than sixty seconds to force us to look at ourselves unmasked.

It brought a destruction of the kind we've only seen in those films of planetary catastrophe where mutilated bodies, buildings, and infrastructure fall on all sides like insignificant little marbles confronted with the anger of an all-powerful giant. A destruction whose magnitude still makes one shudder four months later and that produces a feeling of distress that is exacerbated by the inactivity of the authorities.

Could so many deaths have been avoided? I leave that question to the experts. Some of the contributing factors appear quite obvious: the failings of urbanism, the concentration of the population, the degradation of the environment, the failure to raise awareness in and train the public – there would be so much to say about all these factors that no doubt contributed to making this catastrophe all the more cruel. This earthquake is still so vivid in our memories that a large part of the Haitian population hesitates to name it and speaks of it as "the incident" or "goudougoudou" or "bagay la" as if to mentally distance themselves from it as much as possible or to emphasize its monstrous, unnamable nature; neither case helps establish objective and rational thought vis-à-vis this natural phenomenon whose threat, according to expert opinion, is still present.

But who am I to tell anyone how to survive emotionally the horrors they experienced during those seconds that didn't even last a whole minute? What can one say to the former colleague whose two hands were amputated? What can one say to the young woman who pulled her brother and her cousin from the rubble and, some hours later, dug her father's and her seven-year-old cousin's graves in her garden? What to say to the father who saw his house collapse on his wife and child? To the nine-year-old boy who, with trembling lips, relates his mother's dying words to his father? Who am I to even begin to touch the depths of their pain?

At the beginning of February, I went by my childhood neighborhood. It was the neighborhood where I was born, where I learned to love the sun and trample the earth. Pouplard Avenue's name carries with it my mother's sturdy and reassuring presence and the long speeches of my father, preparing his case for the next day. It was the neighborhood I came back to as an adult, after years of living outside the country, to live in my parents' house while I was waiting to move into my own home with my family. It was the neighborhood that I had left, then, a second time but that still lived on in me. Its contours, from the church bell tower to the familiar walls of the public school, had marked my memory more than any other place. It was the neighborhood that I had been avoiding in order to escape the nostalgia I felt when faced with its irreversible descent into the chaos of urban poverty. But when I saw its streets covered with debris, I realized that the transformation would be all the more painful for me this time. When I saw the site of the public school atop that hill that I had climbed so many times, when I saw the empty space cleanly stripped of its debris, with no trace of that structure which had been a part of my surroundings, I felt a savage and heavy gaping hole open up inside me. Elsewhere faced with the grotesque and terrifying shapes of collapsed buildings, I had already noted the extent of the damage, but suddenly I was asking myself if it wasn't worse to see the spaces cleaned out of all that had existed before, as if an invisible hand had forever removed all physical proof of human existence.

For all that it took less than sixty seconds to erase thousands of lives, the earthquake did not have the power to change the way our society functions. Immediately following the catastrophe, the international press arrived. Having come from Europe, North America, Latin America, and the Caribbean, the journalists surveyed the streets, questioned the local notables, flaunted cameras and microphones in the makeshift camps, and produced articles and news reports. With the lack of nuance they often show in unknown territory, some representatives of the western press denounced the inequalities that characterize Haitian society. Those inequalities have been perpetuated for so long that the minority benefit-ting from economic and social advantages seems to think it has a right to them, to the detriment of the great majority, and gets indignant whenever anybody talks about them. The schematic and reductionist quality of certain foreign news reports does not change the fact that even though all Haitians were effectively victims of the earthquake, the consequences were entirely different depending on one's original economic status. If in some way we have all lost either a loved one, a roof, our confidence in the future, a school, a business, a workplace, a limb, a girlfriend, it remains nonetheless true that the horrors that we all lived through accentuate the already flagrant social divides. The country itself remains the biggest victim of this catastrophe in that the majority of its citizens finds itself in an even more difficult situation than before. Moreover, the number of mortalities and the extent of the material damage for the whole society were worsened by those social inequalities. Recognizing that fact would be only a first step, a very small one, toward the acknowledgement of an unacceptable situation.

After weeks of silence followed by clumsy directives, the national ministry of education at last set the date for the return to school, which took place under uncertain conditions. In the meantime, during that confusing interval when panic-stricken parents and distraught school principals were waiting for clear and direct instructions, the schools had already timidly begun to function. "Children have to go to school, after all," said some. Which children? Which school? Is it mere chance that certain private and religious schools were the first to be cleared from the rubble? Is it mere chance that certain private schools with an upper-class clientele were the first to open their doors, even before the ministry's announcement? Is it mere chance if the ministry seems only to pay lip service to the fate of thousands of children who attend hundreds of modest schools which have, for the most part, collapsed, and which are unable to function? It seems to me that we have missed an important opportunity here – the opportunity to make a decision that would put all children on the same level and would permit children of all social and economic backgrounds to see themselves as little Haitian boys and girls belonging to the same country and being entitled to the same privileges. Instead of starting school in uncertain conditions that only reinforce inequalities, it would have been better to have had the courage to delay the return to school for as long as it took to ensuring a genuine and fair return to school. A return that didn't smack of favoritism and that would have distanced itself as much as possible from the usual practices of exclusion.

The earthquake can remind us that in death we are all equals, but it cannot erase the social, economic, and cultural injustice that has fed the structure of Haitian society for two centuries. The ability of some social groups to ignore the needs of the majority is proving to be more glaring than ever.

The state's inefficiency in helping the victims, its persistence in reinforcing the supremacy of a minority over the majority, its abject capitulation before an "international community" that, more than ever, is concerned with the prerogatives of multinationals whose interests are tightly linked to those of powerful countries – all these elements reinforce the population's feeling that it has been forgotten. More resourceful than ever, it is a population that clings to life and refuses to give up. And in the streets of Port-au-Prince alongside the ruins, the piles of concrete block and sand, the small businesses are setting up shop, the neighborhood quarrels are being taken up again, laughter mixes with insults, life picks up where it left off. And though that fact pays homage to the population's resilience, it also raises concerns insofar as it illustrates that the old social practices of abandonment and exclusion can fall back into place with no difficulty.

Here we are more than four months later and the evidence is piling up, clearly highlighting the fact that this reconstruction we hear so much about is not taking into account the interests of the majority. There are prodigious sums, colossal donation promises, development plans that fall apart then come together only to break down again. There are NGOs that are created with the dollars collected, but we all know that this sum will be greatly reduced before arriving here, in the country itself. We also know that the sums that will arrive here will follow obscure routes, and we ask ourselves what percentage of the country will benefit from this so-called "aid."

It's nearly four months later, and for some, life goes on as if nothing had happened. The earthquake, that noisy and disturbing interlude, has gone and left only echoes of its trembling, which the body, if not the spirit, has gotten used to. Little habits are taken up again: the poorly compensated maid who has no right to paid leave, the worker who must accept a laughable salary that he already owes to the neighborhood businesses before he has even been paid, the supermarkets that raise their prices when they get visitors from big-spending foreign powers. There are some changes to note nonetheless: in preparation for the construction that is going on, the stores selling construction materials and hardware are seeing their revenues go up. On the other hand, the supermarkets are disappointed that the employees of international institutions sometimes get their supplies from their own sources and bypass the national market. Indeed, many of the experts called to help the Haitian population by mapping out training programs or by drafting development strategies live in luxurious spaces such as cruise ships or beachfront hotels that are relatively or even completely cut off from Haitian society. Are they being housed in these places to spare them the spectacle of misery and disarray of the population about which they are supposed to be experts?

It is four months later, and the image of those fateful seconds weighs heavily in my memory. Each time I speak of those seconds, it awakens the same feeling of unspeakable pain because it isn't just my pain; it belongs to a whole people. Every word is laden with fissures and stumblings that recall all those destroyed lives. And when I look upon a ravaged neighborhood, upon streets that now exist only in photographs and in our memories, I imagine them filled with those individuals who departed in less than a minute, quite simply, sometimes with no sounds other than those of disintegrated walls and twisted metal. Thousands of people perished with no sound other than that of the crying of their relatives, sometimes with no sound other than that of the dust one clears away so that life can take its course. When I look upon my destroyed country, I want to salute the memory of all those who for the most part lived muted lives in the hopes that their deaths will not pass silently into history. May their deaths contribute to a reflection on our society, to a reorganization of things, and to a new, fairer, more humane and transparent Haiti.

May 2010

Translated by Robyn Cope

PART II

Politics, Culture, and Society

10

Rising from the Ruins:
Haiti in Two Hundred Years

J. Michael Dash

"This is a country, if ever there was one, that needs to sob and bawl and soak the damaged earth with tears." – Marc Lacey, "In Haiti, a Puzzling Drought of Tears."

Haiti is in ruins today. The earthquake of Tuesday, January 12 has laid bare the nightmare reality of the misery of the Haitian people: few hospitals, inadequate infrastructure, weak state institutions, and the illiterate urban poor huddled in shanty towns or perched precariously on hillsides. What the harrowing images in the media have dramatized is nothing new for the vast majority of the Haitian nation. They have lived this way for more than two centuries. Marc Lacey wrote poignantly in the *New York Times* (January 29, 2010) of the "puzzling drought of tears" after a tragedy in which Haitians died in "jaw dropping numbers," their bodies burned in mass graves, dumped in ravines or simply left to rot in the rubble. He sadly concluded that these "stone faced" people with their blank stares "had become so toughened by the harsh lives" they were "so used to living" that they had bottled up their emotions. They had become "toughened" because the earthquake was just the latest tragedy for a country now impossible to dissociate from the epithet "poorest country in the Western hemisphere." There was a "drought of tears" for the uncounted dead that lay in the waters between Haiti and Florida, for those who were cut down while waiting in line to vote or those who were massacred since 1986 because they opposed one military junta or another, and the list goes on. Lacey was right to look beyond the tragedy of January 12 for an explanation for the pervasive stoicism he encountered. Acts of nature, whether hurricane, landslide or earthquake, can inflict terrible suffering because of human failures: Haiti's tragedy is not natural, but manmade, not destiny but history.

We should not forget Haiti was in ruins on the morning after the declaration of independence on January 1, 1804. For the past two centuries Haiti has stood still. We cannot comprehend this immobility unless we understand that independence meant the beginning of a neo-colonial relationship with the outside world. Haiti's legitimacy was questioned in the aftermath of national independence. Its territorial waters were constantly violated in the nineteenth century. Recognition of the supposedly illegitimate nation, Haiti, meant paying a massive indemnity to France in 1825 and thereby perpetuating dependence on the former colonial masters. By 1915, an American occupation, which lasted nineteen years, meant that Haiti had entered the U.S. sphere of influence. It has not left it. The U.S. marines disembarked to secure American business interests and to limit Franco-German influence in the region. It could well have marked the beginning of a paternalistic American attitude to Haiti, which continued to be seen as an orphaned country in need of external, adult guidance. The U.S.-led intervention of 1994 under President Clinton may have been called "Operation Uphold Democracy" but it was primarily driven by the need to stanch the outflow of refugees and not to restore democracy. It did little to change the discourse of Haiti's infantile dependency. Under President George W. Bush, the bicentenary of Haiti's independence was marked by the U.S. complicity in a coup that ousted President Aristide. The Haitian political crisis of 2004 was not, therefore, settled by a parliamentary vote of no-confidence or impeachment of the democratically elected president. Rather the neo-colonial fathers, France and the U.S., were only too happy to step into their usual paternal roles. Now that everyone laments the weakness of the Haitian state, no one remembers the extent to which lawlessness was encouraged in February 2004 when it suited the powers that be.

If Haiti's present ruin is as much historical as it is natural, we must also take into account those forces within Haiti that have traditionally resisted change and immobilized the country. Haiti perhaps stands apart in the Caribbean in that its society has been formed around a uniquely terrible asymmetry of economic power. If Haitian society cannot move forward and cannot realize the dream of modernity that sparked its revolution at the end of the eighteenth century it is in part because it has had an elite that has lived by siphoning off the country's productivity to support its personal consumption, an elite whose power was consolidated during the U.S. occupation. Time and again we hear about Haiti starting anew. James Leyburn in *The Haitian People* (1941) felt that in 1804 that Haitians had the opportunity to invent "an entire new little world." The "second" independence of Haiti after the Americans left in 1934 was similarly seen by Zora Neale Hurston in *Tell My Horse* (1938) as an event that created stability for "the next hundred years." Haiti's burdensome past is the reason why Haiti cannot simply be made anew. Independent Haiti inherited from a violent and degrading past a sharply divided society of urbanites, made up of an alliance of political rulers and the commercial bourgeoisie, and the *moun andeyo* or people on the outside; that is, the rural peasantry. It ultimately is not the Haitian masses who are resistant to progress. Rather it is often the Haitian ruling classes who are impervious to change. Neocolonialist isolation, we should remember, suited the Haitian elites perfectly as it helped them secure local control of the country as importers and exporters living off the ever-dwindling resources of the nation. The elites formed the state that lived off the peasantry, who constituted the nation. The idea of the nation from which the elites drew their legitimacy had nothing to do with the majority of Haitians, who were never consulted or included in any institutionalized way and had no leverage against the state.

The story of post-independent Haiti is one of increasing ruin due to this unequal social and economic order. The eventual collapse of Jean-Claude Duvalier's ostentatious presidency in 1986 was directly linked to the consequences of this exploitative structure. The normally passive peasantry was roused by the message of social justice spread by the grassroots Catholic Church, or *ti-legliz*. The forces that brought down the dictatorship did not originate in political organizations that the regime had successfully crushed, but in the Catholic Church. By 1990 a return to the previous status quo could only be thwarted by a populist savior like Jean-Bertrand Aristide. His *Lavalas* movement was more of a metaphor for sweeping away the old order than an organized political institution, and Aristide represented everything that the ruling classes hated and feared. They struck back and ousted Aristide, who was returned to power only after a flood of refugees pushed a reluctant President Clinton to use force to reinstate Haiti's first freely elected head of state.

Ever since the fall of the Duvalier dictatorship in 1986, there has been an endemic crisis in Haiti's political culture. The popular anti-Duvalier movement put the ideal of democratic reform within the reach of the previously dispossessed masses but it also ushered in an economic model that linked democracy with free trade. Consequently, the central paradox that frustrates the post-Duvalier transition to stable democracy derives from an explosive combination of laissez-faire capitalism, which favors an elite that dominates the local economy, and democratic elections, which give power to the underprivileged. The mass of the population has been energized since 1986 by issues like constitutional reform in 1987 and the electoral process that resulted in the overwhelming vote for Jean-Bertrand

Aristide in December 1990. The problem faced by the wealthy minority has concerned their need to thwart these democratic demands and to profit from a free-market model. Both sides are by now keenly aware of the stakes of the bloody contradictions of a free-market democracy in post-Duvalierist Haiti.

Such a contest for power has produced two kinds of leadership: either politicians who are aligned with the wealthy few and are viewed with suspicion by the population, or demagogic populists who try to hold on to power by constantly inveighing against the machinations of the business class and its foreign backers. Recent events in Haiti bear this out. Jean-Bertrand Aristide created his "Lavalas Family" in the name of the dispossessed masses and to frustrate the free-market expectations of Haiti's wealthy minority. Eventually state business became family business as the incompetent and corrupt rose to positions of power through exploiting family loyalties. The anti-Aristide opposition had as its ultimate goal the dismantling of the Lavalas family. Their hope was that, once the populist demagogue was safely in exile, their access to state power and a free-market economy could be guaranteed by the murderous elements of the discredited Haitian army that had deposed the Lavalas leader.

In post-Duvalierist Haiti, no presidential candidate can be successful unless he or she represents the mass of the Haitian population. The victory of René Préval is a clear demonstration of the importance of a popular mandate in governing Haiti. Unfortunately, Préval inherited the fallout from the crisis that removed President Aristide from power, a crisis resolved not by constitutional means or international mediation, but by brute force. An abrupt and violent change in government and not a constitutional transition had unleashed in Haiti elements of the disbanded Duvalier army. It also gave renewed confidence to those in the market-dominant elite who wish to govern the old-fashioned way – by force. Préval's ineffectiveness in the present crisis should not obscure the kind of leadership he has provided since being elected. He has tried to build bridges in the wake of Aristide's polarizing politics, neutralize the armed, predatory elements in Haiti, and walk the tightrope between market-based economic reform and social justice, as well as attract aid from an easily distracted international community.

The image of the collapsed national palace constantly replayed in the media is a dangerously misleading symbol. It uncannily reverts to the discourse of the orphaned, illegitimate nation that is in constant need of fathering. The mercy missions to adopt Haitian children that were lavishly covered in the U.S. media may have been humanitarian in intent but they also served to reinforce the old image of a country in need of saviors. Préval's government is certainly in crisis at present as he and his prime minister have been unable to assert themselves in the face of overwhelming calamity. Yet he and his government must be central to rebuilding the Haitian state. He and his prime minister represent a new phenomenon. They are neither part of the old political class nor were they imposed by the army. A strong Haitian state does not mean enlightened dictatorship or some benevolent strongman as some desperate commentators have suggested. Obviously, legislative and presidential elections scheduled for later this year and next cannot be held in the present circumstances. Haiti cannot be rebuilt unless respect for state authority and the rule of law is reinstated. Préval has his work cut out for him, but whether he succeeds or fails is not strictly an internal matter. The international community has a key role in Haiti's reconstruction, but this must not be the paternalistic "helping hand" of humanitarian assistance that we keep hearing about. The United Nations must take the lead on this question but it cannot be just another U.S.-led effort. Canada, Brazil, and the CARICOM states must play a decisive role in Haiti's future. At the beginning of the nineteenth century, Haitians attempted to create a modern state from the ruins of the plantation. Their will was thwarted by a hostile international community. That job still remains to be done. We can only hope that the international community is prepared to end Haiti's historical nightmare.

The Haitian writer, Dany Laferrière, with his usual insightfulness has recently said "there is no need to weep over Haiti. Haiti does not need tears but new kinds of energy." Where can sources of new energy be found? Port-au-Prince may be a massive camp of displaced people at present, but ultimate rebuilding must be directed at those elements of civil society that emerged with the anti-Duvalier opposition and gave a voice to Haiti's resilient, silent majority. No amount of aid or assistance can help Haitians mourn the terrible human losses of January 12. What can be done is to empower Haitians to change their society in such a way that we don't have to be constantly asking whether it can be made anew. On a CARICOM fact-finding mission to Haiti in June 1989, I remember the St. Lucian delegate from the group, Hunter François, asking why Haitians were not being encouraged to grow bananas in order to solve the political crisis of the time. When I heard it, this question seemed both absurd and inappropriate in a country that was as poor in topsoil as in political options. However, on further reflection, I suppose that what he had in mind was that banana farmers were a pillar of democratic political culture in St. Lucia and that no political solution for Haiti could be found unless there were something similar on which to ground Haitian democracy.

This is an idea well worth keeping in mind as Haiti undergoes a seemingly endless transition to something other than authoritarian political rule. Democracy clearly needs to be rooted in basic institutions and practices that preserve democratic values. Not only do Haitians, at all levels, lack these institutions, but the only system of government much of the population has known is Duvalierism, a particularly violent manifestation of state power. Having brought down this absolutist state in the name of democratic freedom, Haiti is left with little or no central control and without the means of creating an alternative to the all-powerful state. The experience of the Aristide presidency has not helped in this regard. Aristide never showed respect for institutions, sometimes justifiably so as his experience with the Catholic Church illustrates. In his sermons he inveighed against institutions that were complicit with the social evils that he sought to eradicate. He ultimately fell into the old tradition of institutionless authoritarian rule and became another *gwo neg*, or strong man, but one without resources to distribute, because of the U.S. embargo, and without the protection of an army, which he had disbanded. Aristide was ill equipped to lead his country into a new era of respect for state institutions. He was removed from power by an opposition that itself had no respect for institutions. This opposition was not interested in building its own political base by capitalizing on the widespread disenchantment with Aristide. They were not interested in having a referendum on the self-destructive incompetence of the president. They simply resorted to the hysterical sound bite "Aristide must go," and showed no signs of embarrassment at the parallel government that they installed in 2001 under the decrepit shadow presidency of Gérard Gourgue.

Haiti cannot be saved by those on the outside, if only for the simple reason that a modern democratic society can neither be imposed by the well-armed nor inserted by the well-meaning. Haitians will have to find the capacity for patience and compromise in order to extricate themselves from their predicament. The radical restructuring of Haitian society can be helped, however, by external forces that are committed to long-term nation-building and not to sending contradictory signals, wittingly or unwittingly, to political elements in Haiti. The international community restored Aristide to power in 1994 and left before any real institutional change was established in Haiti. A more sustained global effort can have an impact on Haiti, a country that is vastly smaller than Iraq and nowhere near the violent collapse of countries such as Liberia and Somalia. It is important as we contemplate the next two hundred years of Haiti's existence to conceive of Haiti as a unique but unexceptional member of the Caribbean community. In 2002 the Haitian parliament ratified the CARICOM treaty and Haiti became a full member of the regional body. This is a beginning, and the political and economic experiences of neighboring independent Caribbean countries can be useful to rebuilding Haiti. The region is now more aware than ever before of the plight of Haiti and that the bonds with the first independent country in the region are not simply restricted to the fault line that runs from Enriquillo in the Dominican Republic to Plantain Garden in eastern Jamaica. The Haitian anthropologist, Michel Rolph Trouillot once noted the importance of seeing Haiti from a regional perspective. "I spent fifteen months doing fieldwork among the peasantry in Dominica," he said, "and I believe that I learned more about the Haitian peasantry during those months than I did during eighteen years in Port-au-Prince." Ultimately, it will be up to Haitians to decide what kind of society they want. As Trouillot suggests they may want to be more like Dominicans than dependent on the whims of messiahs or warlords. They may want to live in a country that does not have to be constantly made anew. Today the words of a St. Lucian politician, who felt that Haiti should grow bananas, have particular resonance. Unless Haiti becomes a "banana democracy" it seems fated to remain a banana republic.

March 2010

II

Religion in Post-earthquake Haiti

Leslie G. Desmangles and Elizabeth McAlister

In less than a minute on January 12, 2010, Port-au-Prince and its surrounding area were devastated by an earthquake so lethal it was pronounced the worst natural disaster in the history of the Americas. Entire neighborhoods were destroyed, more than two hundred thousand people died, and tens of thousands would flee to the provinces. As is common in a crisis, people turned to religion for meaning, answers and guidance, as well as for the material support brought by charity.

Haitian religious leaders were moved by the disaster to provide spiritual and physical assistance to the afflicted by camping with their congregations in makeshift shelters. Religious leaders provided encouragement and faith, served as conduits for food aid, and became advocates for their "flocks." Many were so traumatized by the earthquake and the weeks of seismic aftershocks that there was a widespread fear of entering any buildings. The extensive destruction of Christian churches and Afro-Creole religious temples (and for that matter, most buildings in downtown Port-au-Prince) disrupted customs and led to significant changes in ritual observances. Because so many religious edifices were destroyed, religious services were held outdoors in open spaces and on the streets of the cities and towns in the months after the quake. These makeshift arrangements have engendered a new era in the politics of religion that we can see in the adaptation of rituals to the new settings, in the theological discourses of religious groups, in the interactions between different religious congregations, as well as in the intensified transnational relationships with both the Haitian diaspora and international partners. We will explore the ways in which the theological discourse of religious leaders reconciles their communities to this tragic event. Moreover, we analyze the politics of change in the relationships between the major Haitian religious traditions – Catholic, Protestant, and Vodou – since the earthquake.

In the days after the quake, discourse about the events took on a religious valence in theodicy, cause, and in the logic of response, and formed a framework of meaning-making for the catastrophe. After a tour of the city of Port-au-Prince, the teary Haitian president René Préval remarked that "the pain is too heavy; words cannot describe it." Secretary of state Hillary Clinton said "it is biblical, the tragedy that continues to haunt Haiti and the Haitian people." Many asked: "Why does God allow Haitians to suffer so?" The charitable, humanitarian response was swift: "We must respond to our neighbors in their hour of need," said President Obama, and to the people of Haiti he pronounced: "You will not be forsaken; you will not be forgotten." While Haitian families camped on the streets, sang hymns, and handed their fate over to an all-powerful God, the international community committed itself to providing funds and medical aid for Haiti.

Meanwhile, a Haitian businesswoman living in Florida agreed with Mrs. Clinton about the biblical nature of the quake. She claimed that God spoke to her and revealed that for three days on the one-month anniversary of the disaster, evangelicals were to organize a revival in the Champ de Mars park in downtown Port-au-Prince, next to the National Palace. She inspired a transnational network of Haitian, Haitian-American, U.S.-American, and Latin American evangelicals to organize a massive three-day prayer and fast which scores of thousands attended. The spectacular revival was broadcast live on Télé-Nationale d'Haïti, and millions throughout the diaspora watched through the Internet or listened by radio. The Haitian pastors imaginatively cast the earthquake in biblical imagery: the earthquake was the labor pains of a new Haiti. "We don't need a cesarean because Jesus is the doctor," said one. On the third day the pastors declared Haiti reborn. The visionary sister took to the stage to deliver the nation in a grand pronouncement: "In the name of Jesus I rebuke all evil spirits that want to stand as a barrier to the glory of God. Jesus is delivering Haiti."

Ideas connecting the Haiti quake with evil spirits circulated in the American media as well. The day after the earthquake, the televangelist and former Republican presidential candidate Pat Robertson noted on his Christian Broadcast Network show, "something happened a long time ago in Haiti, and people might not want to talk about it, but Haitians made a pact with the devil; they said, 'we will serve you if you get us free from the prince.' True story." Robertson was referring to an event said to have occurred before the Haitian Revolution in which a group of slaves met for a political rally under the cover of night in a forested place called Bwa Kayiman. They were said to have sacrificed a wild boar to their African spirits, and vowed to fight for freedom. This ceremony at Bwa Kayiman on August 14, 1791, sparked a widespread series of slave insurgencies throughout the colony, which grew into a revolutionary war that led to the departure of the French colonists and the abolition of slavery. Haiti declared its independence on January 1, 1804.

Although the ceremony at Bwa Kayiman has appeared in many written accounts, there is only tenuous historical evidence that it ever occurred. It did, however, become a well-known national myth about the slaves' agency, courage, and freedom. Robertson's statement, then, demonizes the Afro-Creole religion the revolutionary Africans would have practiced, and by extension, Haiti's cherished past. What many who heard Robertson may not have known, however, is that Robertson's views were echoing long-standing evangelical ideas about Haitian traditional culture. American and Haitian evangelicals tend to understand the spirits of Afro-Creole religion as real forces, and since they are not referenced in the Bible, they are assumed to be evil. Historically, the Christian clergy has ensured the absolute loyalty of its parishioners by invoking biblical passages saying that one cannot serve both God and Satan, and required a rejection of Vodou. For many evangelicals, the spirits at Bwa Kayiman were devils. In a paradoxical way, these evangelicals have come to see Haiti as having been enslaved by Satan in this "pact with the devil," just at the same time that it was freed from slavery through the revolution. Now the nation must be freed by and in Christ. Haitian evangelicals constitute a small but vocal minority in the Haitian social sphere and express a salvific message that is appealing to Haitian evangelical congregations at home and in the diaspora. These churches, with their transnational dimensions, are formulating a new national identity. They keep in place the nationalist story of the origin of Haiti, stemming from the Bwa Kayiman ceremony, but invest the story with new moral meanings. They are formulating new conceptions of what it is to be Haitian, and stirring up moral debates about the role of Vodou in Haiti's history. This new narrative runs through the Haitian social sphere, is taken up, debated, sometimes finding agreement, and at other times rejected.

Like Pat Robertson and the businesswoman sister who organized the downtown revival, evangelicals tended to blame the quake on the Vodou practices of their compatriots. This theological interpretation translated into a politics of righteousness in daily interactions in the city. Now that religious rituals – like all of life – were often held in the open air, the proximity of Vodou ceremonies to Protestant religious services led to charged and tense encounters. In one publicized incident, scores of evangelicals armed with rocks, sticks, and whatever they could find went to destroy ritual objects and scatter Vodouists to prevent them from "desecrating space" by "serving" their *lwa* (spirits).

Vodouists spoke out to defend their religious practices in a new way in the aftermath of the quake. Vodou had been the subject of persecution by the Church and the state in the past, and consequently had remained relatively invisible in official discourse. Now, Vodouists were unwilling to remain silent in the face of persecution. Max Beauvoir, Vodou's most vocal elder, criticized the Protestant preachers who "want to establish themselves as if they were the sole owners of the land.... They say that Jesus talks to them and tells them that Vodou is evil and should not be present in Haiti." Beauvoir noted that most American evangelical missionaries working in Haiti studied in seminaries in the southern United States where "they learned hatred and fear." He also publically criticized the distribution of charitable food aid, and claimed that evangelicals were helping converted Haitians to the exclusion of Vodou communities. He added that if Vodouists were attacked, he would advocate that they respond in the same manner. The Protestant and Catholic clergy later condemned their parishioners' behavior and admitted that one should be able to worship freely and without interference. Protected under the Haitian Constitution ratified in 1987, Vodou ceremonies were held and guarded by the police after this incident.

Beauvoir's unequivocal stance may well mark a new era in the relationship between Christianity and Vodou in Haiti. The public affirmation of the widespread presence of Vodou in Haitian society may open the possibility for religious tolerance between the members of both religious traditions.

The earthquake also changed the face of Protestantism in Haiti. It brought to the surface the millennial dimensions of its theological discourse. Often in times of extreme stress caused by disaster, and where a society lacks a strong political structure, millenarian movements may take hold, in which a people can interpret circumstances by invoking vivid images of a better world to come. Charismatic leaders or prophets often arise; they are regarded by their followers as shepherds whose task is to lead them into the New Jerusalem, a heavenly city where all who are saved will be liberated from evil and the fallibility of sin. Millenarian movements regard the world as evil and believe that the final end will consist of cataclysmic events ushered in by supernatural forces that will destroy the world. During a service held on Maundy Thursday, a self-proclaimed evangelical preacher named Guibert Valcin stood before an open area filled with hundreds of tents and announced that Jesus was coming soon and that the devastation caused by the quake was merely a sign of the end. "Everywhere you go, you need Jesus. Jesus is all the power.... Vodou can't take you to heaven, only God can. Jesus when he comes one day, he won't come to save the Vodouists. He will save only those who serve God."

The millenarian vision of a heavenly paradise transforms calamities into sacred events. The vivid image of a transformed and perfect world would explain why so many have flocked to the Protestant services since the earthquake to hear the ministers' homilies and be converted. A Baptist pastor in the Pétionville suburb of Port-au-Prince noted that after the earthquake more than 200 people came to his church to be saved. "God struck the country and they have come to make peace that they be taken in rapture with the Lord in heaven," he said. This message grants believers a sense of hope that God will look upon them with favor as they are ushered into the "heavenly kingdom."

In contrast to the evangelicals' visions of heaven, Vodou's theological teachings offer no such comfort about the afterlife. Indeed, its notion of what happens after death is ambiguous. While its theology varies by region, there is a general scheme. The body contains a spirit that is constituted by two parts characterized by their separate psychic functions. In some ways, the Vodou notion of the compartmentalized self is analogous to psychological descriptions of the divisions of the human psyche. The first compartment of the soul is the manifestation of the Godhead in the body; it is known as the *gwo-bon-anj* (literally, the big-good-angel), which is thought to be the root of being, the inner principle that is manifestation of the divine. The *ti-bon-anj* (literally, little-good-angel) is the personality of the individual, the conscience and the moral side of one's character. It is that which distinguishes between positive and destructive behavior.

At death, both compartments of the self leave the body and enter two separate abodes. The *ti-bon-anj* enters heaven and the *gwo-bon-anj* floats to Ginen, the underworld where the spirits of the dead reside. Vodou's teaching about these ethereal worlds varies. No one is sure what happens to the *ti-bon-anj* once it rises to its celestial abode. Likewise, Vodouists are not certain about the exact location of Ginen. Some say that it is at the bottom of the sea while others picture it deep in the navel of the earth. Still others say that it lies in a past, mythical Africa. Ginen is the home of the dead but, unlike the Haitian evangelicals, Vodouists believe that whatever happens there should be nobody's business, and no one should even conjecture about it.

While most evangelical Protestants saw the quake as part of God's plan, many who "serve the spirits," as Vodouists describe their practice, were less sure of the cosmic significance of the disaster. The spirits are perceived as both afflicting and protecting, and many people were cautious about communicating with the spirit realm to learn why the country had been hit so hard. Some were unable to discern a theological answer for such suffering, and felt abandoned by their protector guides. One Vodou priest, Erol Josue, interpreted the quake as a natural and spiritual result of the mistreatment of the land. He explained that as a mystic, he reads the world symbolically. "The land in Haiti is a person," he said. "We consider it a woman, our mother." *Haïti Chérie*, as the well-known ballad goes. "She wants to know, 'who will make me beautiful, put clothes on me, and take care of my children?' When you mistreat her, and uproot her trees, when you give her too much responsibility, she is like a woman with cancer. The tumor metastasizes, and explodes." For Josué, the earthquake was Mother Nature, the land of Haiti, rising up to defend herself against the erosion, deforestation, and environmental devastation that have been ongoing for centuries.

The Roman Catholic Church was also profoundly hurt by the disaster. This institution historically has been the official religion of the majority of the population, typically in a creolized symbiosis with Vodou. The grand Notre Dame Cathedral collapsed, as did 60 parish churches. More than 100 priests and nuns were killed. There was much confusion, and there were too many dying even to offer the sacrament of the last rites. Roman Catholics searched for God's purpose for the quake just as evangelicals and Vodouists did. Consistent with the teachings of the Church, Catholics struggled to resign themselves to the idea that the earthquake was a mystery known only to God. In some parishes, Catholic pastors led their congregations to consider God's mercy, even in the face of such devastation. Some pastors counseled that God's plan for the world can be found in the community's prayerful reflection on God's clemency on the souls of the living and the dead. One priest said in his sermon, "Our God is a God of mercy. He is not a God who punishes his children. And God does not inflict harm on his children." Other priests reached for scientific reasoning, as the Catholic priests are the nation's primary educators and run most of the schools in the country. "We tried to give some light to the Haitian people about the meaning of what happened. We asked the people to understand how the world works and to understand the laws of physics," said Professor of Liberation Theology William Smart to reporters, sitting in front of his cracked home.

In the face of the enormous struggle to aid survivors, Catholic leaders did not view open-air Vodou ceremonies as a problem worth discussing after the quake. If the Catholic reactions to the Vodou ceremonies have not been as quarrelsome as those of the Protestants, it is because today the Church has learned to coexist with Vodou. Evangelical Protestantism is relatively new to Haiti and dates back to the late nineteenth and early twentieth centuries. Catholicism however, has entrenched itself in Haitian society for over three hundred years and its relatively peaceful relationship with Vodou has been forged gradually over recent decades.

Originating in various parts of West Africa, Vodou was brought to the island during the slave trade (1510–1804). During that time Catholic missionaries worked to extricate it from colonial life and convert the slaves to Christianity, and legally forbade its practice. To circumvent the officious interference of the missionaries in their rituals, the slaves learned to overlay their Vodou practices with portions of the Catholic liturgy and the use of Catholic symbols in their rituals. Embarrassed by the encroachment of "pagan" traditions on its theology, the Catholic Church cooperated with the Haitian government to conduct "Anti-superstition Campaigns" in the 1940s by which Vodou temples (ounfos) and their ritual objects were burned. By the 1960s, following the global movement to indigenize the Catholic religion, the church "haitianized" the liturgy of the Mass with a local, Afro-Creole flavor. Hence, Vodou intermixes Afro-Creole and Catholic traditions, and Vodouists practice two religions simultaneously and give their allegiance to both. Said a Vodou priest (oungan), "you have to be a good Catholic to serve the lwa." In the face of such a terrible disaster, and unlike the Protestants, the Catholic-Vodouist population received no revelation that would point to blame, and no cause for theological strife.

The story of religion after the Haiti earthquake extends well beyond Haiti itself. While the Haitian people struggled to understand the cosmic meaning of the disaster, and some evangelicals named Vodou in a theological politics of blame, religious organizations around the world launched a massive relief effort. The vast Haitian diaspora population tends to maintain close ties to the homeland through village associations and churches, and numerous radio stations operate internationally via short wave and the Internet. Diasporic Haitians mobilized immediately to volunteer in Haiti and bring supplies. Many other organizations abroad were already in relationships with Haitians in Haiti. Hundreds of American Catholic parishes are "twinned" with parishes in Haiti, and Protestant congregations likewise have established "sister churches" across the hemisphere. The Church of Seventh-day Adventists, operating in Haiti since 1904, ran a hospital, a water purification plant, and a radio station. Some said that in the vast suburb called Carrefour, the Adventists had more of a presence than the government.

These religious organizations operating in Haiti form part of the "Republic of NGOs," the nickname coined to signal the fact that there are more non-governmental organizations per capita in Haiti than almost anywhere else in the world – ten thousand groups, according to the World Bank. Groups with a longstanding presence in the country were themselves affected by the disaster, but were generally able to recuperate, respond, and draw on their international resources.

Other religious relief groups mobilized within days, including Catholic Relief Services, American Jewish World Service, Presbyterians, Lutherans, and Baptists. Islamic Relief USA teamed up with the Church of Jesus Christ of Latter-day Saints – the Mormons – to send supplies. Samaritan's Purse, the Billy Graham Rapid Response Team, and Scientologists were all visible. However, a lack of coordination hampered the effectiveness of relief aid, and older groups were critical of new groups for not collaborating with more established missions that would stay in Haiti long-term. And for Christian groups, the politics of salvation created some tensions amidst the already difficult conditions. Said Jonathan J. Bonk, of the Overseas Mission Study Center in New Haven: "The new or short-term groups see themselves as being there to save souls first and lives second. The older, less conservative missions often see it the other way around."

As virtually every church in the hemisphere took up contributions for Haiti and prayed for the suffering victims, attention focused on the most innocent of all: the orphans. Orphans are named in many religious traditions as those most vulnerable and most deserving of charity. A media circus focused on ten Americans, most of them Baptist missionaries, arrested for trying to take 33 Haitian children out of the country without proper documentation. The scandal that ensued when the children were found not to be orphans at all underscored the vulnerability of Haiti's poorest sufferers, and raised fraught questions about the involvement of international religious groups.

Religious dynamics have played a complex role in the aftermath of the terrible quake in Haiti. Haitians have drawn on revelation, prayer, and religious meaning-making to keep body and soul together and to make sense of their suffering. Groups have banded together by congregation in encampments to become mutual-aid societies of spiritual and material support and protection. Some have blamed others for causing the quake through their worship of "false idols." Globally, religious groups have responded with religiously motivated compassion and charity. Organizations have moved to deliver the relief, aid, and ministry they perceive is God's will, some envisioning themselves "to be the hands of Jesus." In the medium- and long-term, it will take a sustained effort to coordinate relief and aid, and transform them into systems and structures that will support the self-empowerment of Haitians on the ground.

*The authors derived their information from telephone conversations with sources in Haiti as well as these news stories:

Jacqueline Charles and Trenton Daniel. "As Unity Unravels, a Battle for Haitian Souls Is Stirring." *Miami Herald*. April 12, 2010.

Paisley Dodds. "Haitians Hold Day of Mourning on Quake Anniversary." *Huffington Post*. February 12, 2010.

Marc Lacey and Ian Urbina. "Missionaries Go to Haiti, Followed by Scrutiny." *New York Times*. February 15, 2010.

Elizabeth McAlister. "Why Does Haiti Suffer So Much?" CNN.com. January 18, 2010.

Elizabeth McAlister. "Voodoo's View of the Quake." *Newsweek/On Faith*. January 15, 2010

Katie Paul. "Churches Respond: How Religious Organizations Are Helping in Haiti." *Newsweek*. January 15, 2010.

M. J. Smith. "Tensions Mount in Haiti After Voodoo Ceremony Attack." *Montreal Gazette*. February 25, 2010.

May 2010

12

Shaken Ground, Strong Foundations: Honoring the Legacy of Haitian Feminism after the Earthquake

Régine Michelle Jean-Charles

Anacaona – the Arawak queen who fought against the Spaniards when they arrived on the island in the fifteenth century. Catherine Flon – who sewed together the flag to create an enduring symbol of Haitian resistance to the French army during the revolution. Défilée – who gathered the scattered bones of revolutionary hero Jean-Jacques Dessalines. These are the names of some of Haitian history's best-known fallen heroines. They are foremothers of a matriarchal lineage that exudes endurance, resilience, and resistance.

Since the earthquake of 2010, in which over 200,000 people lost their lives, more names have been added to this Haitian heritage of female leadership. Alongside the countless numbers of women and girls, three extraordinary *fanm poto mitan,* pillars of the Haitian women's movement, were killed in the earthquake. Magalie Marcelin, Myriam Merlet, and Anne-Marie Coriolan: each one pioneering advocates on behalf of Haiti's women and girls. Understanding the impact of their deaths, remembering their important contributions, and honoring their ancestral feminist spirits means considering the gendered implications of the earthquake from multiple perspectives and ensuring that their memory, their work, and their passions are not forgotten.

Following in the footsteps of ancestors like Anacaona, Catherine Flon, and Défilée, these women entered into a lineage of women's activism that goes back to the pre-revolutionary period. The origins of the formal Haitian women's movement can be traced to the 1930s and the activities of the Feminine League for Social Action, which fought for equal voting rights, among other causes. However, women have been working at the grassroots level since before the Haitian Revolution. Merlet, Coriolan, and Marceline exemplified the type of feminist activism that has occurred at different levels of society and across class boundaries, through grassroots- and government-institutionalized approaches.

The Feminist Legacy: Myriam Merlet, Magalie Marcelin, and Anne-Marie Coriolan

Myriam Merlet was an ardent political activist. She contributed significantly to the "second wave" of Haiti's feminist movement during the 1990s.
Merlet served as the chief of staff for the Ministry on the Status and Rights
of Women, created under the presidency of Jean-Bertrand Aristide in 1994.
She was also the founder of the National Coordination for Advocacy on
Women's Rights (CONAP), which encompassed the efforts of numerous
organizations. Merlet also founded Enfofanm, an organization promoting
women's rights through the media that served as an information clearing-
house on women's issues. Merlet was also responsible for establishing in
Port-au-Prince the first V-Day Sorority Safe House for female survivors of
violence in 2001, the same year that *The Vagina Monologues* was performed
in the country for the first time.

Merlet was best known as the founder of these important organizations, but she was also a feminist scholar. In 2002, she published *La participation politique des femmes en Haïti: quelques éléments d'analyse*, a study on
women's political involvement in Haiti. In her writing, as in her political
work, she expressed her longing for women's participation in political
processes at all levels of society. In Beverly Bell's *Walking On Fire: Haitian
Women's Stories of Survival and Resistance*, she writes that "one should be
able to realize and express one's full potential and not only one's social
condition." Merlet encouraged an all-encompassing, critically grounded
approach to feminist activism, and argued that women's organizations
should not only complain about issues, but understand their root causes.
She embodied this philosophy through her own work and life.

Magalie Marcelin used her public profile to promote women's rights as
a fundamental part of human rights across Haiti. She was the founder of
Kay Fanm, the only shelter for victims of gender-based violence in Haiti.
Her work as a human rights attorney was instrumental in addressing legal
aspects of gender inequality in Haiti. For example, she worked on cases
involving women survivors of rape and domestic abuse and was instrumental in criminalizing rape. Through the creation of Kay Fanm, Marcelin
not only established a safe haven for survivors of sexual and domestic
violence, but she also helped these women initiate steps towards healing
and economic independence through the microloan program. Kay Fanm
worked in four major areas: support and rehabilitation for victims of
assault; promotion of women's rights; protection of democracy; and assistance in income generation for and by women.

Marcelin also used the transcendent power of the arts to advocate for human rights issues. As a performer, actress, storyteller, and comedian she appeared in local programs and events that consistently used culture to tell the stories of disenfranchised members of the Haitian society. Through roles such as that of the protagonist in *Anita* (1980), a film about a girl working as a *restavek*, she used her artistic skills to spread awareness of gender and social issues. The power of Marcelin's contribution lies in her ability to change the terms relating to gender equity and the relevance of women's rights in Haitian society through using a multimedia approach. Magalie Marcelin's investment in theater served her well in the judicial system, and helped her understand the power of performative presence. In one memorable instance, recalled by Haitian sociologist Carolle Charles, Marcelin arranged for a large group of Haitian women to be present in the courtroom during the trial of a political figure accused of domestic violence. Marcelin was not only a pioneer in the courtroom, advocating for rape victims and providing expert testimony for them, but she was also a founder of twenty-first-century feminism, fusing new technologies and artistic endeavors to create social change.

Anne-Marie Coriolan was the founder of Solidarité Fanm Ayisyen (SOFA), one of the country's largest women's advocacy groups. SOFA marshaled the efforts of groups working for women's rights throughout the country. This collaborative, collective vision helped to foster solidarity and to avoid the organizational shortcomings of non-profit organizations and NGOs, which generally lack transparency.

SOFA, Kay Fanm, CONAP, and Enfofanm are remarkable institutions, through which these women helped to advance important feminist agendas that addressed the needs of Haitian women and girls. These groups had a distinctively feminist ethos, fighting for social justice, gender equity, and conceiving alternative models of power. The loss of these women, each one a champion of human rights and fiercely committed to the equality and protection of Haiti's female population, is enormous. The effects will be felt among feminist activists on the ground in Haiti, among scholars working on gender and feminist issues in Haiti (the ministry headquarters completely collapsed in the quake), and it will certainly be felt among the women and girls throughout the country who benefited from the tireless activism of these women.

The loss should prompt us to consider how gender inequalities are playing out in the wake of the earthquake. How can we apply the philosophy they espoused and the lessons they taught us to some of the post-earthquake dynamics in Haiti? To remember the significance of their work, their heart's passion for the gender issues, is to pay close attention to what the earthquake has meant and will mean for Haitian women and girls.

Post-earthquake Gender-Specific Needs

Humanitarian crises usually have calamitous gender-specific results that disproportionately affect women and girls. Natural disasters are certainly no exception. In the aftermath of the earthquake, hundreds of thousands of people were left dead, injured, homeless, and jobless. The circumstances under which many Haitians in Port-au-Prince, Léogâne, Jacmel, Petit Goâve, and surrounding areas have had to live since the earthquake present unique challenges to women and girls that must be addressed in relief efforts, recovery programs, and the reconstruction of the state.

Studies have demonstrated that disaster significantly exacerbates existing inequalities, which is why women and girls have been particularly vulnerable since the earthquake. Take, for example, how gender introduces distinct health-related needs. According to the United Nations about 63,000 women are currently pregnant in Haiti, which, prior to the earthquake had one of the highest maternal mortality rates in the world. These women and the children they bear will require prenatal, labor and delivery, and postnatal care in the imminent future. How will such care be distributed? Will these women's concerns be taken into consideration given all of the pressing medical needs of the country? Likewise, nursing mothers are particularly susceptible to malnutrition and dehydration, which could lead to further mortalities. What other public health issues with gender ramifications are emerging as a result of the earthquake?

On the one hand, as journalist and activist Liliane Pierre-Paul has remarked, women mobilized and displayed extraordinary strength and solidarity in the initial moments after the earthquake. In the immediate rescue period, or first phase of the earthquake response, women and girls were quite visible, being pulled out of rubble, proclaiming the faith that helped them through, and flashing smiles of survival in the face of international news agency cameras that seemed to be omnipresent. They were seen in captivating scenes of hope, marching through the street singing songs of encouragement. However as time went on, concerns mounted about how the effects of gender inequality would translate into the aftermath of the earthquake. Disparities in the distribution of aid, for example, put women and girls at greater risk during humanitarian crises. While the remarkable patience of the Haitian community, many members of whom went days without food or water, must be noted, in the event of food riots women and girls would be more likely to suffer. In those situations, the dominant rule is survival of the fittest; the stronger and faster you are the more likely you are to get food. What would happen to the women and girls scrambling for sustenance in uncontrolled crowds?

Following the rescue stage, homelessness resulting from the earthquake poses unique challenges to women exposed under tents that afford little protection for vulnerable populations. There is a dire need for protection and security for those sleeping in the open whose gender puts them more at risk of sexual assault and predatory advances. The high rates of violence against women that activists such as Merlet and Marcelin worked assiduously to address, prevent, and reduce, further underscore these security risks. In one study conducted by Kay Fanm, it was estimated that 72 percent of Haitian girls have been raped and 40 percent of women were victims of domestic violence. How many more must now be added to this number since January 12? While no statistical information is yet available there have been widespread reports of how sexual violence has spiraled since the quake, and of the especially high incidence of rape in the tent cities. How can Haitians, who have exhibited solidarity and organized mobility in response to the catastrophic circumstances surrounding them, effectively tackle gender inequality in a manner worthy of the Merlet, Marcelin, and Coriolan legacy?

A few programs have attempted to meet some of these needs. The United Nations Population Fund very recently implemented the distribution of emergency medical packs for pregnant women. Likewise, the establishment of a coupon system for food that specifically targets women has been created by a coalition that includes the World Food Program and World Vision. The Haitian minister of women's affairs, Marjorie Michel, also recently announced a "cash for work" program that 100,000 women living in camps will participate in. While we have yet to see the results of these new measures, they do point to the possibility for positive transformation. The next step must be assistance programs that not only meet their needs, but also provide opportunities for advancement and self-empowerment. However, within a few days of announcing the programs, there were already reports of women being attacked and robbed for their food coupons. Continued reports suggest that in comparison to the collectives organized by women themselves, these programs have offered little success.

Perhaps the most important contribution will come from women working collectively and organizing on a grassroots level as Merlet, Marcelin, and Coriolan did before them. Grassroots organizations such as KOFAVIV, the Commission of Victim-to-Victim Advocacy, have had more success in protecting women and girls. KOFAVIV is an organization made up of survivors of the rampant sexual violence that took place during years of political unrest. These survivors now work together to protect and advocate for victims of violence. According to one group leader, Delva Marie Eramithe, the situation in the tent cities has made the work of KOFAVIV all the more essential. Even now in the tent cities, such as one in the Champ de Mars, members of KOFAVIV watch over the tents in the night, helping to protect potential victims. KOFAVIV's endeavors actively demonstrate that the approach Merlet espoused, one that includes bottom-up organizing among ordinary women, is the best approach in bringing about change.

It is true that the earthquake in Haiti did not discriminate based on class, race, gender, or ethnicity. Members of the MINUSTAH perished along-side those who worked for meager wages in the Hotel Montana. However, the realities of class and gender inequality make it such that women, and especially poor women, will have to take longer strides and go a further distance to be brought back to where they were prior to the earthquake. Furthermore, given the link between violence against women and poverty, there should be increased concern for women in Haiti whose race, class, and gender situate them at the nexus of multiple oppressions. Supporting women's organizations and increasing educational opportunities for girls are two important areas that should come with the reconstruction of the Haitian state and that will help to begin to address gender inequality.

The magnitude of brutalities against women and girls all over the globe reveals that this sad fact of life is not only particular to Haiti. While in recent years strides have been made to acknowledge that gender-based violence should be considered a human rights violation, the extent of violence against women in developing and developed countries remains staggering. One out of every three women in the world will be sexually or physically assaulted in her lifetime. The global response to this devastation in Haiti presents an opportunity to include gender-specific analysis and application to humanitarian projects.

Rebuilding Haiti through Solidarity with Women

Placing women at the center of rebuilding programs in Haiti will offer opportunities to address the oppression of women in the developing nation. Rebuilding should draw upon successful endeavors that concen-trate on women and girls, such as microfinance loan opportunities or environmental tree-planting movements, both models that speak to the significance of gender in sustainable development. Relief organizations have to take gender into account as they assess the immediate needs, as must Haitians themselves. They can begin to do so by taking on the causes that were so dear to Merlet and her colleagues as well as championing education for girls, gender equity at all levels of society, and refusing to accept gender violence as a quotidian way of life.

The introduction of I-VAWA, the International Violence against Women Act, into both the U.S. House and Senate a few weeks after the earthquake, further suggests that this is an apt time to consider how U.S. involvement in humanitarian relief can help address and eventually end violence against women. I-VAWA includes strategies for helping international assistance programs to address the needs of women in general and violence against women in particular. The humanitarian agenda in Haiti must include similar attention and sensitivity to the specific needs of women and girls.

Ubiquitous narratives of strength have characterized the contributions of Haitian women from as early as the fifteenth century. They are described popularly as women who walk on fire. They are lauded as *poto mitan*, the pillars of society. In Haitian literature, the resilience of Haitian women has been captured, whether in the defiant resistance of Claire, the protagonist of Marie Vieux Chauvet's *Amour*, who has the courage to kill the local *Tonton Macoute* when no one in the town dare defy him, or the quiet strength of Annalise in Jacques Roumain's *Gouverneurs de la Rosée*, who is left to carry on her husband's legacy. However, these enduring portraits of strength can have a counter effect of dehumanizing the female subject they seek to empower. This type of devaluation is evident in how Rose, the protagonist of Chauvet's *Colère*, who is held captive and raped for a period of fifteen days, comes to be seen as a martyr rather than a victim of rape. Understanding the effects of the earthquake and considering its future implications for women provides an opportunity to complicate our understanding of the foundation of Haitian women's advocacy. The losses endured from the catastrophe, and the possibilities it presents for the future require us to mourn the loss of these leaders and look for ways in which to continue their work. Edwidge Danticat dedicated *Breath, Eyes, Memory* to the brave women of Haiti; as she writes, "we have stumbled, but we have not fallen." We can understand the loss of Merlet, Marcelin, and Coriolan in similar terms; it is a stumble but not a fall for the Haitian women's movement. The tradition of women's advocacy continues through organizations such as KOFAVIV, CONAP, SOFA, Kay Fanm and Enfofanm, and through their commemoration of the lost leaders. Rather than simply viewing these women's deaths as a loss for the movement, feminists in Haiti are honoring the legacy of their leadership by continuing the work. Myriam Merlet once wrote,

> I look at things through the eyes of women, very conscious of the roles, limitations, and stereotypes imposed on us. Everything I do is informed by that consciousness. So I want to get to a different concept and application of power than the one that keeps women from attaining their full potential.... The basis of my work with women is to open them up to other things, give them new tools, give them new capabilities ... give women the opportunity to grow.

The work of Haitian women on the ground since the earthquake demonstrates that in fact these tools are being utilized; growth opportunities are being created, and new capabilities are being formed.

The best way to honor the legacy of our fallen Haitian feminist trailblazers will be to rebuild in a way that includes gender equity, to reconstruct institutions that assist the development of women and girls, and to provide more educational opportunities and resources for women and girls to become agents of transformation. These are girls like the one mentioned in a recent *Miami Herald* article, who stated that she was eager to get back to school and when asked why responded, "because my country is broke and I want to fix it." Indeed, investing in the potential and the projects of girls and women will have longstanding beneficial effects for the entire country. "Only a mountain can crush a Haitian woman," asserts the protagonist of *Breath, Eyes, Memory*. Incorporating gender perspectives into the rebuilding efforts would mean remembering that Haitian women did not fall into the earthquake's cracks, and understanding that they are just as instrumental as they have been historically and will continue to be in the future, as *fanm poto mitan*.

An original version of this article was published under the title, "Cracks of Gender Inequality: Haitian Women after the Earthquake" in "Haiti: Then and Now" by the Social Science Research Council. Special thanks to SSRC President Craig Calhoun for requesting the original essay, and to Paul Price for editing.

March 2010

13

Art, Artists, and the Shaking
of the Foundations

LeGrace Benson

Unspeakable. Giving voice to it, a father keens over the body of his little girl. Unimaginable. A BBC photographer cannot feel anything: it is like looking at movie that will not end – unreal. Haitian photographer Danny Morel stands in the street: "I cannot believe what I am seeing. I cannot believe this." An architect finally reached when the cell phones are working again said,

> I was right there a few hundred yards from the National Palace and it was unimaginable. We would try to run outside and the floor would come up to meet us. Finally we got out. I am back here now. I see the rooms we sat in open to the sky and resting over rubble and underneath the dead. It is unimaginable.

A woman cradles a forelimb in her arms. "I hold on to this," she moans. "This is all I have left of my child." Far away in Cap Haïtien, Bertelus Myrbel goes into a dream. He has lost a cousin. He has to do something. He paints three scenes of Port-au-Prince tumbled into pandemonium. Still and silent, the three canvases come out to show those outside the dream and outside Haiti that the event is terrible beyond imagining. People who have been inside a war would understand.

It had happened before, but long ago. In Cap Haïtien, situated athwart another of Haiti's tectonic fault lines, the Cathedral of Our Lady of the Assumption, newly sanctified in consequence of the Concordat with the Church at Rome, crashed in 1860 along with most of the houses and many of the public buildings. In the previous century there had been three: in 1751, 1761, and 1770. Uprisings that led to the open revolution of 1791 eerily track these dates, beginning with François Makandal's proto-revolution of 1751. Earlier, Louis XIV had authorized the French slave trade in 1670 and by 1685 was obliged to sign the Code Noir with its strictures against the most heinous abuses. In between there were two earthquakes, 1673 and 1684, devastating some plantations and thus reducing economic gains.

87

Even minor constraints against brutality in the Code Noir were ignored in the interest of restoring profitability. By 1697 slaves imitated a revolt. Small and failed for the moment, it was sign of things to come: Makandal's Revolt and the ultimately successful efforts of Toussaint and Dessalines.

The 1770 quake wrenched the ground along the same fault line of the 2010 event, running through Port-au-Prince east to west. Haitian historian Thomas Madiou wrote that the tremor leveled the entire city and afterwards the surviving population pitched tents and scrambled for food and water, a description befitting January 2010. Thus ever and always: an unwitting partnership of earth and a tacit socio-economic contract that elevates a natural disaster into unspeakable human tragedy.

In those distant years there were artists, writers, and musicians among the population of African and Afro-Creole slaves and free coloreds, some of them trained in Paris or Rome, and in service to or economically tied to French colonists. Almost out of sight in the slave quarters and in the nearly impenetrable backcountry, the blacks were creating graphic arts, an oraliture, and a music binding the homelands to the new lands. European observers would disdain these as barbaric expressions. Only under pressure of the U.S. occupation of 1915–1934 and the rise of a new consciousness in Haiti and the wider Caribbean would these "barbaric" Creole expressions emerge into public acclaim. Illustrious dancers, musicians, and visual artists would come to Haiti in the 1940s and 1950s to study this Afro-Creole heritage. The Centre d'Art opened in 1944 and by 1948 the Kreyòl-speaking painters and sculptors would garner international praise. More importantly: artists and latent artists all over Haiti began bringing their works to the Centre, galleries opened, and the streets of Haitian port cities were festooned and muraled with thousands of landscapes, depictions of Vodou *lwa* and ceremonies, market scenes, and beautiful women. The Pearl of the Antilles became its art center.

The day after the earthquake, journalists already there or converging upon a newsworthy horror began to report from Port-au-Prince, Léogâne, and Jacmel. One of those already present and familiar with the country for years related her astonishment as she went through the streets and into the emerging tent cities:

> I couldn't believe it! I tried to get some pictures as we drove by. When we were walking on the street between Comité Artisanal and another gallery we saw this guy sitting there on the sidewalk with all these paintings rolled up. As I eyed his stack he unrolled them and showed me some of what he had.

Art vendor unrolling paintings. Photograph by Tequila Minsky

Tequila Minsky continued,

and when we were driving by one of the tent cities a day or so later I noticed people had their paintings beside the doors. A couple of days after that, driving on that same major artery, there were paintings strung up on the fence that separated the tent city from the street. And there was a house with paintings for sale. It looked like they had already organized a "gallery" and were in business.

Frantz Zéphirin threw his distress and energy into ten paintings, one boiling into visibility after another. A work of his from the 2008 hurricanes was featured on the cover of the *New Yorker*. He depicted the rushing waters rising toward an open door. Every stone of the house is a staring, open-mouthed face. In the door are three skeletons clothed in nineteenth-century garments – the *Gede*, those powerful spirits who guide the living into the land of the ancestors. It was the artist's response to the four hurricanes of 2008, but it fit the new disaster all too well.

Trauma is intolerable. It hastens to sink down below the level of awareness so that one can keep going, keep living. It abides there, perhaps uttered in unrecognized ways as ordinary as snapping at a spouse or child, or as an ever-deepening depression. Sometimes it bides time like the tectonic plates underfoot, straining into a pressure that must be released. The television images of the quake disturbed a woman's dark memory. "I was in the San Francisco quake of 1989," she said, her voice catching in her throat. "I still have nightmares. It was almost twenty years ago." Old ceremonies, songs, and dances help in such circumstances. They can charge the familiar rituals, the singing and dancing, with the task of articulating the burden of inchoate fear. Artists, musicians, poets, dancers, players, and filmmakers offer double assistance, in that they have the ability to eject their own mute and invisible dread into a calculated and tolerable sound and fury and thus provide viewers and listeners with a vicarious release from the terror.

As dark fell on the first wretched night, Richard Morse stood on the porch of his Oloffson Hotel, the historic gingerbread confection miraculously intact while all above and below was in shambles. In the yard a few journalists already in Haiti slept on the ground like everyone else. From the ruins beyond the enclosure came singing. The profundities of trauma found place and voice to call on God's mercy against inexplicable chthonic forces. The members of Morse's musical group had all survived and were out there somewhere in the singing darkness doing whatever needed to be done.

While Haitians at the scene went into action immediately, those at some remove began to respond. A woman in London, just returned from Haiti before the quake, was troubled that she could feel nothing but a programmatic cliché of sympathy. As she crossed Embankment Bridge,

Partially fallen house with art for sale. Photograph by Tequila Minsky

for no apparent reason at all she began to sob and sob and sob. She kept walking slowly, shaking, glad that urban folk mostly ignore the faces of passersby. The British artists who had recently exulted in the success of the Ghetto Biennale held in Port-au-Prince were planning a gathering to celebrate. The celebration turned into a wake. They knew that one of the Atis Rezistans, Louko, of the Grand Rue, was dead under a collapsed roof. They knew that Reggie Jean François, managing artisan for the Brandaid group in the Cité Soleil district, had survived but had spent a wretchedly sorrowful day trying to remove the bodies of his apprentices from under lethal rubble. They heard news that Flo McGarrell from Vermont, who had participated in the Biennale, was setting up an art center in Jacmel and mentoring students in the film program. Flo was at the computers in a hotel when the building buckled and fell to earth. The British group collected funds to enable one artist to go back to the site of the Biennale. She would assess the damage, participate in the salvage and safekeeping of art works, and provide food and medical assistance for the downtown community (or *lakou*) closely associated with the artists. A radio talk show planned as a report on the Ghetto Biennale became a fundraiser that then took on a formal status as Foundry Fund/Haiti. They brought one of the artists to London to spark a campaign to restore the Grand Rue community.

The Ghetto Biennale was conceived of by artists who consciously utilized the detritus of "First World" consumer products dumped in Haiti – old vehicles of every sort, old clothing and shoes ("Why do they think Haitians can use winter boots?"), used oil drums, salvaged lumber, and wire. One of them explained that they recycle anything into something new. He pointed out that the only local material is human skeletons. There will many of these now. And the reason for their incorporation into the sculptures and tableaus of the Atis Rezistans of Grand Rue remains unchanged. The artists honor the deceased with the ceremonial feeding that precedes use in the art works, and thus respect their presence as ancestors. To be in the artwork is, as one artist explained, "to set them on another life journey, and maybe this one will be better than the one they had." It is a recycling in the sense of the great wheel of incarnation and reincarnation. On January 12 the quake destroyed the studios and the art class space for the youngsters of the *lakou.* It buried Louko, whose portrait had been on the entrance to the festival of art. Already they are rebuilding. The children are learning reading, writing, arithmetic, and how to make art from the shards and pieces of disaster. The artist who went to England is back at the site on Grand Rue, recycling trauma into regenerated art and community.

In what may be one of the most active turnovers of art ever, many paintings, sculptures, and craftworks have been on the auction blocks to benefit Haiti. Auctions are happening in Canada, the United Kingdom, France, Germany, the United States, Venezuela, Trinidad, Cuba, Ireland, and other countries. The visual arts of Haiti are in the public awareness as never before, even more so than in the 1950s, when there were exhibitions in Paris and New York. In those years viewers were largely an art market public. Today the work is in the eye of anyone who pays attention to the news or to his or her local church and civic association activities.

The music too has a broader audience now and a wider scope, in that Haitian music today ranges from classical concerts by survivors of the Sainte-Trinité school of music, Pentecostal gospel choirs in Brooklyn and Philadelphia, RAM roots music, Boukman Eksperyans, to music and dance groups such as Troupe Makandal from New York. The day before the quake, RAM musicians were recording the rehearsal for 2010 Karnaval. The name of the song was premonitory: "Earthquake." Now the recording is under debris. The new version is to debut at the first post-quake performance in April. The musicians all survived and on the evening after the quake set the music aside for the rescue effort. Other local groups did likewise. Lolo Beaubrun's Boukman Eksperyans wrote new songs, and played these along with some old ones in a memorial concert held in the garden of their home. Makandal members went to Haiti from New York as soon as possible to put a school back in operation and set up shelter tents for families.

While there the Troupe made music with a local group in some buildings that were still habitable. Such actions continue to be evident. In the meantime the songs everyone knew rose up in spontaneous chorus all over Port-au-Prince and Léogâne. These are actions where the diaspora, friends of Haiti, and quake survivors are working hand in hand now and for the foreseeable future, using long, long musical traditions to create new compositions for raising up a new Haiti.

Visual artists and collections in Port-au-Prince suffered incalculable losses. The Roman Catholic Cathedral of Notre Dame instantly looked like the ruins of Tintern Abbey, its priceless stained glass in shards. Stained glass artist and photographer, Kesler Pierre, grew up in Port-au-Prince but now lives in the United States. He immediately went to Haiti to begin a restoration process. An article in the *New York Times* on January 15 headlines Pierre's work: "The Spirit of Port-au-Prince, Now Broken." This can only refer to the glass. Pierre's presence signifies unbroken spirit.

The renowned murals of the Episcopal Sainte-Trinité Cathedral suffered nearly total annihilation. Philomé Obin's *Crucifixion*, Castera

Bertelus Myrbel, *Earthquake*, January 2010. Photograph by Jon Reis

Bazile's *Ascension*, Rigaud Benoit's *Nativity*, and Gabriel Lévêque's *Angels* in the apse around the main altar disintegrated into colored powders. Wilson Bigaud's *Marriage at Cana* returned to dust along with the murals of T. Auguste, Préfèt Duffaut, and Adam Leontus. Patrimony is held in high regard by most Haitians, so no one was surprised to learn that a group had made special efforts to prevent bulldozers from demolishing the remains before rescue and preservation efforts could begin.

The Centre d'Art where the Creole artworks began their journey into world attention collapsed almost completely. With the aftershocks still quivering, those who knew that some of the national art treasures might still be intact risked their lives to bring them out and pack them into the trucks and vans that would take them to safe storage. The Musée de l'Art Haïtien had withstood the earthquake better, and rescuers immediately went in to salvage treasures. Axell Liautaud held Wilson Bigaud's *Earthly Paradise*, while a *New York Times* photographer took a picture that would bring grateful tears to many. But close by, the Fondation Création collapsed completely with unknown losses. The collection of Issa ElSaieh, whose art gallery was the first to open after the initial success of the Centre d'Art, remained sturdy through the quake, as did the nearby Oloffson Hotel in all its gingerbread glory and its collection of paintings and Vodou flags. But farther up the hill the priceless private collection of George Nader, whose gallery had opened almost as soon as Issa's, was a catastrophe. Nader's son John, photographed in the process of rescuing as much as possible, spoke of several thousand works, many of them now lost or damaged beyond repair. These were the classic works of the artists from the period Selden Rodman called "The Haitian Renaissance." Although privately held, most were on public view and part of public heritage. Many were relieved to see Marianne Lehmann on the Internet rejoicing that a miracle had happened. Buildings all around her had crumbled but the invaluable collection of Vodou religious art in the Fondation pour la Préservation, la Valorisation, et la Production d'Œuvres Culturelles Haïtiennes (FVPOCH) survived. Nearby, the Nader sales gallery also remained standing and the works unharmed. But several galleries, artists' studios, and homes sustained damage, ranging from serious cracks to total destruction. Each artist or gallerist was mourning a relative or co-worker who had perished, and grieving the work of human hands perished.

In Jacmel the Ciné Institut for young film and video hopefuls fell, but the students grabbed what equipment they had at hand or could rescue and took to the streets. They tirelessly documented the loss of buildings, of lives, and of the vivid Karnaval arts for which the city is famous. The mask shops were in ruins, some of the artists dead or severely wounded. Ciné Institut is in the process of reconstituting itself with the help of donors from the outside. With Karnaval – the event that is a major source of income for the city – cancelled, the artists are now living in tents and have no income. Nevertheless, in place of the joyous event they held a spirited wake. Mask maker Onel Bazelais led the parade, holding aloft a caricature of the president. Behind him were all the traditional spoofs of politicians and the famous, power spirits like the horned Bossou, and cadaverous Gede, the death *lwa*. People fashioned costumes from whatever pieces they could cobble up. The drums and horns of rara paced their funereal march from the center of Jacmel to the cemetery. The record of it is there, because the students of Ciné Institut filmed it all.

There are so many stories. Many of them are the same tale: of being in a strange state of detachment then surprised with a tight throat and tears; grieving with the mind only and then with the whole body; singing and praying; picking up pieces; burying the dead, mourning irrevocable losses; helping an unending surge of the hungry, thirsty, and homeless; raising money with songs and paintings; creating new paintings and songs; and making sure the children would have school and be able to make art. They know how to do this, these Haitians. They have been rehearsing and performing this theatre since that first act of earthquake and revolution in 1751.

Yet. Yet. Stories of artists from the past indicate that the loss of a substantial part of a body of work has a serious and permanent impact. Arshile Gorky comes to mind. When a studio fire burned an important group of his works he spoke ruefully of "his beauties" deceased. He cleaned up the damaged studio and created *Charred Beloved* as one of the last works he would do. He went into a deep depression and eventually committed suicide. For Haitian artists and any Haitian who experienced the shaking of the foundations, the unfolding of the trauma lies now and in the future. For any Haitian caught up in the quake the memory of the event lies like seeds underground with a slow germination and a long row to hoe.

April 2010

14

From the Rubble to the Telethon: Music, Religion, and the Haiti Quake

Elizabeth McAlister

Like so many people with connections to Haiti, the January 12 earthquake sent me into a frantic search for family and friends, news, and information. As a music scholar and producer, I also tuned in to the sounds emanating from Port-au-Prince. Friends who live in Port-au-Prince tweeted the evening after the quake that people were singing in groups as the sun went down, as they faced an uncertain night of camping in the streets. So many people had lost everyone and everything. Some were left with only the air in their lungs. Richard Morse, the roots musician from the band RAM, tweeted, "the streets are Haiti's living rooms and bedrooms." Variously, the news media began to report on Haitians' use of music to hold themselves together through the trauma. Mostly they sang Catholic and Protestant hymns. Some understood the quake as the beginning of the apocalypse, and stood ready in that moment to receive their Christ. "Alleluia, Praises to God," they sang.

I stopped in my tracks when I saw a report on NBC: a woman named Janette, who was trapped for five days, *came out of the rubble singing*. Her song sounded like a Protestant hymn that said, "Do not be afraid of death." Several news media carried this remarkable story of a woman brought out singing from the rubble. I wondered: How could someone live through such horror and emerge singing?

In reflecting on this puzzle, I found wisdom in the teachings of two powerful vocalists who have educated me about the cultural work of singing: Mimerose Beaubrun, the lead singer of the roots band Boukman Eksperyans, and Bernice Johnson Reagon, the founder of Sweet Honey in the Rock. In an interview about singing in Haitian culture, Beaubrun told me that

> Singing is a tool we use to manipulate energy. It's also a tool that lets you focus your mind. It's a way of controlling the energy around you, to be able to control the energy in yourself. There is sound, the air that surrounds

you, which is a form of energy. It surrounds your whole body, because your whole body needs air. The air you use in singing is the air that lets you feel what's going on inside you.

Mimerose Beaubrun points us to the idea that music, like religion, orients people in time and in space. Haitian quake survivors used religious music to locate themselves in the midst of the material destruction and psychic disjuncture, to move toward equilibrium. They sang to reconstitute themselves as individuals and as groups – families, congregations, and neighbors thrown together in makeshift camps. They sang to run energy through the body, the individual body and the collective body. They sang to re-form themselves, and to reach to their God to sustain them.

On January 16, CNN broadcast a large group of Haitians walking through Port-au-Prince during the day singing hymns. "Tout bagay deja byen," they sang. "Everything is already fine." Their breath created song, as their song reconstituted their lives. In declaring that things were fine, even in the midst of devastation and chaos, this group broadcast a profound Christian faith.

In an "audio postcard" on NPR on January 20, women and girls sang a well-known hymn in the Haitian repertoire. "Jericho, miray-la kraze" – "Jericho, the walls are crumbling." In deploying this hymn about the ancient city of Jericho, Port-au-Prince became the biblical city, while they became the righteous and sanctified people of God. The lyrics went on to name other troubles – hunger, poverty, sickness – but then declared, "There is nothing Jesus cannot crumble." In the face of the worst natural catastrophe in the Americas, the quake survivors produced their own religious music as a lifeline of hope.

Given that after the quake the city of Port-au-Prince became a space of destruction, where more than 200,000 perished, people in Haiti were singing life back into the space of death. They used religious music to make their spaces inhabitable. Bernice Johnson Reagon of the singing group Sweet Honey in the Rock has said that during the sit-ins during the civil rights movement, when they began singing en masse, the marchers would take space away from the sheriff. She said that a group singing owns and controls its space. So in nightly singing in the many encampments in Port-au-Prince, and in marching through the downtown areas, groups of survivors were mapping space and taking ownership of it. Through song, the Haitian people incorporated the city back in to their lives, for their purposes, and for their use.

I came to understand that in those days and weeks after the quake, religious music was a matter of life and death in Haiti. Meanwhile, the world was seeking to help the Haitians with a different musical undertaking.

In a coordinated corporate response to the devastating January 12 earthquake in Haiti, the "Hope for Haiti Now" telethon on January 22 was the most widely viewed telethon in history. A quarter of a century after "Live Aid," "Hope for Haiti Now" aired for two hours live on all of these channels: ABC, NBC, Fox, CNN, BET, the CW, CMT, HBO, VH1, MTV Networks Worldwide (which reaches 640 million households), and CNN International (which reaches 260 million). It was also broadcast over the Internet, on YouTube, MySpace, and the Huffington Post, which compiled updated tweets from organizations in Haiti. In Haiti, survivors could listen in on the radio – if they had one.

The telethon, proposed by Haitian music star Wyclef Jean, was organized during a January 13 phone call between George Clooney and MTV president Judy McGrath. Like "Live Aid," it turned into a multi-venue event, with Clooney hosting from Los Angeles, Jean from New York, Jay-Z and Bono performing in London, and CNN's Anderson Cooper reporting live from downtown Port-au-Prince.

Musical acts were interspersed with taped pieces from CNN's Haiti coverage, thereby putting CNN in the position of helping raise money for organizations they were covering. The beneficiaries included the Red Cross, UNICEF, United Nations World Food Program, Yele Haiti Foundation, Oxfam America, Partners in Health, and the newly formed Clinton Bush Haiti fund. More than 100 musicians and actors were there to generate the largest donations possible. Most of the musical performances were heavily emotional songs with moving arrangements. The telethon's executive producer said they worked with the artists to find songs that would fit the event's tone. "They'll be singing songs that they have an emotional connection to and that best reflect their feelings about this tragic situation," he said. John Legend sang "I Feel Like a Motherless Child"; Kid Rock, Keith Urban and Sheryl Crow sang "Lean On Me"; and Jay-Z, Rihanna, Bono, and the Edge performed "Stranded (Haiti Mon Amour)," one of the few original songs composed for the occasion and the one that ranked first in iTunes downloads.

The last performance of the "Hope for Haiti Now" telethon was by Haitian superstar Wyclef Jean. Wyclef is arguably both a Haitian survivor of the trauma of the quake (insofar as he went immediately to Port-au-Prince and took it upon himself to help pick up corpses from public space) *and* an American musician bent on effecting the emotions of charitable giving. Wyclef's musicianship in turn served to constitute and orient the large Haitian diaspora, to mourn with the diaspora members living and watching outside of Haiti, but also to encourage diasporic viewers away from despair and towards hope.

Wyclef's song for the "Hope for Haiti Now" telethon was remarkable in various ways. First of all, he was the only musician to sing in Haitian Kreyòl. Wearing a large Haitian flag as a scarf, and backed by his band (including his sister Mekly on vocals and his cousin Jerry on bass), Wyclef began in English, with the iconic Jamaican song "By the Rivers of Babylon." He segued to his own composition in Kreyòl, "Yele," which means "Cry," a moving and evocative song that invites "if you have a voice, shout out, if you have tears, cry out." After a few minutes, he stopped the band short in a rehearsed intrusion. "Enough with the moping, let's rebuild Haiti." Like a cortege of New Orleans jazzmen coming back from the cemetery, the band burst into Rara – the exhilarating funeral music from the Haitian country-side. For most viewers in the United States and around the world, this was probably the first time ever to hear this powerful music singular to Haiti. Rara is a music, a carnivalesque festival, and a religious ritual all wrapped into one, and happens to be the subject of my first book. Its music is exhila-rating, produced by a series of hand-fashioned metal horns, each blown separately to create a melody. Most viewers would be unaware that Rara music is played in funerals in the Haitian countryside, and surely heard it as the upbeat, celebratory sound that it also is. Rara is an opportunity for the artistry of coded speech, and Wyclef that night delivered several poignant shout-outs, first to Anderson Cooper of CNN, next to King Kino, the front-man for the band Phantom, who had been rumored to be dead but wasn't. Wyclef gave a shout out to Jimmy O, a rapper who died in the quake, as well as to Fan Fan and Little Cliff. The performance, while on the global stage before millions, was also an insider affair, whose messages were for members of the Haitian diaspora. The Rara lyric, composed for the occasion, switched back to English. It rhythmically asserted, "Earth*quake*, we see the earth *shake*, but the soul of the Haitian people it will never *break*." Reaching to touch the psychic devastation of so many Haitians, Wyclef's song was at once Haitian to Haitian and American to American, mediating several orientations to the quake and its music.

By the next day, a reported $58 million had been raised, largely through new technology: text-messaged donations and downloaded musical performances for 99 cents (or later, for $7.99 for the whole album from iTunes). This, according to MTV, was a record for a disaster relief telethon. By comparison, the 9/11 telethon – "A Tribute to Heroes" (also organized by Clooney) – and the "Shelter from the Storm" telethon for the victims of Hurricane Katrina each raised about $30 million. The album from the telethon was released soon after to a number one slot on the pop music charts in 18 countries.

Telethons are emotionally moving events designed to funnel compassion into material relief. They now provide a way for a global public to respond supportively during an overwhelming tragedy. Said George Clooney, "The Haitian people need our help. They need to know that they are not alone. They need to know that we still care."

But not everybody is uncritical of the telethon phenomenon. Disability rights advocates such as Joseph P. Shapiro have written about how the annual telethons for childhood disease patients reinforce stereotypes of "pitiable poster child" or "inspirational disabled person," the "supercrip." Similarly, the disaster relief telethon often moves back and forth between images of survivors as objects of pity and survivors or rescuers as sources of inspiration. Emotional music and images wring us psychologically for contributions, because "there, but for the grace of God, go we." Like campaigns for cures for disease, disaster aid telethons tend to present a stark divide between the viewer and the people surviving a catastrophic event, between the victim and the star on stage, between the afflicted and the saved, the unfortunate and the fortunate. When a disaster hits a historically oppressed or colonized population, the stark divide can re-inscribe stereotypes of poor, helpless, natural victims who cannot help themselves and need help and rescue from the strong.

On one hand, telethons achieve the mass mobilization of charitable giving, which is significant when we consider that we are bombarded constantly with routine images of horror and violence, to all of which we simply cannot respond. But on the other hand, telethons flatten a disaster like the Haiti quake into *just* a natural disaster. The telethon oversimplified the underlying structural causes of the high death tolls of the quake. These causes lie in Haiti's inadequate housing, which is a result of poverty caused in part by international debt and inequitable trade deals. Delving into these long-term problems that the U.S. bears responsibility for might make the contributors feel less noble in their role as rescuers. Supporters give what they can, and move on with their lives.

"Hope for Haiti Now" ran according to a familiar model that has by now become a scripted ritual. In this script, innocent sufferers are depicted through photographs and filmic segments in order to elicit the help of compassionate responders. By donating, viewers secure a place among the charitable and the compassionate. By giving, we buy our position as the saved and the lucky. Paul Longmore writes that "telethon donation is a collective rite designed to enable Americans to demonstrate to themselves that they still belong to a moral community, that they have not succumbed to materialism, that they are givers who fulfill their obligations to their neighbors." He goes on: "[T]he ceremonial counterimage to conspicuous consumption is conspicuous contribution." He calls such events "rites of American nationalism" in which we perform our moral standing and our public virtue.

As a religious studies scholar, I understood the "Hope For Haiti Now" telethon as a media ritual, part nationalist American rite and part civil religious ceremony, with neo-colonial echoes. We listened to the music of our super-human beings, the celebrities who lead us in empathetic response and release. We affirmed our moral righteousness as Americans leading the world in the mercy of aid and the might of our military responders. We gave, not understanding how we may ourselves be implicated in the economic systems that contributed to such a disaster. We tune in and find our place in the global system, as sufferers or as compassionate givers, or both.

✳   ✳   ✳

Watching and listening to the reporting on the many forms of religious music people made in response to the quake, I traced how Haitians near the quake and Americans far away used music – particularly religious music – to orient themselves in relation to the devastating event. American musicians singing for presumed American audiences used music as a medium of connection, to cause an affective reaction meant to manipulate listeners emotionally into feelings of empathy, compassion, and charity. American musicians constituted Americans as empowered feelers and givers, as the moral responders to the heartbreaking humanitarian crisis. Haitians caught up in the trauma of the quake used music reflexively, and sang for themselves and for each other, to push back death and to orient themselves with their breath and their songs, towards life. They made the quake make sense by singing it. Wyclef Jean, in both places at once, did both.

June 2010

15

The Writing of Disaster in Haiti: Signifying Cataclysm from Slave Revolution to Earthquake

Deborah Jenson

For slaves and former slaves or descendants of slaves to take on the discourses and mentalities of revolution, as they did from the first weeks of the insurrection in Saint-Domingue (later renamed Haiti) in 1791, was already to explode out of the confined spaces of radical action by blacks: brigandage, banditry, conspiracy, even revolt, but never revolution. Revolution was for whites, who, as it happens, conventionally and without irony considered themselves slaves to feudal structures in Europe or their legacies elsewhere. Jean-Paul Marat's bestseller, *Slavery's Chains*, one of the most putatively radical texts of the French Revolution, used the word *slavery* to describe the citizen "slaves" of European monarchies, but not the literal slaves brought to the New World to satisfy Europeans' economic needs. Yet no one accused the French of aping Africans when they decried their slavery to the king; whereas in Haiti, the first assumptions of secretarial eloquence and radical Enlightenment principles by these multigenerational survivors of the Middle Passage were searingly mocked as the primate-like mimeticism of European revolutionaries. Napoleon Bonaparte spoke with seething resentment of the "gilded Africans" in the military uniform in Saint-Domingue. The storming of the stage of the Public Thing, the ideal of the Republic, by Afro-diasporic communities was a disaster threatening the choreographed invisibility of white Euro-American hegemony.

Disaster and catastrophe were in fact among the most common terms found in titles of pamphlets and memoirs by former colonists of Saint-Domingue in the course of the Haitian Revolution; the emergence of a free black state in the Americas was openly qualified as catastrophe. Colonists, including planters who were free persons of color, wrote to the National Convention to denounce the disaster's causes, authors, and narratives, often citing a terrible analogy between the destabilizations of the French Revolution and the disasters in Saint-Domingue. The Marquis François Barbé-Marbois alone used the word "disasters" more than 40 times in a single 1796 text. One could make the argument that the twentieth-century coinage "the Haitian Revolution" quite directly translates, in the colonial discourse of the period, "the disasters of Saint-Domingue." Remarkably, one colonist, Drouin de Bercy, in his 1814 *On Saint-Domingue: Its Wars, Its Revolutions, Its Resources*, overtly theorized seismological disasters on the same continuum as revolutionary quakes.

> However extraordinary these disasters may be, they are not unique [...] There were, among the ancients as among the moderns, other insurrections of slaves. Surinam was ravaged, and Jamaica too, by the earthquakes that had swallowed up the cities of Saint-Domingue; in the Antilles, in the slaves' milieu, the earth shakes literally and figuratively.

Slave insurrection as figurative earthshaking, seismological upheavals as literal earthshaking, are mixed and matched in the history of representations of Haiti.

In the first decade of the new millennium, a period marked by the bicentennial of Haiti's independence, discourses of disaster again rise prominently to the researcher's eye in texts about Haiti. The expressions "ecological disaster," "humanitarian disaster," "disaster management," and "disaster capitalism" have all proliferated around Haiti, well prior to the 2010 disaster that has reset the bar for the meaning of disaster. A National Risk and Disaster Management system had been established in Haiti after the fall of the Aristide government, supported by the World Bank, the European Union, and other international entities, although participation by Haitian ministries was reportedly weak. In 2008, Haiti ranked highly on the UN Development Program's Disaster Risk index of countries most vulnerable to natural disasters. Among this proliferation of discourses about Haiti's disaster vulnerability, one can find references to "the Haitian disaster" as a kind of metonymy for the Haitian state and its history. These crop up particularly frequently in assessments of corruption in Haiti's political economy, an approach which I find deeply worrisome, as it unintentionally closes the loop with that earlier tradition regarding the advent of a black state as disaster, and replaces a whole national tradition with a kind of apocalyptic signifier, as if nothing were there but what might replace it.

It is not only externally but also internally, however, that the historical genesis and survival of Haiti as an "earthshaking" nation – from the first black republic in the Western hemisphere to the current seismic ruins of a postcolonial state – often have been narrated in a mode one might describe as the writing of disaster. From the alignment of storm with divine retribution in the revolutionary "Oath of the Cayman Woods," to Jean-Jacques Dessalines's appropriation of cataclysm as friendly to decolonization, to the existential *mise-en-abyme* or symbolic redoubling involved in Frankétienne's rehearsal of his play "The Trap" at the moment of the quake, a relationship to disaster runs through Haitian letters. In what follows I will broach comparison of the modalities of Haitian representations of disaster with the antagonistic external commentaries most recently exemplified by Pat Robertson's motif of disaster resulting from a Haitian "pact with the devil."

The phrase "the writing of disaster" echoes the title of a famous 1980 book by French philosopher Maurice Blanchot, *L'Ecriture du désastre*, a meditation influenced by Hegel and Lévi-Strauss and linguistic poststructuralism, and almost stunningly ill-tuned to the disaster of January 12, 2010. Blanchot's book grapples with the limits of conscious experience, the limits of the sovereignty of self and memory, and the threatening absolutes of a reality beyond linguistic transcription. In effect, disaster serves as the mythological testing of the limits of the conceivable and the transcribable. Blanchot describes disaster as the "unexperienced," as the limit of writing, and as something that not only eludes description, but actively de-scribes. This de-scribal mode is of precious little use to a people trying to crawl out from a disaster so overwhelmingly present tense that it acutely continues to threaten survival weeks and months after the moment of what poststructuralists might have called "rupture." And yet we find something similar in early writings of disaster in Haiti, in the sense of the simultaneous animation of nature, the connection of that animated nature to suffering human perception, and the reversal, fragmentation, or phenomenological warping and rearrangement of both. Arguably however, suffering human perception and phenomenological warping are manifest primarily on the world stage in the Haitian imagination, despite their resonance for human subjectivity in the abstract. Disaster in Haitian letters problematizes the abstraction of human subjectivity in the first place, making reversals of experience into new landscapes, rituals and beliefs, and plans of action. There is, in effect, no reason to divide what is literally and figuratively earth shaking into distinct camps.

Disaster was of course the mode of the arrival of Africans in the New World, kidnapped and shipped blindly to a new life of subjugation and what Orlando Patterson described as social death, although survival beyond this social death is the cornerstone of Afro-diasporic history. The disaster-stricken condition of new arrivals was not lost on eighteenth-century physicians. The American physician, signer of the U.S. Constitution, and innovator in the treatment of mental health, Benjamin Rush, contributed to the consideration of slavery as a pathological state in his 1787 article "An Account of the Diseases Peculiar to the Negroes in the West-Indies, and Which are Produced by Their Slavery" in *The American Museum*. Rush described the "*mal d'estomac*" (stomach pain) common to newly arrived slaves in the French West Indies as a somatoform result of the Middle Passage itself, not a result of poisoning, as slave owners often believed. According to Rush, this painful condition generally arose soon after the arrival of Africans in the New World, with symptoms slave owners blamed on intentional self-poisoning or on assisted suicide by other slaves, and was often fatal. But the fundamental cause of the malady was not poison, in Rush's view, but grief, in a pathological form to be laid squarely on the doorstep of the institution of slavery.

For survivors of the Middle Passage in Haiti, *Guinen* (or Africa), both as a place of heritage and as the space of an afterlife, was relocated symbolically, spiritually, and possibly geospatially under the water. Although this belief was associated by slave owners with the problem of slaves' suicidal aspiration to return or pass over by drowning, the vision of the lost country and afterlife under the water, *anba dlo* in Kreyòl, clearly also had sustaining properties. Robert Orsi writes that

> [o]nce Africa is transposed to the bottom of domestic bodies of water, the ancestors (on both sides of the family) are within earshot, and also within range of prayers and supplications. As a result of the transposition of Africa into the New World, [...] the spirits also are within hailing range, hovering just below the surface of the waters.

Witness the words of one of the best-loved Vodou songs: "Anonse o zanj nan dlo / Bak odsu miwa ..." (Announce to the angels [spirits] down in the water / the boats above the mirror ...). Offerings to these *lwa*, sent out on little boats or barks from rafts or boats in a zone about three miles from the shore, are only considered to have been successful in locating passage to the underwater world if the boats sink. Once the boats have disappeared from view, their delivery of offerings is assured. Where normally for migrants, the community of the ancestors becomes geographically distant, and the gods associated with the dead may fade from view, Orsi asserts that in Haiti, history became archaeology, layered in a watery subterranean realm. The space *anba dlo*, so prominent in the work of the Haitian painter Edouard Duval-Carrié, symbolically bridges the cultures of the New World and Africa through the waters that divide them. The Middle Passage in this sense is built into the metaphysics of traditional Haitian spiritual life.

There is a similar rearrangement of natural and celestial spaces and agents in the early Creole (Kreyòl) poetic text, transcribed decades later by the Haitian writer Hérard Dumesle, that stands in the Haitian tradition as the collective ceremonial oath that launched the Haitian Revolution in August of 1791. The "Oath of the Cayman Woods" hints at disaster on a horizon of battling European and African metaphysics.

Bondye ki fè soley, ki klere nou anwò,
Ki souleve lamè, ki fè gronde loraj,
Bon dye la, zot tande? Kache nan yon nuage,
E la li gade nou, li wè tout sa blan fè!
Bon dye blan mande krim, e pat nou vlè byenfè
Men dye la ki si bon, ordonnen nou venjans;
Li va kondwi bra nou, li ba nou asistanz.
Jete potre dye blan qui swaf dlo nan je nou,
Koute la libete, li pale kè nou tous.

God who makes the sun, who lights us up from above,
Who raises up the seas, who makes storms growl,
God is there, you hear? Hidden in a cloud,
And there he watches us, he sees everything the whites do!
The god of the whites orders crime, he wants nothing good for us,
But the god there who is so good, orders us to take vengeance;
He will guide our arms, he will give us assistance.
Throw down the portrait of the god of the whites who thirsts for the
    tears in our eyes.
Listen to liberty, it speaks in all of our hearts.

In the oath, one god – bondye, from "the good lord" (bon dieu) in French – animates nature. Bondye then splits into two gods, a division heralded by the separation of the two syllables of the compound word bondye itself into bon and dye. The god of the whites delivers crime, gives nothing good. The whites' god is indistinctly positioned in the stormy skies in relation to the god phenomenologically centered as there, the god who can be confirmed by the speakers of the oath, the god who sees, who is a witness of the crimes, and who will guide the slaves' vengeance. Even the material icon or portrait of the god of the whites, perhaps hanging on a wall, has a taste for the slaves' tears. The slaves, once they have cast the portrait down, are able to hear the voice of a freedom rooted in their own bodies and hearts. The oath shows a multi-directional and multi-sensory sphere. Portraits thirst, bodies speak, celestial gods act and are watched and split apart, and nature heaves; not a disaster in itself, and yet reminiscent of the unhinging of world bearings that is characteristic of disaster.

The first black leader of Saint-Domingue, Toussaint Louverture, generally avoided such cosmic descriptions of disaster, but he did forcefully describe the personal and governmental disaster of his deportation and imprisonment by the French. In his memoir addressed to the attention of Napoleon Bonaparte from his cell in the Fort de Joux, he described himself as arbitrarily arrested, pillaged, deported, and defamed. These experiences spill pell-mell into a series of visceral metaphors of disablement: he is naked as an earthworm, a paralytic forced to walk, a mutilated mute forced to talk, a living cadaver. In the manuscript passage, written in Toussaint's own hand, readers can see his primarily verbal grasp of French; he was perfectly able to compose and write a complex description of his experience and subjectivity, but he was unfamiliar with where words in French began and ended. "M'envoyer nu comme un ver de terre" was thus "man voyer nu comme ver de ter"; "couper la langue et lui dire 'Parlez'" was "coupé la langue et loui dire parlé." When Napoleon Bonaparte received Toussaint's memoir, he was angry enough to order that all writing implements and paper be removed from Toussaint's cell. The text below was found wrapped in Toussaint's headscarf after his death, his literary protest and self-defense clinging to his body like a second skin:

> Arresting me arbitrarily, without hearing me out or telling me why, taking all my possessions, pillaging my whole family in general, seizing my papers and keeping them, putting me on board a ship, sending me off naked as an earth worm, spreading the most atrocious lies about me ... and after that, I am sent to the depths of this dungeon. Isn't this like cutting off someone's leg and saying "walk," isn't this like cutting out someone's tongue and saying "talk," isn't this burying a man alive?

Jean-Jacques Dessalines, a revolutionary general and the leader of the new nation of Haiti from 1804 to his assassination in 1806, communicated a sense of the dangerous destabilizations inherent to states in military crisis in his first independence proclamation. This proclamation, which preceded the document we know as the Haitian Declaration of Independence, was co-signed by generals Christophe and Clerveaux after the final victory against the French at Vertières in November of 1803. Dessalines, despite his lack of formal schooling, had a compelling literary voice and political worldview that came through consistently in his proclamations, which were transcribed by a variety of secretaries from among the ranks of Haiti's highly educated mixed race elites. (Dessalines was hardly unique in dictating his thoughts to secretaries who would render them into formal political texts; this was a standard mode of military and political correspondence in the Western world.) In the November 1803 proclamation, Dessalines came close to apologizing for the impossibility, in the "crisis" of the Haitian Revolution, of avoiding all unwarranted violence against whites. Crisis begets disorder and excess, he reflected; but after the storms of appalling war, after a world "shaken up" by civil discord, it was time for Saint-Domingue to show a new face. At the same time, he seemed able to justify apocalypse itself to prevent the restoration of slavery and colonization:

> Were they [the Haitians] to cause rivers and torrents of blood to run; were they, in order to maintain their liberty, to conflagrate seven eighths of the globe, they would remain innocent before the tribunal of Providence, which has not created men to watch them groaning under a hard and shameful servitude.

After all, he reflected, "Nothing has a price, and everything is permitted, to men from whom one would steal the most fundamental of all privileges." He was eager to reverse the category of slavery and apply it as a label precisely to those who would impose it on others, rather than those who had been its victims. Persons who might be "slaves to a criminal pretension, blind enough to believe themselves privileged and destined by heaven to be our masters and tyrants," would only find, upon arrival in Saint-Domingue, "chains and deportation."

The colonial notion of catastrophe in Saint-Domingue continued to permeate Haitian consciousness of an independent historical trajectory after Haitian independence. In 1824, Dessalines's former secretary Juste Chanlatte (with Bouvet de Cressé) would borrow the terminology of colonial memoirs in the title of his *History of the Catastrophe of Saint-Domingue*. This strangely hybrid text was in effect a history of the Haitian Revolution and its aftermath, in the form of a narrative of the Haitians' misfortunes. But the intended meaning of the term "catastrophe" is marked by continuous slippage, from the brutalities of the French, to the massacre of the remaining French by the Haitians, to the continuing and looming crisis of the commercial and social isolation of the Haitians in the postcolonial period. Despite the emphasis on disaster, the book opens with an eloquent treatise in defense of blackness and of African achievement, dating back to the "cradle of the world," and justifying the line from the Song of Songs, "I am black, and I am beautiful." Ultimately one might situate the "catastrophe" of Haiti in this text as precisely the signification of

African ethnicity in Western nationalist modernity. In 1824, the year before Haiti's agreement to the payment of a disastrous indemnity to France to buy French recognition of Haiti's independence, one cannot help but wonder if the use of the term "catastrophe" to describe this complex and troubled history does not reveal a defensive and vulnerable self-positioning of Haiti.

As Haiti's literary and historical traditions continued to develop, description of natural disasters plaguing the Caribbean entered Haitian narratives, just as they have in the contemporary "epic" novel form in Guadeloupe and Martinique, where earthquakes, insurrections, volcanic eruptions, fires, and plagues punctuate time in novels like *Texaco* by Patrick Chamoiseau or *L'Isolé Soleil* by Daniel Maximin. Caribbean natural disasters also are featured prominently in texts published in the United States, notably in the francophone novel *Le Vieux Salomon* about the February 1843 Guadeloupean earthquake and ensuing Caribbean migration to New Orleans. In the middle of the nineteenth century, Haitian historian Thomas Madiou looked back at the devastating earthquake of June 8, 1770, an event that quite closely paralleled the area and scope of the recent quake. It entirely flattened Port-au-Prince from end to end, as well as the towns of the western province, he wrote. Throughout the whole night, the earth floated. Residents traced that inability to find their footing or safe ground to a fault or source quite similar to the epicenter of the January 12 earthquake. Madiou referred to it as the place we call the abyss (*Le Gouffre*), at the mouth of the rivers of Cul-de-Sac and Léogâne. He noted that several times before the day in question, subterranean detonations had issued from this site. Madiou also described water-related seismic sequellae with almost Old Testament or mythological intensity: Grande Rivière went dry for about 16 hours, and then exploded back with violent floods. Similar floods – not tsunamis but river-based events moving from inland outward, and from mountains to valleys – had been observed after the 1692 earthquake in Jamaica. After the 1842 Haitian earthquake, many explosive water events were described, including the release of torrents from mountain springs onto lower plains and the division into two separate parts of the Yaque river, one of which suddenly rolled back to flood into the other. Interestingly, Madiou noted that in that in the aftermath of the 1770 quake, after several months of living in tents, the inhabitants rebuilt the capital in safer wooden rather than mortar structures, and within a year the visible traces of catastrophe had been erased. Cycles of devastation by catastrophe and erasure of catastrophe are evident throughout Haitian historiography.

Journalistic accounts state that when the earthquake struck in Haiti on January 12 the writer Frankétienne was rehearsing his play "The Trap," which (like several of his other texts) represents ecological Armageddon. The play featured two characters trapped in a crumbled and devastated space with no exit. "No outside, no inside," says one. "No day, no night," replies the other. "No black, no white," the first rejoins. "Wherever 1 am, 1 Babylon and reimbabylon myself terribly. From the depths of the abyss, to the kingdom of nothing. The hegemony of nothing." More collapse and catastrophe ensues, until crushed bodies are everywhere, and pain finds a home in the viscera of the speakers, who outline dialogically: "The planet oscillates.... No light in the collapse of the cities, the slums, the palaces and castles all in one cacophonic hecatomb." In a shared refrain, the characters shout, "The opera of gangrene! The rats' *opera macabre*!"

The conditions for the literary staging of this devastation in precise coordination with its realization in life have been in place since the early descriptions of the former slaves' national life as the colonial death of the French, and since the earth first began to lurch and float through dire nights in Port-au-Prince and Léogâne and Petit Goâve. It was easy in the colonial era for Haitians to associate disasters such as the yellow fever that decimated the French army or earthquakes that ruined colonial cities with an animated omnipotent force of anger over slavery; Madiou noted that in the devastation of Port-au-Prince the anger of a Supreme Being, like celestial fire, had passed over the face of the tyrant and had struck it with a long agony. Such correlations now sometimes recur in the form of angst over karmic imbalance in Haiti, unfortunately often associated in the Protestant tradition with Vodou and with condemnations of founding cultural scenes and texts such as the oath of the Cayman woods. Even aside from the distribution of blame that can be a part of the strategic claims of organized religion, a fundamental psychological interrogation of misfortune, as in Marie Chauvet's narrator's exclamation in *Love, Anger, Madness*, haunts Haitian letters: "So then we are cursed! Hurricanes, earthquakes, drought, nothing spares us."

The task now is precisely to recognize how the *sekous*, the quake in the Haitian world, has rearranged not only heaven and earth but Haiti and its geopolitical neighbors in shattered slabs of international relations, how it has repositioned the faithful, *Vodouisant* and/or Christian, with regard to "god who is *there*," how to claw the future out from the debris, all without wrongly and prejudicially consigning Haiti, its state and its history, to disaster. In the midst of crisis, we need to repeat and repeat to ourselves something simple: that Haiti, dear Haiti, no matter how tested and remapped by disaster, is *not*, in itself, disaster.... *Haiti is not disaster.*

Further Reading

Bercy, Drouin de. *De Saint-Domingue*. Chez Hocquet, 1814.

Blanchot, Maurice, and Ann Smock. *The Writing of the Disaster*. University of Nebraska Press, 1995.

Cressé, Auguste Jean Baptiste Bouvet de, Juste Chanlatte, and Henri Christophe (King of Haiti). *Histoire de la catastrophe de Saint-Domingue*. Librairie de Peytieux, 1824.

Madiou, Thomas. *Histoire d'Haïti: 1819–1826*. Editions Henri Deschamps, 1826.

Orsi, Robert A. *Gods of the City*. Indiana University Press, 1999.

Vieux-Chauvet, Marie, Rose-Myriam Rejouis, Val Vinokur, and Edwidge Danticat. *Love, Anger, Madness*. Random House, 2010.

April 2010

PART III

History

16

The Legacies of Pre-revolutionary Saint-Domingue

John D. Garrigus

In 1790, French Saint-Domingue was Europe's most profitable colony. In this territory the size of Belgium, nearly half a million enslaved black workers grew and manufactured the sugar and coffee that were changing the way Europeans lived. This extraordinary society fascinates scholars of world history for three reasons. As a colony from the 1640s to 1803, Saint-Domingue had an important economic and cultural impact on France, which in turn transmitted those legacies to other slaveholding powers and to its nineteenth-century empire. Second, beginning in 1791 it produced the Haitian Revolution, the most successful slave uprising of modern times. Third, in 1804 its leaders created Haiti, the first independent state in the Americas in which people of non-European descent were the majority population.

For those who want to understand modern-day Haiti, Saint-Domingue is even more central. At least five elements of Haiti's modern history are deeply rooted in the colonial period: the military nature of national governments; the country's current environmental crisis; its long experience within the global economy; its extraordinary culture, especially Haitian Vodou; and the stark division between rural and urban populations. In the remainder of this essay I will explore each of these elements in turn, and suggest some of the ways in which they have shaped the history and present-day reality of independent Haiti.

Military Government

France's claim over what is today Haiti began in the 1640s. Around that time, officers of the French crown managed to assert control over an international population of buccaneers living on the western coast of Santo Domingo. Spanish authorities had evacuated this part of the island to stop the ranchers who lived there from trading with Dutch smugglers. But the problem of control was not limited to the Spanish. Long before 1697, when

Spain officially recognized French possession of western Santo Domingo, Versailles's emissaries discovered how difficult it was to administer this mountainous territory, ten times the size of Martinique and Guadeloupe combined, with its long coastline.

As in other French colonies the navy administered all levels of Saint-Domingue society, from the governor general's office right down to the local parishes. A parish commander, usually a retired military officer appointed by the crown, oversaw every aspect of local government. Planters complained bitterly about being subjected to these officers' unchecked personal power. Such a "despotic" system may have been appropriate for the buccaneering 1600s, they argued, but in the 1700s it led successful colonists to flee Saint-Domingue as soon as their estate revenues could sustain them in France. These absentees drained wealth from the colony, and their managers abused slaves and skimmed profits for themselves. Only when civilians ruled under an established legal framework, colonists argued, would planters remain in the colony and become loyal defenders of the French empire.

However, the military tradition did not end in the eighteenth century or with Haitian independence. From the national to the local governments, the Haitian army played a central role in governance and administration throughout most of the period from 1804 to 1994. In Haiti, as in much of Latin America, there are many reasons for the historical prevalence of military governments. A significant part of the country's authoritarian experience is however rooted in the long colonial period. French officials did experiment with civilian government in the late 1760s, but within a year they decided to reinstitute the military system, in part because they were concerned that colonists' drive to protect their estates would trump their loyalty to France, if, for example, the British attacked.

Environmental Damage

The extraordinary wealth Saint-Domingue produced for France was based on the exploitation of enslaved Africans and the colony's land and water. But to what extent can Haiti's contemporary environmental crisis be traced to the colonial period? The answer is quite complex. First of all, the country's topography is quite severe: slopes of 20 percent or greater cover 60 percent of the territory, making erosion a threat for the farmers who cultivate these lands. Second, Caribbean trade winds blow from east to west, and rain clouds release much of their moisture over the eastern slopes of Hispaniola's mountains, leaving Haiti, on the island's western side, in a permanent "rain shadow." Finally, a century before the French arrived, Hispaniola had already experienced severe environmental trauma with the near extermination of the island's Taino people and the introduction of European crops and especially livestock, which roamed in large herds by the 1600s.

Nevertheless, French colonists observed dramatic environmental changes caused by deforestation and understood that the expansion of plantation agriculture was to blame. By 1764 planters complained that they could only find wood suitable for building on mountain summits. Versailles envisioned a reforestation program, but the governor informed the minister that "the nature of establishments here does not permit the planting of the required trees." Colonists were too eager to profit from sugar and coffee to invest in the far slower business of growing timber. In 1790 one French sugar expert observed how rainfall had diminished markedly in regions where coffee planters had cleared trees from the hillsides. These "sterile" mountains lowered the level of nearby rivers and had reduced sugar yields in the plains of Gonaïves, Artibonite, Cul de Sac, and Léogâne.

By this time, colonists had already begun to remake Saint-Domingue's waterways. Understanding that well-watered sugarcane was sweeter, beginning in 1731 planters built dams, levees, and canals in Saint-Domingue's alluvial plains to prevent floods caused by water rushing down from denuded hills and to distribute water to sugar estates. By 1789 the colony had dozens of such complex systems, several in nearly every coastal plain. Control over water allowed many plantations to construct water-powered sugar mills, which were far more efficient for large estates than mills powered by oxen.

In many parts of Haiti today, water still runs in the irrigation works traced by French engineers and dug by enslaved Africans. But the water that flows from Haiti's bare hills has now far exceeded the ability of any colonial construction to block or channel it.

Proto-industrialization

This extraordinary investment in irrigation works amazed visitors from the British West Indies, all of which combined did not produce as much sugar as Saint-Domingue. Moreover, Saint-Domingue's export economy was more diverse than that of any other Caribbean colony; in addition to sugar, it shipped 60 percent of Europe's coffee, as well as large amounts of indigo dye and cotton. Size was one reason for this productivity; the

French colony was two and a half times larger than Jamaica, its closest rival. But massive investment was another.

The colony's African labor force was at the heart of that investment. Enslaved workers made up 90 percent of Saint-Domingue's population. But reproduction rates were low and on an average plantation overwork, malnutrition, and disease killed between 4 and 10 percent of workers annually. The appalling conditions, and the ongoing extension of coffee-planting into virgin mountain territory, fed demand for the slave trade. By the end of the eighteenth century, tens of thousands of men, women, and children were arriving in chains from Africa every year. In all, Dominguan colonists bought approximately 800,000 Africans, nearly as many as the total slave imports of all Britain's 13 North American colonies combined.

The conditions of Saint-Domingue's proto-industrial plantation system also explain another of Haiti's modern environmental problems: micro-farming. Many Haitian peasant farmers support their families on less than two acres (0.75 hectares) of land. French slave law, the Code Noir of 1685, obligated owners to provide their slaves with a specified minimum amount of food. By the mid-1700s, however, Saint-Domingue's planters had discovered it was cheaper to give slaves garden plots and let them grow most of their own provisions. These plots became vital to the survival of enslaved workers, allowing some to escape malnutrition and even to enter the local economy. Slave gardeners produced much of the food available in colonial markets. Gardens became synonymous with autonomy, even freedom. After the great slave revolt of August 1791, as rebel leaders tried to negotiate with colonial authorities, their primary demand was not emancipation, but three days a week to work in their gardens. The end of slavery in 1794, Haitian independence in 1804, and the end of the threat of a French invasion in 1825 produced an exodus from the plantations. Because of the country's size and political independence, former slaves were able to establish themselves as peasant farmers, unlike newly freed people in many other Caribbean colonies, where colonial planters retained control of the land after slavery.

After the revolution, for the first time, Haiti's population began to grow, putting some pressure on farmers as peasant families divided their land among their children. By 1918 the population had reached an estimated 1.9 million, up from roughly half a million in 1790. Over the course of the twentieth century the country's population quadrupled again, growing to an estimated nine million today. The kind of agriculture that made Haiti a peasant's paradise in the 1800s cannot support the many millions more families that have been added over the last hundred years.

The very different kind of agriculture that made Saint-Domingue so profitable for France in the 1700s did not come cheaply. A planter needed approximately 2,500 livres (pounds) to purchase a man from a slave ship, a sum that was equivalent to the life savings of most working people in Paris at the time. A viable sugar plantation was said to require at least 100 workers, whose slave-market value far exceeded the net worth of most provincial French nobles. And a plantation needed land, buildings, livestock, and sugar processing equipment, as well as managers, refiners, bookkeepers, and other employees.

Such massive investment could yield high returns for this era. With over 200 workers, the Leroux plantation near Les Cayes produced 8,400 livres a year of revenue for its owner, a return of 11 percent on an estate that was valued at 734,000 livres in 1756. At the same time, over a fifteen year period the value of the plantation's land, workers, and installations increased by 40 percent, to 1.2 million. To reap such profits, however, a plantation manager would have to be vigilant about planting and harvesting, timing the actions of his workers so that the mill and refinery would have a steady flow of ripe cane; he would have to watch carefully over the maintenance of irrigation channels, the efficiency of his harvest, and the expertise of his sugar refiner.

A successful Caribbean sugar planter, therefore, was as much a manufacturer as a farmer. Some historians argue that Saint-Domingue was a proto-industrial society in which slaves were not peasants working for a lord, but rather capital assets whose owners carefully measured their productivity and costs of acquisition and maintenance. By this measure Haiti is not an "undeveloped" country, but one that is still recovering from its first experience with the global economy.

Slavery, Resistance, and Culture

Most experts believe that Haitian Vodou did not form a coherent belief system until sometime after 1791. But it seems likely enslaved plantation workers shaped Saint-Domingue's pre-Vodou spiritual culture in reaction to the "modern" nature of plantation work. We know little of this culture, but the practices we do know of helped to forge bonds among Saint-Domingue's diverse African and Creole people and allowed them to cope with a dehumanizing plantation regime.

Most scholars trace the roots of Vodou in Saint-Domingue to the spiritual practices of West Africans from the so-called "slave coast" of the Bight of Benin, who composed 60 percent of the workers imported during the colony's first quarter century of major slave trading, from 1700 to 1725. By the middle of the century, however, slave traders were drawing more heavily on the Congo River Basin, and elements of that region's religious cultures began to appear in Saint-Domingue. To this day, the Vodou *lwa*, the spiritual mysteries at the heart of the religion, are divided roughly into two pantheons: the Congo; and the Rada, from Allada, a major slave-trading power in the Bight of Benin.

Christianity was an aspect of the lives of many enslaved Dominguans, especially those from the Congo region, where Portuguese missionaries had been active since the sixteenth century. But Saint-Domingue's planters were notoriously lax about evangelizing their slaves and even the religious orders owned large and profitable sugar estates. The Jesuits did teach and preach to slaves, however. The order's expulsion from Saint-Domingue in 1763 was partly motivated by its members' refusal to testify in the investigation of the so-called Makandal poisoning conspiracy of 1757–1758.

The Makandal affair is often evoked in discussions of why Saint-Domingue, known for its revolution, did not experience the repeated slave revolts that occurred in neighboring Jamaica in the 1700s. Some have suggested that pre-Vodou spiritual practices served as a psychological safety valve, drawing the focus of enslaved people away from armed revolt. Others have pointed to the Makandal episode, in which over 6,000 people died suddenly and mysteriously, as evidence that enslaved Saint-Dominguans did fight the planters before 1791, just not with machetes, guns, and fire.

A closer look at Makandal reveals that this dichotomy between revolt and submission is overstated; the reality of this famous case was somewhere in between. François Makandal was a maroon (escaped slave) who was burned at the stake in Cap Français on January 20, 1758. His arrest after as many as eighteen years of illicit freedom was the climax of eight months of colonial hysteria that began when an enslaved man named Médor began spontaneously confessing to having poisoned scores of people, including his master's family. Before he died, apparently by suicide, Médor claimed Saint-Domingue's free and enslaved blacks had a powerful "secret." He named at least a dozen others, slaves and free blacks, who either supplied him with "poison" or used these substances. As colonists began interrogating – and brutally torturing – the workers he named, they became aware of two frightening realities. First, there was a network of black men and women in the hinterland of Fort Dauphin, Cap Français, and perhaps Port de Paix who were making and trading esoteric substances, and using them on other people. Second, in this same region – and nowhere else in the colony – large numbers of people and livestock were dying myste-riously. Administrators believed that 6,000 to 7,000 people and tens of thousands of livestock died in the space of roughly 18 months. Many colonists concluded that Médor's "secret" was a vast poisoning conspiracy against the whites.

Makandal was such a charismatic figure that when whites finally captured him, with the help of enslaved informants, they were convinced they had found the master poisoner. After boasting that whites could not kill him, the ex-maroon momentarily escaped the stake before a large audience assembled to watch him burn to death. Although the execution proceeded, this image of a deathless enemy of the master class became a powerful legend. Twenty-five years later a Parisian journal reported that Makandal's name still struck terror in the hearts of Saint-Domingue's planters. Today his memory survives in Haiti as the essence of Haitian culture and resistance.

The legend of Makandal must be separated into two parts, however: the conspirator and the spiritual leader. The notion of a secret plan to drive the whites from the island does not easily square with the fact that 90 percent of the people Makandal allegedly poisoned were slaves. White planters concluded that he was eliminating their workers to bankrupt them, but even with 6,000 victims, Makandal and his accomplices would have killed just 10 percent of the enslaved population of the North Province.

I have argued that Makandal's victims probably succumbed to some other killer, for during the very months of the poison investigation the colony was under an unprecedented British blockade, as part of the Seven Years' War. Smugglers bringing food and livestock into the country may have introduced new diseases. Although unprovable, it is quite possible that slaves ingested spoiled grain that smugglers introduced into the North Province, which was especially dependent on imported food. An epidemic introduced by imported livestock may have killed the tens of thousands of animals.

What the Makandal incident incontestably demonstrates is that Saint-Domingue's population of free and enslaved men and women included many whose spiritual abilities attracted worshippers or clients. Makandal was one of those individuals. After torture he revealed his "secret" to colonial judges; it consisted of the techniques he used to create spiritu-ally powerful bundles known as "gris" or "makandals." Carried under one's hat, they would jump around, provide luck and help predict the future. He never admitted to making poison. Other slaves generally agreed; Makan-dal's bundles could not cause death or even illness, only good or bad luck.

Nevertheless, colonists who had seen black spirituality as benign superstition up to this point now embraced the idea of a network of black poisoners. In the absence of another explanation for the thousands of deaths, blacks as well as whites accepted the theory. In the 1790s, Toussaint Louverture feared poison terribly and he began Haiti's tradition of black leaders who attacked Vodou as a malevolent force. In the national period, Haitian leaders not only criticized Vodou as a sign of cultural backwardness but accused Vodou practitioners of crimes, including cannibalism. This persecution continued well into the twentieth century, especially when foreign institutions, like the Church of Rome or the U.S. government, demanded it.

Separate Rural and Urban Societies

Another legacy of the colonial regime in Haiti is the stark divide between country and city that has existed through most of the country's independent history. Although the French founded Port-au-Prince and made it their colonial capital, they did not initiate its dominance in modern Haiti; the fact that today approximately 20 percent of the country lives in the greater Port-au-Prince area is a legacy of the U.S. occupation of the 1920s, which centralized government and business affairs there.

In the French period, rather, the difficulty of overland transport led to the emergence of three main coastal cities. Port-au-Prince was the official capital but Cap Français (now Cap Haïtien) on the north coast was the leading port, the largest city, and the most European of all the cities. Les Cayes on the southern coast had its own local elite, port, and cultural center. By 1789 Cap Français, with close to 19,000 residents, was larger than Boston, but Saint-Domingue's total urban population amounted to only about 8 percent of the colony.

In the years after 1763 French colonial authorities took measures to transform the nature of urban life in this overwhelmingly rural society. As I have argued elsewhere, this was motivated by the fear that the French empire would not survive another conflict with the British. In the Seven Years' War Saint-Domingue was France's only important North American colony not to be captured by this rival empire. Imperial officials believed that planters in Guadeloupe and Martinique had rapidly capitulated to the British in 1759 and 1762 because they were more concerned with the survival of their plantations than preserving these islands for the French Crown. In an attempt to build loyalty after the war, Versailles briefly experimented with abolishing Saint-Domingue's hated militia system and replacing the parish commanders with elected officials. But the French navy relied on the militia to reduce defense costs and it restored this unpopular institution in 1769, provoking a minor revolt.

In the years following that revolt, the colony's free population experienced two kinds of social transformations. First, the colonial administration began building new ports, government offices, military installations, fountains, parks, and encouraging the development of theatres, cafes, dancehalls, and other social spaces. The colony's first printing press had arrived in 1763, and Saint-Domingue soon had its own newspaper. Many of the social and cultural institutions that had become part of enlightened urban society in France now appeared in the colony. These changes, in my view, were part of an attempt to create a new "white" cultural identity that would unite French and island-born colonists.

The problem lay in defining which of these island-born colonists were truly French. For nearly one-half of Saint-Domingue's free population were *gens de couleur*; some of them were free blacks but even more were of mixed European and African ancestry. Beginning in 1770 – mere months after the anti-militia revolt – officials began to enforce the color line that separated free people of mixed and pure European genealogy. Discrimination had formally begun in the early 1730s with laws barring free people of African descent from leadership roles over whites. But in practical terms, officials counted planters' legal or common-law wives, including many free women of color, as white in censuses; notaries drafting formal documents involving such women – including marriage contacts – did not mention their racial identity. Unlike in French Louisiana, interracial marriages were never prohibited in Saint-Domingue. Up to the 1780s, 17 to 20 percent of all religious marriages in the colony's south province involved white men marrying women of color. Up to the 1760s and 1770s, the children of such unions were also considered white, especially if they were wealthy and light-skinned.

After 1770, Saint-Domingue's institutions took a new approach to racial identity. Notaries were required to ask wealthy, freeborn, French-educated men and women of color to show documents proving they were not slaves. Colonial elites began to describe such people, some of whom could be called "elite" themselves, as *affranchis* – ex-slaves. A law in 1773 even required that all free people of color with French family names take new names of African origin. From the 1770s French authorities and colonists insisted that racial genealogy was a natural dividing line in society and that it had always been observed as such. Not coincidentally, the new social spaces being built in Saint-Domingue's cities – dancehalls, theatres, and the like – were racially segregated by law, a development that thrust French and Creole whites together, while separating island-born free people on the basis of skin color.

In similarly large sugar plantation societies like Jamaica and Brazil, elites commonly treated the wealthy descendants of prominent planters as "white," despite their African ancestry. But after 1770 Saint-Domingue broke with this pattern, partly because of concerns about imperial loyalties. This ensured that obstreperous island-born whites would never side with free people of color in a kind of Creole coalition against French rule. The events of the revolutionary 1790s showed that colonial whites would even disregard the danger of a slave rebellion in order to repress the free coloreds' desire for equality.

In the 1780s, this new emphasis on a genealogical rather than social or cultural definition of race had a profound effect on the colony's several hundred wealthiest free men and women of color. Their desire to be recognized as members of the elite led them to scorn their black ancestors. In 1784, for example, the wealthy indigo planter Julien Raimond, a man of one-quarter African ancestry, proposed that the government make a new social class of "New Whites" – to be composed of free-born wealthy people of one-quarter or less African ancestry. Under such a system, Raimond would have been a New White; his freeborn mother, wealthy in her own right, would have remained a woman of color. Vincent Ogé, another wealthy free man of color who advocated early in the French Revolution for expanded voting rights, told colonial authorities that he did not even know any free blacks.

These concepts of color hierarchy and the self-conscious separation of Europeanized urban spaces from the more African culture of the countryside had an enormous effect on Haiti in the nineteenth century and persist to this day. Urban Haitians still call country people "moun andeyò" – literally, "people on the outside." While undeniably linked to the country's history of sugar plantation slavery, these features of Haitian society are rooted in the specific policies of the French colonial administration.

※   ※   ※

It would be absurd to suggest that a century-and-a-half of French rule and plantation slavery created all the challenges facing Haiti today. The whole point of Haitian independence was that a people that liberated itself from slavery could make its own history. And yet, in the ways I have outlined – the militaristic nature of colonial governments; the colonists' abuse of the natural environment; the early implication in the global economy; the development of a remarkable culture of resistance and survival; and the deliberate, stark divisions created between rural and urban populations, and between different class and color groups – we can sense that certain important elements of colonial Saint-Domingue did not simply disappear after the revolution, but continued to have a haunting, but also very real, presence in independent Haiti.

Further Reading

Blackburn, Robin. *The Making of New World Slavery: From the Baroque to the Modern, 1492–1800*. Verso, 1998.
Garrigus, John D. *Before Haiti: Race and Citizenship in Saint-Domingue*. Palgrave Macmillan, 2006.
Geggus, David P. *Haitian Revolutionary Studies*. Indiana University Press, 2002.
McClellan, James E. *Colonialism and Science: Saint Domingue in the Old Regime*. Johns Hopkins University Press, 1992.
Moitt, Bernard. *Women and Slavery in the French Antilles, 1635–1848*. Indiana University Press, 2001.

March 2010

17

Reckoning in Haiti: The State and Society since the Revolution

Jean Casimir and Laurent Dubois

The catastrophic earthquake in Haiti in January 2010 quite literally turned many of the buildings of the Haitian state into rubble. Reconstructing the Haitian state, and doing so in a way that helps assure that the state will be able to address the serious problems in Haiti, is clearly a vital priority in the wake of the earthquake. The current political order in Haiti, with its dispersed power that resides in various poles – the UN mission, the "Republic of the NGOs," foreign governments and their representatives, the different ministries and poles of authority in the Haitian state, and a wide range of civic and religious institutions – has shown its limitations in many ways in recent years, and during the recent catastrophe.

At the same time, of course, the society has remained remarkably organized in the face of the magnitude of the catastrophe. People have mobilized, often quite effectively given the limited resources at their disposal, to rescue neighbors and friends, to find solace, and to gather together to begin to plan for the future, while others have left the city to seek the solidarity and assistance of family in the countryside. If a similarly catastrophic event – resulting in no state infrastructure, no communication, no active security forces, and overwhelming destruction of the built environment – took place in a North American city, the level of social chaos would likely have been, it seems to us, much greater than it has been in Haiti. That is probably in part because of the ways Haitian society is largely independent from, and indeed in some ways in opposition to, the state.

This is a moment of reckoning for the Haitian state, but it should also force us to grapple with the longer history of state and society in Haiti. For we need to both admit and think about the fact that state-building has in fact been a focus of a great deal of effort and attention in Haiti for many decades, indeed for longer than that. The calls for reform and reconstruction, in other words, were part of Haitian politics for much of the twentieth century. And yet the Haitian state continues to operate in a very problematic way within the society. How might today's calls find a different outcome, and create a different future, than others that have come before? And how can history inform our understanding of what should happen next?

It is, we would submit, useful to go back to the beginning. From the moment of the Haitian state's official creation with independence in 1804, those who have embodied and spoken for it have confronted a very particular set of circumstances. On the one hand, the existence of Haiti was predicated on a radical refusal of, and a radical break with, French colonial control and slavery. That refusal of control is the bedrock, the foundational "social contract" of Haitian political life, and one that no Haitian politician could ever truly afford to reject, at least openly. One of the main pillars of this refusal was the constitutional article that banned foreign whites from owning property in the island. Foreign merchants found ways to get around this article, notably by marrying into Haitian families, but Haitian politicians who suggested repealing it did so at great political peril. The United States, however, rewrote the Haitian Constitution during the occupation to remove this stipulation. In a broader sense, however, a strong strand of Haitian politics has long been defined on one level by a powerful sense that foreign control inevitably means exploitation. The specter of a literal return to slavery, or of a return to forms of labor that resemble slavery, consistently haunted politics in Haiti in the nineteenth and early twentieth centuries.

At the same time, however, the Haitian Revolution brought together, and at times powerfully unified, very different currents of political aspiration. The motor of the revolution throughout its history was the resistance of the enslaved, a majority of them African-born, who drew on their own experiences on both sides of the Atlantic in conceiving of and struggling to create a "counter-plantation" system. This was a refusal not just of French control and chattel slavery, but also of the plantation system itself, and involved the creation of a very different way of living, one focused on production for oneself and for surplus within a local market.

But within the revolution's leadership, which was composed of individuals who were already free in 1791 and of others who had liberated themselves from slavery and rose into the high ranks of the military during the insurrection, many were committed to the maintenance of the plantation economy, and focused on the need for Haiti to continue to have outlets in the global market. While they refused French control and colonial racial hierarchy, they also believed it was necessary for independent Haiti to occupy a global economic niche much like that of colonial Saint-Domingue.

Both groups developed their political projects and their vision for the future in a context deeply constrained by the situation within Haiti and beyond it. In a sense, they had no option but to pursue the approaches they did. And both approaches were driven by very strong, and quite justifiable, fears and hopes. Those who refused the plantation model and created something else in its place did so because they rightly understood that any form of plantation labor, even paid, would be exploitative and deeply constrain their autonomy in ways they found unacceptable, especially given the recent memory of slavery. Those who wanted to maintain the plantation system, though, saw that if Haiti did not have a source of foreign exchange it would be deeply weakened. If they had in mind their own profits, they also had a serious and well-justified concern about defending Haiti from the prospect of invasion and developing a strong state in the face of such a possibility. Although these fears might seem, in retrospect, unfounded, in fact in France in the early nineteenth century there was an outpouring of pamphlets and proposals from individuals convinced that the nation could re-conquer its former colony and return it to its previous state as a productive plantation colony.

The contrasting and indeed contradictory social and economic visions that shaped Haiti's nineteenth century are best understood when situated within the broader story of post-emancipation societies in the Americas. In all the societies where plantation slavery existed, emancipation failed to fully deliver on its promises. In the U.S., Brazil, and the Caribbean, the abolition of slavery did not bring full equality and dignity to former slaves and their descendants, who continued for generations to face extreme forms of political, social, and economic exclusion, as well as structural inequalities that shape these societies to this day. In some ways the situation in Haiti paralleled the broader failures of post-emancipation societies in the Americas. Elites in Haiti, like those in other countries, marginalized the majority of descendants of slaves and continued to exploit their labor when possible and to exclude them from political and economic control.

The descendants of slaves, however, struggled in many ways successfully to refuse the forms of economic exploitation the elite sought to carry out, insisting on and constructing in their own communities a social order predicated and passionately insistent upon equality. And they were able to construct a social order in the countryside in which their quality of life was in fact significantly *better* than that of descendants of slaves in other societies. They owned land, produced for internal and external markets, and experienced a cultural autonomy and social dignity largely refused to people of African descent in other societies in the nineteenth century.

But Haiti's elite also faced a particularly challenging set of circumstances, one that distinguished their situation from that of other elites in the Americas. First of all, while all of the difficulties and challenges of creating a post-emancipation society burdened post-independence Haiti, most of the capital accumulated through a century of extremely profitable plantation agriculture ended up outside of the nation, in France as well as North America, which profited enormously from trade with the colony. In most other societies, the economic inequalities that shaped the lives of the formerly enslaved and their descendants existed within a broader economic matrix that encompassed the fortune of their former owners. In Haiti, while there were some former plantation owners of African descent among the post-independence population, for the most part the planters and merchants who had profited from slavery had either died or fled, and much of the capital produced by the plantation complex had in any case accumulated in French port towns and in Paris among merchant and planter families. The Haitian Revolution also destroyed towns and plantations and left perhaps 100,000 residents of Saint-Domingue dead. The nation not only faced the challenge of building a new order on the ashes of a plantation system, but did so in a context in which they inherited the legacies of massive and violent labor extraction without inheriting any of the capital that this extraction had produced.

Haitian leaders also had to deal with the fact that many foreign leaders saw the very existence of their nation as a serious, and seditious, threat. Although responses were far from uniform – some British abolitionists championed Haiti and worked with Henri Christophe to set up schools in the country – no nation acknowledged Haitian independence for two decades after 1804. Haiti's early regimes, meanwhile, poured a great deal of money into the construction of an impressive series of forts built along the spines of the mountains of the country, meant to assure that the Haitian army could withstand and ultimately repel a new invasion on the part of the French. This sapped the already limited resources of the new state. After a series of unsuccessful negotiations between Haiti and France, during which the French proposed on several occasions that they actually retake some form of control over their former colony, in 1825 the leaders of the Haitian government drew up a deal in which they would pay an *indemnity* of 150 million (later reduced to 60 million) francs in return for recognition from France. They were, with some reason, optimistic about potential productivity, especially of the coffee economy in Haiti, and saw the deal as a way of securing better access to the global market for plantation products.

Because of this deal, Haiti not only inherited the burdens of a century-long process of extraction, but actually had to then pay their former colonizer for the right to be recognized as independent. This money went to placate former planters, who had long lobbied the French government for a new conquest of Saint-Domingue, and instead received payments from the French government for what they claimed to have lost during the revolution. What they had lost, of course, most of all – what comprised the greatest part of their investment in Saint-Domingue – were human beings who, now citizens of an independent nation, were made to bear the burden of paying an indemnity to the French.

Since the Haitian government could not pay at the time, they took out loans – helpfully offered by French banks – and entered into the spiral of debt so familiar to postcolonial nations in the twentieth century, which has continued to this day. Combined with the fact that economic elites were, not surprisingly and certainly not uniquely, focused on extracting the maximum profit from their own holdings, this created a situation in which state institutions and the elites who controlled them heavily taxed rural production as well as coffee exports produced largely through peasant agriculture, with much of this money going to service the debt for the indemnity rather than to assist the construction of infrastructure within Haiti itself. While coffee production in fact thrived impressively during the nineteenth century – St. Marc coffee was the high-end gourmet coffee of its day – the profits from that production were sapped and diverted from projects within Haiti itself.

This story is important not simply because it illuminates some of the reasons for poverty in Haiti, but also because it helps us understand what the state has been, and perhaps might become, in Haiti. The functioning of the colonial state and different regimes in post-independence Haiti gave many in the country good reasons to see the state mainly as a source of actual or potential exploitation rather than as a source of support or a site of proper representation. Twentieth-century experiences in Haiti, notably the U.S. military occupation of 1915 to 1934, tended to confirm the suspicion that in many ways it was best to avoid the state. Though politics in Haiti have long been predicated upon appeals by political leaders to represent and speak for the masses, the conduits through which the demands of the population could actually profoundly shape the functioning of the state remained relatively limited, and popular demands often found themselves thwarted or expressed in uprisings rather than through procedural processes. None of this, of course, was particularly unique to Haiti, but it took on a particular form there, with important consequences.

The United States' occupation of the country in the early twentieth century represented an important turning point in its history, notably in the way that it transformed the place of Port-au-Prince within the country. As Georges Anglade, one of the victims of the earthquake, described well in his remarkable work *Atlas Critique d'Haïti*, the occupation represented a turning point in the geopolitics of the country. Through the late nineteenth century, the economic order of Haiti was organized around a large number of smaller towns and ports, most of them important ports during the colonial period, through which products, particularly coffee, were exported. Among the most successful was St. Marc, but throughout the country these poles produced their own economic activities and bureaucratic and economic elites. While in principle all men in Haiti served in the army, this operated essentially like a kind of militia service, and local leaders could and sometimes did call up forces to descend on the capital in various struggles for power over the central government. But the regions were largely autonomous in their functioning.

The U.S. occupation helped to change that. Economic activity was centralized in Port-au-Prince as the smaller ports were closed, and the political order was centralized as well. The town, from colonial times on, had been comparatively smaller and less significant as a port (especially compared to Le Cap in the north), but that had begun to shift in the early twentieth century (when the Port-au-Prince Cathedral, demolished in the earthquake, was built), and especially after the 1915 occupation by the United States. It was during this occupation that many of the buildings of the Haitian state that collapsed in the recent earthquake, including the National Palace, were built. This change was part of a larger process over the course of the twentieth century in which increasing environmental pressures in the countryside, the decline of the rice industry in the 1980s, and other factors drove massive migration to Port-au-Prince.

Why tell this story now? It is, it seems to us, crucial that we begin to think in a very historical way about the Haitian state, and see to what extent that can help us think about what it actually is and how it functions. Whatever will be built in Haiti will have to be built from its existing institutions, governmental and civic, and will have to be rooted in and make sense within the political landscape and vision of Haitians, which has been shaped and refined through their historical experience. This experience includes, we would argue, all that is necessary for the construction of a better future, so history can be both an inspiration and a caution. The remarkable social organization demonstrated in the wake of the earthquake suggests one of the impacts of the history of the Haitian state, which is that Haitians have largely become extremely adept at functioning without its assistance, even in times of catastrophe and crisis. Obviously, it would be better if they did not have to. But the fact that they do, and in some ways prefer to in the existing situation, is telling.

In a sense, the argument about how aid should be deployed and channeled in Haiti will very likely follow the two paths it has long followed. While many advocate forcefully, and for good reason, that the major effort should be toward the establishment of a functioning Haitian state that could most effectively deliver necessary services, many others are skeptical that this can be accomplished. In the meantime, the "Republic of NGOs" is driven by the idea that people desperately need certain services – health care, nutrition, legal representation, agricultural assistance – and that in the absence of a Haitian state capable of delivering these services it is a moral responsibility to deliver them. Each approach is, in its way, completely logical and completely correct. They are also, theoretically and practically, incompatible. But we live right now, and what we face now is a massive crisis, a toll of suffering that is difficult to even know how to count, or name.

As we try to grapple with the overwhelming disaster and what looms ahead, with the many mountains to climb in the coming years, we will need historical clarity and imagination. How can we assure that Haiti can rebuild both as quickly and as effectively as possible? Whatever the approaches taken, whether they are channeled through the Haitian state or through NGOs, they will only be successful in the long term if they are predicated upon the empowerment of the Haitian people to reconstruct their world in ways that promise to respond to their pressing and long-deferred aspirations. This empowerment could take different forms. One crucial zone of action is in the area of language. Notwithstanding the Constitution, which acknowledges Kreyòl as an official language, French is and will likely remain for some time the primary language of the state, as the language of education and the judiciary system in Haiti. While the expanded use of Kreyòl in official contexts is unavoidable and necessary, it is also true that spreading mastery of French will expand access to power and institutions in Haiti, and therefore aid in the enfranchisement of the population.

Giving people more access to communication will also assist the recovery effort. Projects to distribute cell phones and make their use afford-able would, in fact, have an immediate and useful impact on reconstruc-tion efforts, allowing people to communicate, strategize, and act. And the more reconstruction efforts can depend and draw on the knowledge and skills of a broad swath of the population, the better they will work. If there were some way, for instance, to funnel building materials into the market in Haiti, not precisely as donations but as a heavily subsidized infusion of such materials – particularly lumber – into the country at affordable prices, this would allow the many who are skilled carpenters and builders to provide shelter for the many who have lost it. These structures would be built much more quickly, and perhaps more effectively, than might be done otherwise, and with the benefit of allowing people to do paid work and participate directly in the reconstruction of their neighborhoods.

A new kind of state and political order will emerge in Haiti only if the people are empowered. And they need to be empowered as they are. If far too many are poor and illiterate, they are no less ready to think and act for the future, just as their ancestors did during the Haitian Revolution. That revolution began an irreversible process that has constituted the political and social organization of Haiti today, which is the only foundation for the future.

This is an expanded version of an article that appeared at the SSRC Online forum "Haiti, Now and Next," available at http://www.ssrc.org/features/view/haiti-now-and-next.

May 2010

18

Uprisings, Insurrections, and Political Movements: Contemporary Haiti and the Teachings of History, 1957–2010

Patrick Bellegarde-Smith

"We could have done much better," said my mother to me, a ten-year-old child, in Port-au-Prince in 1957. Her veiled, disconsolate, acerbic tone still haunts me. Though spoken in French, that phrase was as multilayered, as rich as if she had spoken it in the Haitian language, a tongue famous for its double-entendres. Dr. François Duvalier had just been selected by the military officers of the High Command of the Armed Forces against the favorite son of Haiti's light-skinned elite, Louis Déjoie. Much later, the United States government was forced to admit that the election had been fraudulent, and that Déjoie had won the presidency.

In subsequent long conversations my mother had plenty time to amplify her thought, unraveling her statement into its component parts, which became a rich interpretation of Haitian history itself. She treated me as an adult, and I resented it. As the Duvalier dictatorship unfurled, too much knowledge became a burden. Fear accompanied my waking moments, as I spent my life sheltered in the vast and moist gardens inhabited by the family patriarch and his descendants, in the decay of central Port-au-Prince. "We could have done much better," was my mother's reflection upon Duvalier's accession to power. Later, I realized that it was meant as a rebuke to the Haitian upper classes that had denied the smallest shreds of dignity to common Haitians, or to the country's middle classes for that matter. Governments had failed to follow through, in major and minor areas, even in those areas where victories could easily be achieved, such as the eradication of illiteracy. Mother had spoken eloquently of a Puerto Rican nation that had achieved cohesion, "even in skin-tone," a feat that had eluded Haiti plagued by black, brown, and beige class divisions. These were the discussions, "a long conversation," that marred my childhood, and that were my entrée into a sociological discourse that marked me for life.

Small events matter later as their meanings become clear, but big events seem to matter more in national life. The Duvalier dynastic presidencies of 1957–1986 were such an event. In hindsight, Duvalierism should have been predictable. Its ideological roots were anchored in raised expectations formed by an earlier middle-class government, that of Dumarsais Estimé, 1946–1950. And that government was the result of progressive administrative policies undertaken by Haitian ministers of education during the U.S. occupation in the 1920s that expanded the middle class. It was also the result of economic growth in that same period. But most importantly, the surge in middle-class consciousness was due to the relentless and unrequited search for power sharing, arising early in the twentieth century in struggles that, at times, had turned violent. Haiti had entered "its" twentieth century through the dislocation ushered in by the U.S. military occupation that did not resolve Haitian social problems, but instead aggravated them. The United States had had a different agenda, distinct from Haitian concerns. While Haiti sought to survive increasing American hegemonic power in the Caribbean and Central America, the United States sought to challenge German commercial interests, and to control the natural resources of the region for American corporations. The Americans were quite naturally drawn to favor Haiti's light-skinned elite, and opposed all efforts to dilute the latter's power by darker-skinned insurgents. In effect, the net impact of the American intervention was antidemocratic in the extreme, as it muzzled the press, dispersed the legislature, undertook fraudulent elections, scuttled the supreme court, and killed armed insurgents in droves.

Ostensibly intervening to install political stability in order to protect property, American designs over smallish nations had been crassly economic, in support of private industry. Since the early part of the twentieth century, American racism had increased exponentially. Its presence would be felt in all U.S. interactions with Latin American nations. Even the road networks established by American authorities were largely for military incursions in the provinces where resistance to the occupier was fiercest. The U.S. Marines would see that all possibilities of rural uprisings against the central government would disappear ... permanently. As it departed in 1934, the United States left an all-powerful Haitian military, officered by light-skinned elite men. That new army would act as the arbiter of national political life. The post-occupation period saw the reinforcement of U.S. hegemonic control, and also a recrudescence of internal strife based on class lines. It was a rich period in Haiti's political discourse.

Once before, the middle class had asserted power with the legislative election of Dumarsais Estimé, the "peasant from Verrettes," in 1946, but his government proved too progressive for the United States. The American occupation had spawned a black consciousness movement, *indigén-*

isme – the precursor of worldwide negritude – together with a guerrilla movement in the countryside. The latter was painstakingly eliminated by the United States with about 50,000 Haitian deaths, but the former survived and flourished. Politically progressive, the Estimé government was unable or unwilling to break the economic stranglehold of the upper classes and their foreign allies. Estimé displeased the Americans and the Haitian oligarchs who exercised their option for regime change, via the army. Estimé's health minister, the physician François Duvalier, worked for the return of the middle class to power, *la classe*, under his brand of black power, called *noirisme*. He would claim to rule in the name of the vast peasantry and the urban working classes, in the name of the black masses, but approximately 30,000 citizens died in the consolidation of his rule.

All this mattered. By the time Duvalier assumed power, the United States had had a change of heart. Other Anglophone Caribbean states were coming into political maturity and into independent life, away from British colonialism, under the leadership of their middle class. Cuba and the Dominican Republic had also experimented with middle-class rule and pro-western dictatorships. Furthermore, Latin Americanists at U.S. universities had made a case for middle-class political leadership, based on American governmental experience, in order "to ensure stability." Soon, a plethora of newly independent African states would come to the fore, all under the rule of their middle sectors. Haiti seemed ripe for Duvalier, and Duvalier seemed acceptable to the United States. The next three decades, 1957–1986, saw great U.S. financial and political support for the Duvaliers. For one, the Haitian government supported the U.S. cause against Cuba and international communism; it also decimated the Haitian communist party. *Noirisme* or Black Power, seemed more palatable to the United States than class struggle and forms of radicalism based on social class.

What Duvalierists called the Duvalierist revolution became easily the most venal, brutal, corrupt, and personalized of all Haitian dictatorships. Though it allowed the expansion of the middle class into the body politic, it otherwise had no redeeming value. In that part of the world, heightened foreign intrusion into industry and commerce often results in increased corruption on the part of national elites shut out from financial gain by outsiders. By the time Duvalier came to power, the only way to make money seemed to be in politics. Cuba exhibited a similar outcome pre-1959. What then develops in Haiti is a grand alliance between the middle classes and the upper classes, whose symbolic unification was the marriage of President Jean-Claude Duvalier and Michelle Bennett, in which seven million U.S. dollars were spent. Subsequently, when the urban working classes and the peasantry attempt to join in the governing of the country, they are met with strong and unified opposition by the old and the new bourgeoisies, and their foreign backers. To their credit, the Duvaliers' governments did not denigrate the Haitian language, by favoring French, nor did they actively persecute or disparage the Haitian religion, Vodou.

Just as there were seven governments during the 1911–1915 period that preceded the U.S. occupation, there were five interim administrations in the 1956–1957 period immediately before François Duvalier came to power. The existence of so many provisional administrations before a strong regime comes to power shows dissent in the ranks of dominant groups as factions jostle for power, and dissatisfaction in the population at large. It is at these moments in Haitian history that foreign support, favoring one group over the other, one solution over another, matters most. Democracy was never in Washington's best interest.

My mother's words, "we could have done much better," haunt me still decades later. Although my family backed Louis Déjoie – he visited the family compound at 10 p.m. one night, in his black Cadillac and with his bodyguards – I thought intuitively, that it would be "best" to join forces with the middle class for a rejuvenated Haiti. I was ten years old. The Duvaliers and their particular crowd, were the wrong *éléments* (as is said in Haitian French), for that grand alliance. And when in 1959 Fidel Castro entered Havana, many Haitians, myself included, thought that freedom for Haiti was nigh. During the years of the dictatorship until I left Haiti in 1964 at sixteen, my "job" had been to intercept all news on Haiti from Radio Havana and the Voice of America in several languages every day, type an accurate report, and distribute it "upward" to adults in my family and to trusted outsiders. I had received as a present a manual German typewriter, which had the French diacritical marks necessary for this work. I always typed one original and several carbons. My fear of being discovered increased substantially – other fourteen- and fifteen-year-olds had already been "disappeared" by Duvalier's secret police, *cagoulards* and *Tontons Macoutes*.

Over and over, the United States came to the rescue of the Duvalier regimes, anytime either "Papa Doc" or "Baby Doc" needed American support. Like all Haitian presidents (and all Haitians), from the beginning of the twentieth century, the Duvaliers assumed that their government would not survive without active U.S. support. The American anthropologist Sidney W. Mintz wrote, "Another political effect of the occupation was the importance it imparted to the United States ambassador, whose political opinions thereafter would matter significantly in the transmission of power of the Haitian governmental system." It was assumed by successive American administrations that Haiti could not do better than what it had with the Duvaliers. In the course of two hundred years of national existence, Haiti had gone from colonialism, a brief period of independence (1804–1890s), and almost seamlessly into neo-colonialism – even before the term was invented. *Could we have not done much better?*

Political stability for economic growth, rather than development, had been the leitmotiv of American plans for Haiti. Social justice was never an issue. A non-ambitious plan for enclave export assembly industries was to be Haiti's salvation, according to American economists. The agricultural sector would be decimated, both in production and its labor, to sustain the urban industries. But the world's cheapest workforce did little for rapidly underdeveloping Haiti. Schemes for Haitian development increased Haitian poverty. There were uprisings, small-scale invasions from abroad, passive resistance, and large migrations abroad, both from professional ranks and later from impoverished peasants and urban workers. The Haitian diaspora is one of the largest in the world. As usual, university and secondary school students did their part. Many were killed. Over time, even the Roman Catholic Church in its liberationist *Ti-Legliz*-based community organizations, the Vodou associations (organized around the *ounfò*), the temples, the spoken media, and written press all did their share. Jean-Claude Duvalier was deposed, and he departed the country after a phone call to him from the U.S. ambassador, on February 7, 1986. The Americans had pulled the plug on a comatose government.

Less than 1 percent of Haitians receive about 44 percent of all income, but pay only 3.5 percent of taxes, leaving the overburdened majority with the rest of the bill. In Haiti as elsewhere in other capitalist states, wealth inequalities fuel social discontent that results in political instability, as inherently weak governments become dictatorial just to maintain the status quo. The repressive apparatus of the state increases to meet dissatisfaction and insurgencies of all kinds. The national security state favors narrow, sectarian interests, and fewer resources are available to meet the demands of a dispirited population. Governmental foreign aid and foreign charities are then expected to assuage these populations, in the absence of a rational plan for national development. In this, we face *un capitalisme sauvage*, a rudimentary form of capitalism in which majorities starve and the rich become consequently richer. At least, this is the observable pattern outside the center, in peripheral regions of the globe, but it is equally observable internally in rich countries in their ghettoes, barrios, favelas, townships, reservations, and bantustans.

As stated earlier, in terms of the impoverishment of the Haitian bourgeoisie that became a clientele elite, the neocolonialism that entered Haiti in the 1890s impoverished all Haitians further. Soon after independence in 1804 the Haitian peasantry had the highest standard of living in the Americas after the United States. Now it has the lowest. The interactions between weak and strong states, domestic and international elites, the evolution of power structures in the international system, and international capital are the only plausible explanations for the plight of Haiti in the world. The knowledge of history is fundamental in seeking explanations.

How many times does a phoenix rise from his ashes before being given a "pass?" The popular movements that preceded the uprisings that led to the overthrow of the Duvalier dynasty were widespread. Their roots ran deep into the rich soil of insurgency.

The deep, perennial concerns for democracy are illustrated in the struggle to enact the new constitution. Haitian constitutions are small literary masterpieces, and paragons of liberal thinking at its best. Though seldom respected, constitutions nevertheless provide a "snap shot" of an ideal Haiti. The Constitution of 1987 provoked enormously positive public reaction: in the intense discussions it elicited at all levels of society there was an indication of uncanny political awareness; in the referendum that saw its adoption with a 99 percent approval rate; in its provisions that went beyond previous documents. It decriminalized Vodou, placing it on par with other religions, as it withdrew "state religion" status from Catholicism; it raised Haitian as one of two official languages alongside French; it decentralized power, devolving much to the provinces, in contradistinction to policies dating from the U.S. occupation; it declared public education and health to be basic rights. It was no longer a matter of bad versus good presidents, but of institutionalizing power and turning away from personality cults, and of achieving an equilibrium between branches of government. It split executive power by creating the post of prime minister. The Constitution countered the tradition of a strong, often despotic executive. Peasant groups submitted their desiderata to the *Assemblée Constituante* for the first time in Haitian history. The Constitution of 1987 dared address issues of economic democracy. But the document remained liberal, reformist, not the radical or revolutionary document some wanted. The Constitution heralded a *prise de conscience*, not a different political culture, just the initial possibility for such a cultural change.

African-American social thinkers Harold Cruse and Maulana Karanga had both argued that cultural oppression may indeed precede political and economic oppression, as cultural control facilitates the other two. Cruse continued that analysis, arguing that "there can be no real ... revolution ... without a cultural revolution as a corollary to the scheme of 'agencies' for social change."

However, as there were gaps between political culture, historical traditions, and popular demands as a result of the execution of power across five centuries, there was an unbridgeable gulf between Western-derived, established state structures and national institutions, the latter springing from the deep yearning for cultural autonomy and democracy, stymied by the former. During the national debates, more progressive elements within the Catholic Church accused the United States and its religious "private sector," of doing its best to stop the poor from "taking over." It was an accurate reading of the popular mood at that time. I returned home in February 1987 to see how I might assist the new Haitian government, and I heard or overheard many such comments from the poor themselves, indicating that they were insisting on being a part of the political process, as they had been two centuries earlier in forging a new Haiti.

Duvalierism had not died with the end of the Jean-Claude Duvalier presidency. Now controlled by middle-class elements, the national army remained the absolute arbiter of Haitian politics, as the United States had intended in 1916. The army's unbending will was counteracted by massive demonstrations in which scores of individuals died. It was later learned, via the American press, that most or many individuals of the army's High Command had been paid assets of the United States, starting as young officers. Army-sponsored death squads intimidated a citizenry that refused to be intimidated. As demonstrators were killed, more demonstrations were fueled to protest the killings, leading to more killings. There were devastating attacks against the media, particularly radio stations, since many Haitians are illiterate and received their news from that medium. Peasant associations were persecuted. Hundreds of Vodou priests were murdered at the urging of some Catholic and Protestant clergy.

The popular cry was picked up by a populist priest, Jean-Bertrand Aristide. The episcopate tried to silence him repeatedly. The bourgeoisie and the United States feared the worst when Aristide declared, "we have the steering wheel of Haitian history in our hands ... and we must take a left turn." There were to be 13 attempts against Aristide's life; he survived them all. Seeing that Aristide had survived these assassination attempts and imbued by their faith, many Haitians dubbed him Moses – who spoke truth to power – and Danbala or Legba, the Vodou deities, powerful symbols in the Haitian cultural matrix.

But before fair elections could be entertained, there would be continued death and mayhem at the hands of the army and the remnants of the Duvalierist Macoutes. A number of provisional military governments took over after consultation with the United States. In February 1988 in flawed elections, Professor Leslie F. Manigat was named president for a five-year term that lasted only five months. The army deposed Manigat, and ruled again directly. Manigat had been "played," and he was unable to convince his countrymen that, all the while, he was a sheep in wolf's clothing.

There were coups d'état within coups d'état, inside the army itself, when one general would replace another, then another. The army remained fractious, but unlikely to act alone, without the support of some faction or the other of the commercial-industrial elite, or of the United States embassy. That commercial-industrial elite consists of Haitian and non-Haitian wings, going back to patterns established in the 1890s, while foreign military interference was well established from the mid nineteenth century. General Henri Namphy resigned the presidency; General Prosper Avril also resigned as president; General Hérard Abraham resigned as president to hand over power to Madame Ertha Pascal-Trouillot, the first woman judge at the Cour de Cassation, Haiti's supreme court, and the widow of my Haitian history professor in the late 1950s. Her sole function was to give the country fair elections, which resulted in Jean-Bertrand Aristide attaining the presidency for a period of five years that ended a mere seven months later in September 1991.

At this point, Haiti had had – much like as in previously unsettled historical periods – seven governments in four years. These periods of anarchy followed by lengthy dictatorships (or the U.S. military occupation) indicated the level of popular dissatisfaction with the status quo. However, it was clear that democracy does not occur under military rule, as the United States believed during that period. When Aristide was brought back from exile by President Bill Clinton in 1994, he proceeded to the dissolution of the Haitian army in April 1995, against the advice of the United States. And on the eve of transmitting power to his duly elected successor, on February 6, 1995, Aristide "recognized" Cuba diplomatically, annoying the United States greatly.

From the outset, President Jean-Bertrand Aristide, who had emerged as the conscience of the nation, found an unmanageable situation. He was a thirty-seven-year-old Catholic priest when he came to power with an overwhelming mandate, with almost 68 percent of the votes, and with substantial majorities in all nine Haitian departments. The next highest vote getter was World Bank economist, and U.S. favorite, Marc L. Bazin, with 14 percent of the votes. And contrary to the first election with universal suffrage in 1957, that election was fair.

The new president was despised by the upper class (a peasant in power); feared by the middle class (he might move against corruption and nepotism – the middle class occupying the state bureaucracy as is generally true in Latin America); and disliked by the Church (he had challenged the episcopate and the Vatican). He was distrusted by business (he would raise wages and attempt to collect taxes); he worried the army (he could move against the drug trade and contraband at the border), and he was opposed by the United States (he was a socialist, liked by French President François Mitterand). Born in the peasantry in Port Salut (Port Salvation) in Haiti's south, he did not see the peasantry as a special interest group, but as the maw from which sprung all things Haitian. Conversely, he saw the Haitian bourgeoisie as the reason for the impoverishment of Haiti's poor and for their own wealth. The "revolution," he claimed, was political in nature before it could become a social and then an economic revolution. What was there to fear? No one wanted that, except perhaps 90 percent of the Haitian electorate. Poverty, he argued, was the ultimate violence, robbing women, men, and children of all human dignity. *Tout moun se moun*: all people are human beings! Was he really intending to raise abysmally low wages so that Haiti could travel the road from abject misery to abject poverty, an improvement over conditions as he found them? Aristide, as it turned out, was feared by the "right" kind of people, hence the coup d'état in September 1991 and that of January 2004. The first coup was from the Haitian army; the second, by invaders that came from the outside wearing "spiffy" military-styled uniforms.

The lasting legacy of Aristide might well be the creation of a mood and the belief now engrained in common Haitians that they must be empowered. They have become stakeholders in affairs of state, taking Haiti's motto seriously: *liberté, égalité, fraternité*. It was a foregone conclusion that Aristide had to go. He was unwanted and unloved by the people that counted politically, perhaps 10 percent of the population. At the height of his powers, the president was able to ensure a transfer of power to a now friend and ally, René G. Préval, in 1995. Re-elected in 2001, Aristide tried hard as he may, not to implement his vision, but to merely stay in power. He faced increasing violence, and responded with violence of his own. At his ignominious departure from power in 2004, an unimpressed population re-elected Préval, now no longer a friend, for a second five-year mandate. Aristide remains in exile in the Republic of South Africa, where the United States wished him to be, unable to come closer because the

United States threatened the Jamaican government that seemed to want to give him a berth. Jamaica – and Saint Thomas, Danish Virgin Islands – had been the traditional, historical lands of exile for Haitian presidents.

I have argued over the past three decades that in Haiti the issue is not about majority rule and minority rights, nor about mere civil rights, or even – as Americans would say – about pluralism and diversity. It is instead about control of the state apparatus and access to power, control that is exercised and maintained through cultural, social, economic, religious, and linguistic hegemony. (Are the last two elements, religious and linguistic hegemony, coming to an end?) Though weak, the Haitian state has nonetheless been a powerful tool to impose a "vision," a state against the people over which it rules, and for the benefit of a predatory elite and its foreign friends. At heart and at the core, it is still a struggle between Franco-Haitian and Afro-Haitian variants of that culture. Democracy would be an Africanizing process by definitional necessity, as state structures come to embrace and harmonize with national cultural institutions.

Elected twice legitimately but without much enthusiasm, President Préval no longer "sits" in the National Palace, the ultimate symbol of Haitian statehood, nor does he sit in his house in a respectable part of Port-au-Prince. Both the Palace and his home, and about 60 percent of the capital's buildings, were destroyed by the earthquake that ravaged Haiti. The "Goudougoudou" – as we now derisively call the earthquake – of January 12, 2010, killed upwards of 200,000 souls, and rendered homeless about one-third of Haiti's population, about three million. This is the equivalent of 103 million people in U.S. terms. The government is destroyed – more inefficient than it was the day before, on January 11, 2010 – and the Haitian leadership seems despondent. The whole world has come to Haiti's rescue, but will it follow through? After all, the world powers had disempowered the Haitian government, bit by bit, over the last fifty years. This was done partly through the introduction of about 11,000 non-government organizations, the NGOs. Foreign governments and world financial agencies ostensibly feared Haitian corruption, choosing to demote the Haitian government, and deciding instead to promote private NGOs, whose agendas are limited, murky, and more in tune with what world powers seem to want for Haiti.

Can foreign powers, domestic elites, and international capitalism take a chance in strengthening the Haitian government when the Haitian people might insist on *not* electing the "right" presidents? I am reminded of two similar if not identical statements made by U.S. President Gerald R. Ford and U.S. Secretary of State Henry Kissinger about the events of September

II, 1970, when the democratically elected President of Chile, Salvador Allende, fell to a coup d'état, and died in La Moneda. Kissinger said: "I do not see why we have to let a country go Marxist just because the people are irresponsible."

Since the Haitians residing in poverty are hell-bent on applying the state motto, *liberté, egalité, fraternité,* might Haiti's salvation come from using all forces in the nation, the rich as well as the semi-rich, applying Haiti's legend, emblazoned on the national flag, *L'Union fait la Force* – In unity there is strength? It will surely mean a change of heart on the part of social and economic elites domestically, which have long enjoyed the benign neglect of the United States. Since the Goudougoudou of January 12, 2010, and events small and big that have transpired from my homeland, I have had ample time to ponder my mother's statement, "we could have done much better." As a member of Haiti's upper class, she seemed to have understood.

Further Reading

Bellegarde, Dantes. *Histoire du peuple haïtien.* Lausanne, Switzerland: Collection du Tricinquantenaire, 1954.

Bellegarde-Smith, Patrick. *Haiti: The Breached Citadel.* Toronto: Canadian Scholars' Press, 2004.

Bellegarde-Smith, Patrick. *In the Shadow of Powers: Dantes Bellegarde in Haitian Social Thought.* Atlantic Highland, NJ: Humanities Press, 1985.

Bellegarde-Smith, Patrick and Claudine Michel. *Haitian Vodou: Spirit, Myth, and Reality.* Bloomington: Indiana University Press, 2006.

Dupuy, Alex. *Haiti in the New World Order: The Limits of Democratic Revolution.* Boulder, CO: Westview Press, 1997.

Fatton, Robert Jr. *Haiti's Predatory Republic: The Unending Transition to Democracy.* Boulder, CO: Lynne Rienner Publishers, 2002.

Florival, Jean. *Duvalier: La Face cachée de Papa Doc.* Montreal: Mémoire d'Encrier, 2008.

Michel, Claudine. *Aspects éducatifs et moraux du Vodou haïtien.* Port-au-Prince, Editions Le Natal, 1995.

Plummer, Brenda Gayle. *Haiti and the Great Powers.* Baton Rouge: Louisiana State University Press, 1988.

Renda, Mary A. *Taking Haiti: Military Occupation and the Culture of U.S. Imperialism, 1915–1940.* Chapel Hill: University of North Carolina Press, 2001.

Smith, Matthew J. *Red & Black in Haiti: Radicalism, Conflict, and Political Change, 1934–1957.* Chapel Hill: University of North Carolina Press, 2009.

Trouillot, Michel-Rolph. *State against Nation: The Origin and Legacy of Duvalierism.* New York: Monthly Review Press, 1988.

May 2010

PART IV
Haiti and Me

19
Haïti Chérie

Maryse Condé

I "discovered" Haiti in the 1950s when I was a student in literature at the Lycée Fénelon in Paris. With Jacques A.... , a friend who was studying history, we founded a club, the Luis Carlos Prestes Club, named after a Latin-American revolutionary that I don't know anything about anymore. This club had numerous cultural claims and prided itself on livening up the student life of the Antilleans. Jacques A.... wanted to show a documentary about Haiti.

One can measure the alienation in which I grew up by the fact that I had hardly ever heard anything about Haiti. I was unaware of its glorious history. I had never heard the names of Toussaint Louverture, Dessalines, or Henri Christophe. I knew nothing of the wars of liberation that made this country the first black republic, victorious over the armies of Napoleon Bonaparte. This will not surprise those who have read my childhood memoirs, *Le Coeur à rire et à pleurer* (Tales from the Heart: True Stories from My Childhood). My parents never spoke to me about slavery. I had but a faint idea of my origins and my past.

I've forgotten virtually everything about the documentary that was shown. Only one dazzling image remains in my memory today. A black president (was it President Magloire?) majestically descended the steps of a staircase. O stupor! Remember that in those years all of Africa was in chains. Kwame N'Krumah had not yet transformed the Gold Coast into Ghana. Could a state thus be free, independent, and governed by a black? I was overcome and hurried to see my older brother, who served as my educator. He gave me a history lesson which he stopped – conveniently, I realize now – at the year 1805, and gave me a book to read by one of his friends, Edris Saint-Amand, titled: *Bon Dieu Rit* (God Laughs). I could not judge the literary merit of this novel. All I know is that it opened for me the doors of a fascinating and unknown world: Vodou, the wisdom and oppression of the peasants of Haiti, the problems of the past, the present, and the future. All of a sudden, I had a passion for Haitian literature. I devoured pell-mell essays and novels: *Gouverneurs de la rosée* (Masters of the Dew) and *La Montagne Ensorcelée* (The Enchanted Mountain) by Jacques Roumain; *Ainsi Parla l'Oncle* (So Spoke the Uncle) by Jean-Price Mars; *Thémistocle Epaminondas Labasterre* by Frédéric Marcelin; *La Bête de Musseau* (The Beast of the Haitian Hills) by Philippe and Pierre Thoby-Marcelin; to cite only a few. I was initiated into the antiquated charms of Justin Lhérisson's "odiens," his traditional-style novellas, set in the Haitian countryside. One book dazzled me: *Compère Général Soleil* (General Sun, My Brother) by Jacques-Stephen Alexis. This work introduced me to the complexity of social realism, marvelous realism, and a kind of poetic, political engagement. I became close to Haitian students and during that time met our great Toto Bissainthe, who was not yet a singer but an actress in the company "Les Griots." Everything was going wonderfully between us when a considerable danger arose: my new friends were violently protesting in the streets against the candidacy at the next presidential election of a certain François Duvalier, a doctor, black like the great mass of the Haitian people. Thanks to Aimé Césaire, I was a fervent follower of Négritude, and perhaps without knowing it, of Duvalier's *noirisme* too. Didn't a political leader judge himself above all else by the color of his skin and his social origins? My Haitian experiences were to cease suddenly, however.

Indeed, I had just met my first husband, Mamadou Condé, a Guinean actor whom I had admired at the Odéon in the play *Les Nègres* (The Blacks) by Jean Genet. He brought me into the tumult of the African independences. At his side, my understanding grew ever deeper. Sekou Touré and the Boiro camp taught me that to limit oneself only to one's skin color leads to dangerous aberrations. A black leader can become the torturer of his people. Personal dramas added themselves to the prevailing situation, and marked the beginning of some dark years. My sister's husband was called back from his post as ambassador to Liberia under the pretext of an imaginary plot. He was thrown in prison without being tried. We would never see him again. During those years, I never forgot Haiti, whose *banderillas* had solidly implanted themselves in my heart and in my soul. I also became friends with Haitian writers, who were numerous at the time in Africa and especially in Senegal: Félix Morisseau-Leroy, Gerard Chenet, Jean Brierre, and above all the incomparable Roger Dorsinville, author of, among other things, *Mourir pour Haïti* (To Die for Haiti), *Renaître à Dende* (Reborn in Dende), and *Un Homme en trois morceaux* (A Man in Three Pieces). A quasi-filial friendship was born between Roger and me. I had him read the manuscript of the novel I was working on: *Heremakhonon*. Its "negative heroine" and the iconoclastic and provocative nature of the text did not please him very much because he was in favor of a much more traditional form of political activism. He told me this straight and ... I took no heed of his remarks. With my Haitian friends, I discussed the delusions, the traps of African socialism. They revealed to me the crimes of Duvalierism. The doctor of the poor, sworn enemy of the tropical skin infection yaws, had very quickly thrown off his masks. Jacques-Stephen Alexis, the unforgettable author of *Compère Général Soleil*, had been arrested and tortured. Duvalier's private militia, the *Tontons Macoutes*, was slaughtering entire families. The country's population was decreasing; the intellectuals were fleeing en masse. I learned, painfully, about the division between the discourses adapted by political leaders to fit given circumstances and the reality that they force their people to live.

I believe that I came to Haiti for the first time in the 1970s with my second husband, Richard Philcox. I had since come back to Paris after those mournful years. At the time, I was working at the journal *Présence Africaine*, which the Senegalese Alioune Diop had founded. I had a very bad reputation there because, informed as I was by my personal experience, I refused the convenient myths in use at the time, the sugarcoated words hiding the materialism and the corruption of the so-called political elite. Alioune Diop gave me a message for one of his friends, René Piquion, author of a work titled *Les Trois grands de la Négritude* (Three Great Men of the Negritude Movement). Given his reputation as a man of the government, I was careful not to go looking for him. To my surprise, he came in person to the modest bed and breakfast we were staying at and asked us to stay in his home, since life in Port-au-Prince, he told us, was not easy. I realized that one must not reduce a man to his ideological positions, which were often dictated by contradictory reasons. A Duvalierist could turn out to be human, civil, and friendly. René Piquion's wife was losing her vision and was going blind with a grace and a dignity that astounded us. Once again, my preconceived ideas were overturned. The Piquions' home was a veritable museum; overflowing with African and Haitian works of art, it taught us the proximity that exists between these two places of creation. On a personal level, the couple illustrated the complexity of the soul of certain Haitian people. In their garden stood a little Vodou altar, yet they were perfect Catholics, pillars of the Sunday Mass. They were generous to the point of caring about the well being of two unknown people. At the same time, some "restaveks" (unpaid domestic laborers from poor families) lived in their home, and they were treated not with brutality, perhaps, but with the most perfect indifference. The stories and memories of these "restaveks" were the inspiration for my first children's book, *Haïti Chérie*

(Dearest Haiti), re-baptized a few years later as *Rêves amers* (Bitter Dreams) by the publisher Bayard Jeunesse.

A few steps from there lived the grammarian Pradel Pompilus. What a paradox! I, who knew nothing about Guadeloupian Creole, was interested in Haitian Kreyòl, which to me seemed harmonious and hermetic. It was there that I first heard of the debate that later would become all the rage: Créolité. Should one write in the language of the people, a language forged by the plantation and which possesses, according to some, a certain "something extra" in terms of its expressiveness? Should one write in French, a language imported and imposed by the colonizers? Pradel Pompilus invited me to meet a writer by the name of Frankétienne, who was shaking up Haitian literature. With his friends, he had founded a literary movement, Spiralism, but he was known above all else for his virulent plays in Kreyòl. Unfortunately, all of our attempts to meet failed. I keep a luminous memory of this stay. I also keep in my memory my following trip to Haiti, when I met Roger Dorsinville, who had returned from exile in Dakar. He lived, I believe, at the end of a courtyard. The moon lit up a part of the sky above our heads. Someone was reading excerpts of his memoirs, *Accords Perdus* (Lost Agreements). It was a perfect moment.

These trips were followed by many others, over the course of which I visited Jacmel, Les Cayes, and Cap Haïtien. When I went to Cap Haïtien, the French-built northern road had just been completed. It was a Sunday. Men and women in their best clothes, a mass of peasants, were all heading toward their places of worship. The austere beauty of the landscape, the energy of its inhabitants, all of it made for a dizzying kaleidoscope. Once I arrived at the Cap, I visited on the back of a donkey the ruins of the Palais de Sans Souci and those of the Citadelle La Ferrière. The place had been taken over by thorn bushes, giant cacti, and above all, phantoms. What was left of this past? Nothing. I saw it, Negritude had held itself up for an instant, the time of the rebel generals' victory, then it had fallen to the ground, vanquished. Was it defeated by the rancor of the French colonizer? By the dangerous proximity of American capitalism? By the greed and the negligence of the local despots?

My last voyage to Haiti was in 2007, when I was invited to Michel Le Bris' Etonnants Voyageurs festival. This trip was completely different from those that had preceded it. Since then, Haiti gone through the complicated years of Aristide: the only leader who sincerely loved his people, said some; a cruel dictator, more bloodthirsty than the Duvaliers, said others. Haiti was on the verge of political division, trampled by gangs of armed thugs. It had just returned to democracy with René Préval. People spoke only of kidnappings and prostitution, and there were murmurings of pedophilia. I don't know what to think about these rumors. What is certain is that I didn't recognize Port-au-Prince; the city was saturated to the extreme, overpopulated, and almost intimidating. Reuniting with the numerous Haitian friends that I had made over all of those years did not help me overcome a feeling of strangeness and dispossession. Haiti was no longer in Haiti. I left this land very determined to go back there to try to see things more clearly. I didn't have the chance to do so.

I found myself in New York City on January 12, 2010, when the horrible news broke about the terrible disaster that had happened. I could not imagine a crueler feeling than finding oneself in a comfortable and protected apartment looking out on the Hudson and on the beautiful riverside trees, their leaves shed for the winter, and witnessing minute by minute the devastation striking Haiti. I felt like a pitiful voyeur. For once I did not reproach CNN for its taste for the spectacular and the morbid. I absorbed everything: the dead, scattered throughout the streets; the injured pulled out painfully from the rubble; the homeless; the collapsed monuments; the destroyed homes; all of that suffering. My friends who were in the process of adopting Haitian children informed me that they had already prepared everything to welcome these young ones: bedrooms, toys – in a word, nothing was lacking – but the orphanages were practically destroyed and the papers had disappeared. Other friends, Haitians this time, were without news of their families. I myself sent emails here and there and received no response. I learned that Jacmel, a place of so many fond memories, was destroyed, and despite myself tears came to my eyes.

Sometimes, more mundane thoughts came over me. I was writing a novel composed of three stories, one of which took place in Port-au-Prince. Since my work was based on the information that I was receiving at the time, the story's end was optimistic. The country was said to be entering a period of relative peace and prosperity. The kidnappings had practically ceased. The gang leaders had all laid down their arms. Now that the country had to be rebuilt, I had to rewrite everything. Or at the very least change the final pages. After two days during which I lived the disaster in my mind, weary of feeding on all of those misfortunes, I turned to TV5 Monde and learned that Eric Rohmer had also passed away, but by less painful means, I think. In homage to the director, the television network was showing a film: *Ma nuit chez Maude*. I was upset with myself for taking so much pleasure in listening to the film's illuminating dialogues once again, in admiring the acting of Françoise Fabian and Jean-Louis Trintignant. Alas, human beings are thus made, complex, multifarious. At the end of the film, I returned to my images of destruction. Obviously there were absurd, preposterous moments. The pastor Robertson harked back to the curse of Haiti, which supposedly had signed a pact with the devil in order to free itself from French colonialism. The extreme-right commentator Rush Limbaugh advised not to send a cent for Haiti because President Obama, whom he detests, would make it his personal project. On another station I learned that Brad Pitt and Angelina Jolie pledged a million dollars of their personal fortune to help this unfortunate, stricken country. Other celebrities also did their best. As for me, I could give only my sorrow and my profound sympathy for this country that I have loved for so many years.

The famous song "Sometimes I Feel Like a Motherless Child" that opened the concert "Hope for Haiti Now," organized by George Clooney and Wyclef Jean and broadcast on all of the American networks, expressed the sadness and the despair that we were all feeling. That night, no millions were donated by celebrities, who found themselves caught between compassion and the search for personal prestige. This concert was aimed at the ordinary citizen. One couple donated one hundred dollars to Steven Spielberg, seated modestly behind a telephone. A woman made a gift of 25 dollars to Julia Roberts, who thanked her warmly. For the moment, all concerns were focused on the future of the children.

A few months ago, one of my daughters adopted a baby from Mali who had been abandoned on a road in the north of the country. Since then, our family has surrounded this little miraculous survivor, who does not yet know where she comes from and from what hell she escaped. It may be this adoption that made me aware of the problems of the orphans in Haiti. There are thousands of them. A little boy remained buried for eight days under the rubble, next to the corpses of his father and his mother. He came out without a scratch but with eyes full of the horrors that he lived through, trapped in his stone coffin. A young girl was also pulled from the pile of concrete blocks, unharmed but dehydrated, her skin cracking like a leaf of paper. Strangely, she raised her arms in a gesture of victory. We learn that 57 children, whose adoption papers were in order, landed at Pittsburgh airport, 30 in Paris, 100 in Holland. Soon, the administrative services of the different countries assure us, all of the children whose papers are being processed will leave to join up with their host families. One might wonder what will happen to the others, all the others who live in the tent villages with what remains of their families, practically without water or food.

A lot is said about the reconstruction of Haiti. But there is the fear that the different countries that come to its aid will be guided excessively by their own interests and their own perspectives. To be beneficial, the reconstruction of Haiti should be the work of the Haitians themselves, supported with advice and opinions, if necessary. My dream, alas it is but a dream, would be that this catastrophe would bring to an end the old demons of selfishness, corruption, and materialism so that the children of Haiti will one day be reunited with a land that will welcome them and permit them to fully blossom.

If I had to sum up, I would say that Haiti played a key role, as key as that of Africa, in my personal development. The episodes of its history dictated the nature of my political engagement and of my ideological choices. However, for me its essential contribution lies elsewhere, in its incomparable cultural richness. Some twenty years ago, outraged by the classification of Mali amongst the 15 least advanced countries in the world, I wrote the novel *Ségou* (Segu) to demonstrate that one must not confuse material poverty with cultural poverty. Haiti is the resounding proof of this truth. The newspapers call it the poorest nation in the Western hemisphere at every opportunity. However, none of them would dare deny that it overflows with other riches. In 1975, on the eve of his death, André Malraux journeyed there and fell in love with the painters of Saint-Soleil. In *L'Intemporel* (Timeless), he consecrated a few of his most beautiful pages to them: "Another few kilometers," he writes,

> another cemetery, a cross with raised arms, tombs painted with a furious freedom, but not in a childlike way: a Merovingian cemetery colored by the Ensor of *The Masks*, the goddess Phantasmagoria and her god Carnaval: it's the cemetery of Saint-Soleil.... Framed by the stone arch that dominates the entrance, the fierce hills bristle with little plots of land, like photographs from a travel book. They draw nearer. Looking into the sun, the binoculars make out paintings on easels, which hide the chests and the heads of painters who carry them. The thin vegetation of trees and shrubs is called, I believe, savannah, but exoticism has no place here. A foreign land, in itself. Towards the haunted bazaar of the cemetery and towards us, intermittent throughout the semi-forest, the paintings converge like nomadic tombs.

The musical rhythms of Haiti, as traditional as they are modern, are appreciated throughout the world. Its literature is not only rich, but also serves as a model and stimulates thought. How does one properly blend political ambition and the art of entertainment? Must one always be politically correct, or conversely, be facetious and a bit risqué like certain of its authors? What is the role of history? What is its place in a work of the imagination? Since Edwidge Danticat and Myriam Chancy began to write in English, the new, pressing question is that of the novelist's freedom to choose a language. Perhaps neither a maternal language nor a language of colonization exists? Perhaps a writer has the ability to freely change language? Perhaps all that matters is that which best expresses all the facets of one's self and one's creativity? The phrase that I repeat over and over today – "I write neither in French nor in Creole. I write in Maryse Condé" – came to me as I reflected on the work of these two women writers.

In the great unresolved debate over whether art can "save the world" I am not one of those who respond affirmatively. I admire political action and struggles with physical, real stakes. I think there must be green revolutions, successful agriculture, irrigation systems, and for the children mosquito nets to protect against malaria, in order to change the world in which we live. When it comes to Haiti, however, my opinion is slightly different. Fifteen days after the catastrophe, the rescue teams were still pulling men and women from the rubble, dehydrated but apart from that unscathed, visibly animated by a furious desire to live. I believe that this extraordinary resistance can be attributed to a profound cause. The magic of the local creators – painters, sculptors, artisan iron-workers, novelists, poets, musicians – compensates for the ugliness and misery of the everyday and instills in each individual a precious energy. Artistic beauty exhibited in great abundance serves as an antidote to the real.

February–March 2010

Translated by Leslie Kealhofer

20

7.0 On the Horror Scale:
Notes on the Haitian Earthquake

Beverly Bell

*F*ollowing is the log of Beverly Bell during the first ten days after the earthquake in Haiti.

*Beverly first went to Haiti as a teenager. Since then she has dedicated most of
her life to working for democracy, women's rights, and economic justice in that
country. She founded or co-founded six organizations and networks to support
the Haitian people, including Washington Office on Haiti and the Lambi Fund
of Haiti. She worked for presidents Jean-Bertrand Aristide and René Préval, and
is author of the PEN-New Mexico award-winning* Walking on Fire: Haitian
Women's Stories of Survival and Resistance (*Cornell University Press, 2001*).
*Today she runs Other Worlds and is Associate Fellow at the Institute for Policy
Studies. She resides in her hometown of New Orleans.*

January 12, 2010

4:12 p.m. 7.0 EARTHQUAKE ROCKS HAITI. I read this email subject line
several times. My brain can't make sense of it.

January 13

8:44 a.m. The quake's epicenter was the town of Léogâne. Léogâne was my
old stomping grounds. More precisely, its hospital was.

When I was nineteen and running a grammar school in a village, I made
frequent forays to that hospital with people with diseases that our little
village clinic could not treat, like tetanus, typhoid, meningitis. I also ferried
many babies and young children in the final stages of starvation. A lot of
my trips were to collect the corpses of those little ones – wrapped in a sheet
when we had one, folded into a cardboard box when we didn't – to bring
back to their mothers.

Most of those trips to the hospital should never have happened. They
were a consequence of centuries of plunder by colonial and postcolonial

power. They were a consequence of systematic policies by foreign states, the International Monetary Fund, and the World Bank, which undermined the capacity of the Haitian state to provide basic public services. And they were a consequence of a historic disregard of the Haitian state and elite for the people.

A half hour down the road in a *taptap*, those crazy-painted jitneys, and then a 30-minute walk down the path was my home in Bwa Gran Rivyè, Big River Woods. There live hundreds of people whom I love profoundly. I am sick with worry over their fate now. They never had access to a cell phone or email back in what we never thought would be seen as the good old days.

Then I realize that my friends in Bwa Gran Rivyè are safer than most. Their sad little houses of sticks and mud never kept the rain off them and didn't last very long. But the structures were so minimal, they most likely didn't crush people when they collapsed. This may be the only instance when being poorer is better.

3:03 p.m. Hearts are cracking open everywhere. Friends and colleagues in Haiti circles are employing the word "love" for each other. Everyone wants to know what they can do.

Friends I haven't spoken to in years are calling and writing to offer condolences and support. Even my ex. I have heard from him only one other time in the eight years since we split: after Hurricane Katrina.

I write him back a grateful note and close it with: "Given that your notes come only after an apocalyptic crisis in an area where I have a primordial connection, I hope not to hear from you for many more years."

January 14

6:38 p.m. The disaster was natural. The resulting suffering is not. The quake was so destructive because more than three million people were jammed into a city meant for a quarter million, with most living in extremely precarious and overcrowded housing. This is partly due to the demise of peasant agriculture over the past three decades, a result of so-called free trade policies, which forced small producers to move to the capital to enter the ranks of the sweatshop and informal sectors. It is also due, in part, to the fact that government services effectively do not exist for those in the countryside. I.D. cards, universities, specialized health care, and much else is available exclusively, or almost exclusively, in what Haitians call the Republic of Port-au-Prince, forcing many to visit or live there to meet their needs.

9:11 p.m. Camille Chalmers, coordinator of the Platform to Advocate Alternative Development in Haiti, emails me to outline the priorities, which include: "Structural solidarity: activities and investments that will allow people to rebuild their lives in better conditions, making it possible to: (a) overcome illiteracy; (b) build an effective public school system that is free and that respects our history and culture; (c) overcome the environmental crisis and rebuild Haiti's watersheds; (d) construct a new public health system; (e) reconstruct a new city based on different logic; (f) construct food sovereignty based on comprehensive agrarian reform; (g) destroy the dependency ties with Washington, the European Union, and other forms of imperialism. Cut ties with the international financial institutions."

January 15

10:51 a.m. Everything has gone weird. Can't remember if a conversation transpired a day or a week ago. The message/response function of my brain is malfunctioning, such that I open my mouth to speak and instead start crying.

However, I awakened today with the firm orders: "Deploy yourself, Bev."

I am grateful to have so much to do, the hours and concentration involved keeping me soldiering forward. Most of my energy is spent trying to direct aid to support communities and movements. Am connecting offers up with need, speaking to journalists, responding to hundreds and hundreds of email and phone requests. It's already clear that the focus will soon shift from helping people meet their basic needs to strengthening their capacity to determine their own future.

The work today is in equal measure trying to ensure that the aid does good and to stop it from doing harm. Partisan politics are emerging in shameful ways. Scoundrels and conmen are slipping out of every alleyway. So many people are looking to gain a buck and some power out of this.

1:16 p.m. Pay back a post-quake $100 million loan to the IMF, with interest?

Most government buildings have been destroyed. The president is walking around the streets with his cell phone in his hand. *Before* this earthquake Haiti's destitution was a marvel on the planet. The poet Jean-Claude Martineau said, "Haiti is the only country to have a last name. It's 'the poorest country in the Western hemisphere.'"

From where will Haiti generate an extra $100 million to pay back the bankers in Washington? The only resources the country seems to have right now are cadavers, homeless people, and cement rubble. It's not obvious how revenue can be made off of any of those.

6:17 p.m. Found one more alive! The network is cranking with all of us sharing delighted news of our findings with each other, and inquiring about hundreds more from whom no one has heard.

I take strength in news of each survivor. I take strength, too, in the fact that this crisis, like all, opens a space in which the masses realize that all strangers are their sisters and brothers. What can we do so that tenderness and commitment towards humanity continues long past the disasters?

11:49 p.m. I recorded funding requests from something like a dozen different institutions today, some of which have no experience in disaster relief or Haiti. The Democratic Congressional Campaign Committee? The Clinton Foundation?

The poor are such excellent business.

But there are also the compassionate ones, who are everywhere wishing the best for what Haitians call *Ayiti Cheri*. They are less powerful, but more numerous.

January 17

8:13 a.m. Sunday. I had resolved to take today off, but despite myself, I connect to the Internet. I want to go back to the list of survivors I had been so excited to find, to search for additional names.

The last entry was made more than 24 hours ago, and it was mine.

Many of the names of dead we'll never learn because they were shoved into holes with bulldozers and covered with dirt. Perhaps they'll stay flattened in those buildings until they become unrecognizable.

Most of our losses we may just slowly come to discover through process of elimination. Our survivors' names will appear on a list or we'll get a text message from them. A friend will relay the name of a lost colleague in a teary phone call. And the rest we'll just figure out on our own. Someone will be sitting in a bathtub a couple of months out and suddenly remember Mimose. She will fill with grief and think, "Oh my God, Mimose. She must be gone, too."

1:14 a.m. Talking on a street corner, a woman says, "All we're seeing on TV from Haiti is the same thing we saw after Katrina: people looting, doing violence. Is there anything else going on?"

I tell her about people collaborating to get survivors out, digging with their bare fingers, teaming up to carry strangers to medical care. About the streets full of people singing together, praying together. About folks organizing to get food to the hungriest. Of the strength I am seeing among Haitians and the hope I have heard, even in this most hopeless of moments. I quote to her Haiti's minister of tourism Patrick Delatour, who said, "This is bad today, but one must remember that we have the historical memory of slavery here. What can be worse than that?"

Haiti has a powerful tradition of people fighting against the bleakest conditions to create just social and economic alternatives. It's not yet clear how they'll get out of this, but I have no doubt they'll somehow emerge through their resilience and resourcefulness.

For them to get on the path to where reconstruction serves all, though, the government needs to be allowed to take charge of its own country. And the people need to have participation in the process. We'll all have to throw ourselves into stopping the elite decisions made in secret, especially by outside forces, especially by the U.S. government.

7:17 p.m. Philippe emails: "I seem to have gone numb – can't laugh or cry."

Struggling to find a way to encourage him, I write: "Be strong. Hang in there. Someday it will get better. Someday the survivors will sit around a cookfire on hot nights and recount the sad stories for their grandchildren, who may hear them in the same way that I as a child heard stories from the Bible – ancient, epic, apocryphal. Someday, just maybe, it will be inconceivable that the U.S. could come in and force an airport to be officially turned over to it. Someday Haiti may signify something beside 'failed state' or 'progress-averse' to the world."

January 18

8:53 a.m. Just learned that a sister, Magalie Marcelin, perished. She was a fierce defender of the rights of women, notably poor women. She was at the forefront of the birth in the 1980s of the contemporary women's movement in Haiti. She started Kay Fanm, or Women's House, Haiti's first shelter for battered women, which was also a hub of feminist and anti-violent activities. She was instrumental in passing laws for women's equal rights in marriage, and for the criminalization of rape and domestic violence.

We worked together to fight attacks against women during the 1991–1994 coup d'état, and traveled together to South Africa on an economic justice exchange. She'd been urging me to translate *Walking on Fire* and offered to coordinate the project. I had turned over to her hundreds of tapes of women's interviews that I had collected for the book so that she could make them part of Haiti's patrimony. I wonder if those tapes are gone, along with Magalie.

10:18 a.m. Doctors are *re*-amputating limbs. Turns out that, in the absence of the requisite antibiotics, the original amputations are turning gangrenous, so they are cutting again higher up.

Six days later, there is still no food or water reaching most of the two million people estimated to be in need in Port-au-Prince, even the most central parts. What the hell? There is tons of it at the airport, as there are lots of doctors and medical supplies waiting, not yet dispatched.

People are reportedly putting toothpaste on their upper lip in an attempt to block the smell. It's coming from bodies rotting inside the buildings. You see the pictures of the buildings' stories now compacted into tidy layers of cement, and you know that inside them are tens, hundreds of bodies flattened like balloons after the air has gone out.

One journalist describes those buildings pancaked all over the cities and towns as mausoleums.

How can our little human hearts handle so much grief, all 7.0 Richter degrees of it?

2:53 p.m. Eramithe Delva sends this text message from the center of Port-au-Prince. She coordinates the Commission of Women Victim-to-Victim (KOFAVIV by its Kreyòl acronym), the anti-child slavery and anti-women's violence organization. "So far, we've found about 300 of our members who are lost. For the majority of women of KOFAVIV, their houses are destroyed and they've lost all they had. Right now many of the women are sleeping in Champs de Mars [a downtown boulevard], with the sun beating down on them, with rain soaking them. They were already people who had nothing, now hunger is ready to kill them. We've lost many of our family members. KOFAVIV's office was destroyed. Our school was hit, too, and we have many dead children.

"If there is not some intervention soon for those who are still alive, the situation will get a lot worse."

8:15 p.m. Strength. It's one of the things about Haitians that has always impressed me most. Friends in Haiti keep sending me text messages urging *me* to hold strong.

I watch my friend Yolette Etienne, director of Oxfam Great Britain-Haiti, on British TV. She is so beautiful and courageous, standing there telling about the work before them, not even mentioning that her mother was killed and her house destroyed until the journalist asks. Yes, she says, we buried my mother in the garden early, before I had to go to the staff meeting.

She concludes the interview by saying, "We only can have hope and we are sharing hope."

January 19

4:08 p.m. We're coordinating with two women from Boston and Lagos who are going to Haiti in the next few days, who have agreed to carry down the money we've raised for KOFAVIV and find a safe street corner where they can transfer it from hand to hand. It's all very complicated, figuring out the logistics of getting the money across four points to the final hand-off in Port-au-Prince.

One of our two courier friends says she hopes the sum we want to send isn't too high; she admits she's nervous. I respond: "If it makes you feel better, I once carried $9,000 in cash in my bra and underwear to P-au-P – the very first allotment of money the Lambi Fund ever got."

She replies, "I've already got too much [money to carry for people] so it's just a matter of not attracting any attention … and wearing big underwear."

The second woman texts, "of course i can take that amount. i remember underwear sneaking cash mama. the things we lugged to haiti … i once brought shock absorbers and a drive shaft. and wore cute underwear."

9:16 p.m. People are organizing distribution of available food (yes, from abandoned stores, for starving people, what journalists love to call "looting"). Folks are stepping up to make their own lists of the living and the dead in the camps.

Philippe reports that small groups of Haitians have organized themselves to do their own triage and, through mutual respect, decide who should get treated first. They have signs asking the foreign aid workers to leave them alone except to give them supplies, rather than taking over and running things.

12:14 a.m. Learn of no new deaths of my peeps and that Tibebe is alive. By current standards, that makes it a good day.

January 20

9:26 a.m. From Washington, Marie Racine tells me the number of family and close friends she has learned to be dead reached 75 several days ago. Then she stopped reading email.

4:07 p.m. The Haitian grassroots is starting to organize itself. Receive notices from a workers' rights organization, a peasants' association, and an alternative development group. They are shaking the cement dust from themselves already to announce their plans to organize for grassroots voice and power in determining the direction of the country. They are denouncing Haiti's militarization by the U.S. and calling for all international debt to be cancelled – a debt they've already repaid many times over.

5:44 p.m. Gas is up to $25 or $50, depending on where you are. Other costs are, too, in disaster capitalism. But here comes this dispatch from Haiti: "While stores have raised their prices, the street vendors have not raised theirs, in solidarity."

6:39 p.m. Armed guards in tanks are keeping the hordes of injured out of the General Hospital. More than 1,000 people are waiting for surgery at the hospital, said a spokesman for Partners in Health.

Another risk from the earthquake's injury is "crush syndrome," in which damaged muscle tissue releases toxins into the blood, causing possible kidney failure and death. To treat it, you need dialysis machines. Doctors Without Borders is trying to get these machines in. Two of them were on planes that the U.S. military blocked from landing three times on Sunday.

Meanwhile, a little girl's hand is amputated with an insufficient amount of anesthesia. An elderly woman's badly broken ankle is set in a cardboard splint.

January 21

9:29 a.m. The Haitian minister of communications encourages citizens to take photos of bodies on their cell phones. That's the identification system.

They're burying people in Titanyen. They're just dropping the dead in shallow ground, bulldozing right over their bodies, and then digging more pits. Body parts are protruding everywhere, heads lie around under the flies.

This horror requires no explication. What is not obvious is the way that this is the most perverse insult on top of injury. The mere name of Titanyen strikes terror in the heart of most any Haitian. It is the potters' field outside Port-au-Prince favored by the Duvaliers for their victims. During their reign from 1957 to 1986 (that reign heavily supported by the U.S. government), bodies were regularly dropped off in the night to rot in the next day's sun.

This dumping was a criminal action then. It is a criminal action now.

11:26 a.m. The U.S. now has 20,000 ground troops in Haiti. The UN has 12,500 troops.

That's just about the right number of health care workers who should be flying in. But they can't, because most of the 120 to 140 flights per day that the airport can handle are filled with military personnel and their equipment. In fact, according to Air Force General Doug Fraser, more than 1,400 flights of aid and relief workers have been blocked from getting in.

Aside from the medical care being denied, can you imagine how much food and water is being diverted from a starving population to feed strapping U.S. and UN soldiers? You know those guys aren't eating uncooked wheat and drinking gutter water, like a whole lot of Haitians.

Furthermore, just what are they doing there? People are lying on the ground with crushed bones and their response of choice is *guns*?

6:47 p.m. The Heritage Foundation posted this in the earthquake's aftermath: "[T]he U.S. response ... offers opportunities to re-shape Haiti's long-dysfunctional government and economy as well as to improve the public image of the United States in the region."

This "shock doctrine" response to disaster is reminiscent of an op-ed that Milton Friedman, the father of Chicago School free-market capitalism, wrote in the *Wall Street Journal* after Hurricane Katrina: "This is a tragedy. It is also an opportunity to radically reform the educational system."

It's been said by many since last week that this earthquake might represent a wonderful opportunity to construct a different kind of nation. But constructed by whom? For whose benefit?

One man's disaster can be another man's profit.

January 22

1:51 p.m. I am rushing out the door to borrow cash from a friend to take to the Western Union office so it can hit our friend's account in Lagos in time, so she can get it before flying and put in the KOFAVIV women's hands. As I hustle toward my car, a man approaches me. "Excuse me; you're probably in a hurry. Are you connected with Haiti?"

My eyes grow big. "How did you know that?"

Someone told him, "I think there's a woman on your block working with Haiti." He says he's spent the whole week trying to find me.

I apologize that I can't stay to talk but explain that I am indeed in a hurry, and tell him why. He responds, "I'm a silversmith. I sold some jewelry at a trade show in south Florida last week and told everyone I'd give 10 percent of the sales to Haiti. I saw so much money being wasted after Katrina that I wanted to wait to be sure I had the right place. So I've just been holding the money meanwhile." With that, he opens a little bag and pulls out $250 in cash.

I tell him I have nothing on me to show that I am legit. I don't have any receipt I can give him just now. He says, "I trust you," and places the money in my hands. We exchange a big, tight hug.

He is already ambling down the street as I thank him once more, tell him again I can't believe his gesture.

He calls back over his shoulder, "It all flows according to the divine."

10:45 p.m. One night when I was living in Bwa Gran Rivyè, someone knocked frantically at the door of my little house. It was a woman, clutching to her chest a baby in the final stages of dehydration and starvation. Not having a car to drive her to the Léogâne hospital, I instead wrote a note to the staff. By virtue of my knowing them all through many visits there with children such as this, and of my U.S. citizenry and white skin, this was guaranteed to give the infant quick access to health care.

The next morning, a neighbor came to tell me the baby had died. "Died?" Her admission was good to go and the treatment was free. "Didn't they connect her to an IV?"

"No," my neighbor told me. "The mother didn't go to the hospital. She couldn't come up with the *gourde*" – at that time, 20 cents – "to take the bus there."

I have thought about this tiny girl hundreds of times throughout my life. She is an indicator of our pathetic failure as a global society. I have also wondered about the woman she might have become. I always imagine that she would be fighting to create a new world in which no one dies for lack of 20 cents.

Today, I like to think, she would be out there working hard to ensure that the Haiti that is reconstructed doesn't look anything like Haiti before the earthquake, because that society served very few. She'd be making sure that the rebuilt Haiti is based on justice, rights, and equity.

January 2010

21

Art in the Time of Catastrophe

Madison Smartt Bell

I first got involved with Haitian art when –
– already, though, there's a problem. Wrong pronoun for the topic.
The egoistic "I" keeps isolating itself, merely by existing, so it would be
preferable to use the Kreyòl "nou," which can mean both "we" and "you."
Or maybe the Rastafarian "I and I." But in sad fact these locutions, the
sensibility they represent, don't properly belong to me, not yet, so I have
to begin as a solitary, First World "I" adrift on the vast sea of Haitian
consciousness.

About two weeks after the earthquake reduced most of Port-au-Prince
to rubble, LeGrace Benson, a long-time connoisseur and scholar of Haitian
art, reported the following:

Going from west to east across the city:
1. Roman Catholic cathedral. Some walls still standing but building
    unsafe. Funeral services for the Archbishop was held in plaza in front.
    Nearly all windows in shards. A Haitian artist with expertise in stained
    glass is gathering the pieces for possible restoration. A few windows
    intact.
2. Sainte Trinite Episcopal cathedral. Most of the school buildings either
    down or uninhabitable. Cathedral itself mostly rubble although some
    walls remain. From satellite photos I saw some of the mural walls may
    still be up. I am told a group was able to keep the bulldozer people from
    pulling everything down.
    There are efforts to mount a rescue and restoration.
3. MUPANHA is mostly underground. Cracks and some probable damage
    to art and historic artifacts. It is said to be risky to do full investigation
    but people are hopeful that works remain.
4. Musee d'Art Haitien. Still mostly standing. Looks less damaged in
    photos than it actually is. Some works rescued including the great
    treasure, Wilson Bigaud's "Paradis Terrestre" I saw tha in a photo in NY

166

Times, wrongly noting it was in Centre d' Art. Thank goodness it was
NOT.

4. Fondation Culture Creation building next door is totaled.
5. Centre d' Art has largely collapsed and much of what is standing may
    collapse at any minute. In the photos I can see many paintings that
    are probably OK except for dust. I am told that there are attempts to
    protect what is there until a real rescue can begin.
6. Issa Gallery I am still trying to find out. They had jusr redone it after
    Issa's death and it was lovely. I am waiting to hear from Sharona Issa.
8. Just below Petionville Reynald Lally's home and collection collapsed,
    staff were hospitalized but he was in Montreal. I had seen the collection
    in December and had arranged for photos. I hope there are some.
7. In Petionville the big George Nader gallery collapsed as did his museum.
8. I am trying to find out about the nearby Marianne Lehman collection.
    Much of the best of that is on tour in Europe so its safe.
9. On South side of downtown the Grand rue studios and biennale artists
    lost some folks, and most of the buildings are unstable. Much of the
    art survives and they need to get it to shelter before the bulldozers
    arrive.

This message is a snapshot of a certain moment; Ms. Benson has
allowed me to retain even her typos, while noting that some of the information later proved inaccurate, or changed. At the moment that I type
this sentence there is heavy rain all over Haiti; when much of the population of the capital still lacks adequate shelter (not to mention food and
clothing and medical care), it's hard to imagine that priority can be given to
salvaging artwork from such ruins. So a great part of the heritage of Haitian
art is simply getting washed away. How much does it matter, next to two or
three hundred thousand dead? Opinions on that point will certainly differ,
as they have done, in similar cases, for centuries.

On the wall of a beach resort hotel near Cap Haïtien in the north of
Haiti, there's a wicked little cartoon by a well-known French artist whose
name I do not recall: a cheerful *blan* (foreign) customer is purchasing art
from a couple of Haitian artists or artisans who are sawing off suitably sized
sections of typical Haitian scenes from a plank, or a sort of endless *bande
dessinée*, that recedes on trestles all the way to the horizon and probably
beyond. The satirical intent of the drawing, of course, is to show that a lot
of Haitian art is no more and no less than a market commodity. How bad,
how diminishing, is that? The inexhaustibility also implied by the sketch
might, at this point in the history of disaster, be encouraging.

Scholars and connoisseurs recognize a difference between fine art on the one hand and craft, *artisanat*, on the other, with perhaps some sort of continuum or gray area between them. And to some degree they create that difference, by exercising their knowledge and taste. The collections of artwork now destroyed or endangered in the wreckage of the capital were canonized by having been collected. Certainly those works must have an aesthetic value, however recognized and defined, superior to that of the run of the mill craft artwork that will continue to be produced, inexhaustibly, no matter how many individual producers are slain, whether by being crushed under an earthquake or by less exceptional causes of death such as violence, disease, and starvation.

That begs the question of why they make the stuff in the first place. My answer is that I don't know, but to know that one doesn't know is a kind of beginning.

I first got involved with Haitian art in 1995, during my first trip to Haiti, pursuant to researching a series of novels about the Haitian Revolution and its first catalytic leader, Toussaint Louverture. At that time I knew a great deal about Haitian history between 1791 and 1804 and otherwise practically nothing at all. My ignorance of the culture and the realities of daily life was so complete as to be astonishing.

In the bar of the Mont Joli Hotel in Cap Haïtien I made the acquaintance of an artist who was a friend of the barman, Guidel Présumé. I was traveling with a European artist and in the course of the conversation Présumé took out a few small paintings to show. I wasn't enormously impressed at the time but for some reason the images stayed with me afterwards. I bought one of the paintings, a waterfall scene, through the mail. This act was a first step onto a slippery slope that led to my becoming a very small-time, pro bono Haitian art dealer.

The older part of Cap Haïtien is a beautiful colonial town, renowned at the end of the eighteenth century as "the Jewel of the Antilles." During the Duvalier period the town had a prosperous tourist trade, which nourished a great many artist-craftsmen. After the restoration of the democratically elected government in the mid 1990s there was a reasonable hope that tourism would resume. That hasn't exactly happened so far, but for the rest of the decade there were enough journalists, NGO types, and strays like me around to keep the artistic wheels turning.

Présumé introduced me to an association of young painters (mostly younger and at a more apprentice level than he) called AJAPCA. At that time the group had a sizeable studio-gallery space in the center of town. The work was a feast to my inexperienced eyes. Most of it was the sort of thing the French cartoonist represented as being milled off that endless plank. All the typical Haitian subjects: history paintings, country pastoral, Vodou scenes, imitations of the Douanier Rousseau, generic surrealism (never my favorite), and some scenes of recent political events, as they were expressed on the streets.

The history paintings attracted me first. These were visual representations of the very scenes I was trying to write. In oral-history cultures, of which Haiti is one, there is a curious foreshortening of time, and all historical events feel like they happened yesterday. Most of the AJAPCA artists were of high-school age and the history paintings were not tremendously well-informed, indeed they were sometimes peppered with ludicrous anachronism, but their immediacy was striking.

Next the images of daily life. These, I guess, were sort of generic if you looked at too many of them for too long. But they were, even the least of them, better than photographs. The Haitian panorama can be overwhelming to the eyes of the new-come *blan* and to my mind at least there was no part of it that could be fit inside a camera. But these little paintings somehow got it, got some of it anyway. They captured, as a photo could not, something of the living spirit of the place.

I had the impression that these young artists all trained each other, in a sort of guild system. They all painted closely similar subjects and tended to imitate each other, as artisans in a guild would also do. There was no consciousness of poaching or anything like that. If you were making chairs to sell in the market you wouldn't have a sense of plagiarizing the other guy's chair. Indeed your chair was expected to look and operate the same as the other guy's chairs.

This attitude was perplexing to my European artist friend, who made several trips to Cap Haïtien with me. At one point Présumé (who was older, more experienced, and more sophisticated than most of the AJAPCA painters) said with a certain satisfaction that while most painters only knew one style, he himself had mastered several. My friend quite naturally replied: "But what is your own individual style?" To Présumé this was not a meaningful question. Whatever the purpose of art was to him, it was not self-expression. In spite of the fact that his best paintings have a strong numinous quality to them, this quality does not seem to come from the individual self, in the way that it would from the hand of a First World artist marking territory with a particular "I."

For several years I bought as many paintings as my baggage would hold. I'd pay a Haitian price for them and if I could sell them Stateside I'd give the full difference to the artist on my following visit. This activity made me

rather too popular, since tourists persistently failed to materialize in suffi-
cient numbers. Eventually AJAPCA lost its space and the artists scattered,
though I still represent a couple of them: Emalès Délis and Armand Fleuri-
mond, as well as Présumé, artists who stood out, individually, to my eye.

It was necessary for me to exercise some sort of judgment in choosing
paintings to bring to the States. At the same time I had to take something
from every artist present at our annual meetings in the AJAPCA. An egalitarian strain in Haitian culture made it truly unthinkable to do otherwise,
though if a painter seemed not very interesting I would only take one small
piece. Past that, since I have no training or any special aptitude as an art
critic, my choices were all purely intuitive. Though I recognized a force of
collectivity in all the paintings – the aggregate whole of the production – I
was still trying to choose paintings that in some way stood out, that had
some special inspiration to them. There was one young painter (impaired
in some way – he seemed to be mute) whose work struck me more forcefully than the rest. He had an otherwise ordinary Haitian pastoral painting
with a composition that made the eye of a little donkey become a sort of
central vortex, and I remember trying to explain to the other painters, in
extremely fractured Kreyòl, why this painting was superior. The spirit is
there, I said to them, right there in the eye of this *bourik*. I'm sure they all
thought I was bughouse nuts. Perhaps I was.

Craftsmen know they are serving a market, making a product someone
will buy. Fine art painters, the successful ones anyway, do the same, though
the market they serve is smaller, wealthier, and more delicately nuanced
in its decisions. Still, the difference is one of degree. *L'art pour l'art* is a
beautiful concept but it doesn't make anybody eat.

I struck a deal with Présumé's barman friend to swap a printer for four
small paintings. When the exchange was accomplished I found one of the
paintings to be no good for my purposes. The artist was one I was known
to admire (I had kept some of his best paintings for myself) but this one was
a truly undistinguished depiction of a Vodou grotto, a smudge of muddy
black adorned with a random arrangement of sloppily daubed skulls.

I had a long inconclusive discussion with Présumé and the barman
about this problem. They insisted that the painting was perfectly good
because it was a very strong subject. As it happened, Présumé had recently
given me a much better painting (his own) of a similar subject, so I
compared the two works at some length on their visual merits and defects,
an exercise that had no effect whatsoever. For the two Haitians, the value
of the two paintings was the same, solely and absolutely because of their
representational content.

I didn't understand it at all.

Several years later I had an extremely fortunate opportunity to sell a couple of Présumé paintings to the newly constructed U.S. Embassy in Port-au-Prince. The purchasing office felt some anxiety about the content of the images – whether they might be disturbing or offensive to any visitors to the Embassy. I was able to reassure them convincingly enough that they asked me to vet some other work for them, which I was happy to do. However, by this time I had internalized enough of Haitian culture that I was giving them, without consciously realizing it, a Haitian response. That is, the only thing to worry about was that they might mistakenly purchase a *pwen* – a spirit power bound into an object – when they meant to acquire a simple work of art. Like genies in bottles, the spirits in *pwen* endure a form of slavery, and so they are apt to turn on their purchasers.

I had learned this distinction the hard way. Some years before, a Baltimore art dealer to whom I owed a favor had asked me to get him a piece by a certain Port-au-Prince artist who had become very collectible and who was also well known as a Vodou priest – a *bokor*, in fact, one who works with the left hand, trafficking with the more sinister powers of Vodou.

Vodou as practiced by most Haitians is not like that at all, but rather resembles charismatic Christianity in that it releases its followers from the prison of the self. Ginen, another word for the bright side of Vodou, is an extremely benign power in the Haitian world. But all religions project their dark inversions, as Christianity projects Satanism.

This artist made relief objects involving fabric and dismembered bits of dolls, and it was apparent to me, from their appearance, context, and the eerie radiance of them, that they were also *pwen.* At this point I was an inept and ignorant novice practitioner of Ginen and so I knew I had no business handling such things; however, I repressed that knowledge and set out to deliver the favor for the Baltimore dealer, as if I were buying an ordinary work of art.

It did not go well. First of all my friend and guide couldn't find the "artist," though I knew his name and approximate location. We spent a fruitless hour wandering the Marché de Fer. Finally something snapped in my brain and I admitted I was looking for the *bokor* of the same name. My friend led me directly to him. I made a tentative arrangement to purchase an object such as the Baltimore dealer desired. After this visit, everything continued to go wrong. A bad day in Haiti can be a Very Bad Day Indeed; moreover my dream life went so deeply awry that I was in a blue terror for longer than one day.

A more knowledgeable person had once explained to me that if you err in ignorance the spirit will pardon what you have done, but if you do wrong knowingly it is a different matter. Such was the problem I had created for myself. The only solution was to renounce the whole affair. I did so, and also carried out an elaborate *renvoi*, a ceremony to repel a spiritual attack. No one had taught me how to do it, but somehow I seemed to know.

For First Worlders, most of us, the unconscious is internal and personal, an aspect of the inner space of the psyche. In Haiti, as in Africa, the unconscious is external and thus a shared space. From this reservoir arise both angels and demons. The wisdom of one's choices determines what sort of visits one will receive.

Despite the success of my *renvoi* I continued to feel somewhat uneasy about having troubled the waters in which the artist/*bokor* resided. I would not enter the presence of his artwork, and would not mentally pronounce his name. These feelings did not abate when the *bokor* died, as in Haiti death is only a translation of state.

Some years later, friends took me to visit an artist in Miami. She invited us to see a work by the gentlemen in question, which she kept in a back room. I demurred at first but then she explained that the *bokor* had installed the work for her with a ceremony that, so to speak, stabilized it. So I spent a moment in the presence of the object and afterward felt that my problem with the spirit of the *bokor* had been reconciled once and for all.

Before doing me this great favor, the Miami artist had served each of us a pickled scorpion from her refrigerator. Coincidence, possibly, but in Haitian life there are no coincidences.

As for the U.S. Embassy, I eventually inferred that their concern was that art they displayed not outrage the sensibility of Protestant evangelicals who automatically perceive all representations of Vodou as Satanic, but that is another story, and a sadder one.

In the late 1990s Présumé introduced me to an artist acquaintance who hoped to sell me some work. This person was painting large canvasses, which I found inconvenient to carry, in a surrealistic manner I didn't much care for. I told him the work was too large for my purposes. In a week's time he brought me 40 freshly painted small paintings on board, in several different styles, all impressive. I couldn't comprehend how he had done so much so fast, though later it dawned on me that he had most likely subcontracted the work and signed his name to all of them. Another collective enterprise, though in this case claimed by an individual, as in the case of the European Renaissance *ateliers.*

One especially talented hand had produced several images of Vodou ceremonies in which the heads of the *serviteurs*, all bound in brightly colored head cloths, were positioned together so that the colors, and the heads inside, all seemed to hum together like a hive. These were the most vivid images I had seen of the concept of *têt ansanm*, heads put together – the tight compression of collective consciousness, which in ceremonies usually precedes possession.

I still don't know much about museum-quality Haitian art, but no doubt some of those artists have the same aesthetic goals and the same motives of self-expression as artists from the First World are supposed to have. In the case of the craft painters, a world I have come to understand a little better, I still think some paintings are a whole lot better than others. Inspiration makes that difference, and as for any artists anywhere, inspiration comes and goes. In the case of the Haitian art I do know, it seems to me that inspiration is less likely to spring from the individual self of the artist and more from a shared, collective unconscious.

The presence of a shared unconscious creates an opportunity for the soul to be freed from the self, from the egoistic limits of the "I." It makes extraordinary communal experiences not only possible but likely. The ordinary meaning of *têt ansanm* is comparatively mundane: cooperation of combined intelligence for the common good. In Haiti it's an extraordinary force, one with which the First World is no longer familiar; the force which has brought and will bring Haiti back from the worst of disasters.

Si "noula," se NOU ki la. Non sèlman "mwen."

March 2010

22

What Is This Earthquake For?

Bill Drummond

"Haiti is run by guys who would like nothing more than a real disaster to hit our country, like a massive hurricane or even better an earthquake." – Rodrigue, December 15, 2009

January 13, 2010

At 11:13 last night I received a text from Tracey Moberly telling me there had been an earthquake in Haiti. I went directly to the BBC site to see what I could learn.

This morning I'm sitting at my screen starring at the photographs of school children we (John Hirst and myself) were working with the week before Christmas, in a school in Port-au-Prince, Haiti. And I'm wondering what has happened to them. But it does not take much wondering to know that their lives, if they still have one, will never be the same again. Those warm welcoming smiles may never return to their faces.

The night has brought a fresh fall of snow. I'm in my usual seat; the window beside me looks down onto the road below, where the local youths of the London borough of Hackney are heading for school. The usual jostle and banter, shrieks of laughter, snowballs being thrown. But in front of me on the screen is this photograph of six young people, who as I write these words will be going through the darkest night of their lives, literally, and in whatever metaphorical sense you want to force. It is three hours before dawn for them and whatever electrical supplies Port-au-Prince has will be down and darkness in whatever way you want to imagine the word to mean, will be total.

John Hirst and myself were in Haiti for less than a week (December 13–19, 2009). We were there as part of the first Ghetto Biennale. This was to be a biennale with a difference, one where artists from the "developed" world would work and exhibit alongside artists from Haiti. It took place down in the Grand Rue area of the city. The Grand Rue being the poorest

174

area in the old part of the town. The celebrated sculptors of the Grand Rue were our hosts.

Leah Gordon, the co-curator of the Ghetto Biennale, had invited me to lead a performance by The17. And if you do not know, The17 is a choir, but a choir that is made up of different singers every time they perform. And the singers can be anybody, of any age. And it does not matter if they have not sung since they mumbled along at school assembly. And the music sung by The17 uses no words, rhythm or melody. And The17 is never recorded for posterity. You will never hear The17 on radio or TV, they will never make a CD, and you will never be able to download their music from the Internet.

Since The17 went public in early 2006, they have given over 260 performances. But our performances in Haiti were the first in the Americas.

In November we had led a performance of The17 in a large comprehensive school in the English east midlands town of Corby. The school was called Kingswood; it had been my school as a teenager. I had hated it and loathed everything I perceived it stood for. The performance of The17 at Kingswood in November involved over 500 pupils and was considered a great success. It had been planned that this performance would be twinned with a performance of the same score in a school in Port-au-Prince. None of the students in Corby had heard of Port-au-Prince or had very little idea of where Haiti might be. We told them that we would come back in the new year to tell them how it went.

The school that we were working at in Port-au-Prince was called L'Ecole Guillaume Manigat; it was a lot smaller than Kingswood. The age range seemed to be about eight to fourteen and we were working with only about 60 pupils altogether. Without laboring the point too much, it was a school in the heart of one of the poorest districts in the poorest country in all of the New World.

In Kingswood, John Hirst and I were paid a good daily rate to work with the pupils. In Haiti we had to provide a pencil, exercise book, and school bag for each of the pupils taking part. The thinking being that if some white bloke from the United Kingdom has got the money to fly to Haiti, stay in a *luxury* hotel for the week and expect us to do what he wants, then he can pay for the privilege. The pencils, books, and bags were the agreed fee for this privilege. It was well worth the price.

We arrived in Haiti on the Sunday evening and were driven to the Hotel Oloffson – via a Vodou ceremony. The Oloffson is a classic Gothic gingerbread mansion, straight out of an American horror movie. It was also the inspiration for the Hotel Trianon in Graham Greene's novel *The*

Comedians. Over the years it had been a bit of a hangout for the jet-setting bohemian crowd. It seems that Jackie O. and Mick and Bianca used to hang there in the '70s.

Early in the morning following our arrival, a bloke called Louko drove us down to the school. Louko was one of the Grand Rue sculptors. His English was broken and our Haitian *Kreyòl* non-existent, but that did not stop him from telling us all about what he did, why he did it, what his ambitions were. More of Louko later.

At the school we met up with Rodrigue, who was to be our translator. Haitians speak a *Kreyòl* that is part eighteenth-century French mixed with the traces of various West African languages. Rodrigue was a tall good-looking man in his forties. He had gone to university in the U.S. but got himself in trouble and was kicked out of the place. Now he worked as a translator, mainly for the UN. He was full of life and eager to get involved with the job in hand. More of Rodrigue later.

The teenage me would have loathed and despised what I am about to say – and remember that this school is in the middle of an open-sewered, lawless slum. The young people at this school were the best turned out, politest, most eager to learn, and brightest school pupils that I had ever worked with. They were open, un-cynical, sang with fervor (and in pitch), came up with creative ideas, helped with the practical things in getting set up. And there was their handwriting – they may not have had exercise books to write in but their writing was the best I had ever seen. Mrs. Clements, my primary five teacher, back in 1962, would have wept at the beauty of it. The performance they gave of The17 was certainly one of the most rewarding for me.

We had brought with us a large print of a photograph of the pupils in Kingswood school. It had been taken at the end of the two weeks that John Hirst and I had been working there. The pupils in this Port-au-Prince school wanted to know all about these other young folk. Who was the best at singing – them or us? How did the girls do their hair? Were the boys any good at football? What kind of music were they into?

We spent two days working with them. On the second day my friend and fellow Ghetto Biennale artist, Tracey Moberly, came down to the school and took photos. It is her photos that I am looking at right now. I wanted a formal photo of them all; John Hirst suggested the one of them holding the photo of the Kingswood lot; Tracey wanted to take some informal ones. Then afterwards the members of staff of L'Ecole Guillaume Manigat wanted a group photo of themselves done. All were taken.

Afterwards Rodrigue, John Hirst, and I got talking. Rodrigue was keen to emphasize that these kids had nothing, that although they came to school all clean and well turned out, they may not have eaten anything in the last 24 hours. And however bright they were and whatever they achieved at school, there were probably no prospects for them after leaving school. That the unemployment rate in Haiti was massive, way above 80 percent. And those that got good jobs did so because the family already had jobs and they were in a position to sort it out for them. Hirst and I suggested that we should try and do something for the school, maybe get together with Kingswood and set up a fund that could raise money for this school to have the very basics. Hirst suggested that it maybe should be to raise money to cover the costs for them having a school lunch every day. Rodrigue then told us that this is all very well, but the problem would be how to get the money to the school, with all levels of corruption between whoever is donating the money and the kid getting something to eat.

The conversation drifted. Rodrigue told us of the nation's history of despotic rulers. How the rest of the world was not interested in Haiti and Haiti only had itself to blame. We asked him what Haiti had that the rest of the world might want. I mean did it have any mineral wealth?

"No."

"What about sugar cane or bananas or … ?"

Then Rodrigue told us how Haiti used to be a green and fertile country, but they had chopped down all the trees for charcoal. And once the trees had gone, the rains swept away all the fertile soil. Nothing was left. They now cannot even grow enough to feed themselves. Everything has to be imported.

"Well what about sweat shop industries?"

"It is too politically unstable here for us to make our way as a sweatshop to the world in the way that Taiwan did."

"Well you must have something?"

"I will tell you what we have got – poverty. That is our one industry."

"What do you mean poverty an industry?"

"Some of our people get very wealthy out of our poverty. The last thing they would want is for the poverty to go. These are the people who run Haiti."

"How does that work?"

"Simple. The people who run this country go to the rich countries and say – look at our poverty, we need aid – the rich countries give aid and the people who run our country put most of that money into Swiss bank accounts. Then a few years later, they go back to the same rich countries or the IMF, or the World Bank and ask for more money in aid, to help with all the poverty and then they do the same again. If the vast majority of the people of Haiti were not in poverty, there is no way that these wealthy Haitians could carry on doing this. That is why it is in their interest to keep the country the way it is. Per head of population we have one of the biggest debts to the World Bank. And we have nothing to pay it back with, not even the interest. And none of that money came to the Haitian people that you are meeting. It is all in Switzerland. But the World Bank, the IMF and all the international aid agencies have got wise to what is going on. We supposedly owe over $850 million. And this is why they will not wipe the debt, because they know the money is still there locked up in vaults. Why should they slash the debt?"

This was all a bit beyond my comprehension. I was used to accepting the U.S. and us in western Europe as the baddies. That it was us fucking them over. Rodrigue thought my thinking almost patronizing in its naivety.

"What about that debt to France from 1825 that I read about? I thought it was that which had kept this country down ever since?"

"Those that run this country keep harking back to that. And our glorious revolution in 1804. Some revolution when all that happened was Dessalines crowned himself Emperor of Haiti. If George Washington had done the same after the American Revolution, they would have ended up like us. Washington put proper government into place; we got ourselves a dandy dictator. That is when it all started to go wrong. And we are supposed to see Dessalines as a hero when he was no better than Stalin. People use history as a get-out clause for taking responsibility for their lives in the present day. In most wars people use history to justify what they are doing. Every despot will try and hold onto power by appealing to his people's sense of their own history. They want us to keep thinking it is you in Europe or the U.S. that are at fault, so we do not see it is them, our rulers. Look, it is this bad, Haiti is run by guys who would like nothing more than a real disaster to hit our country, like a massive hurricane or even better an earthquake. It was their last big pay day when we were hit with Hurricane Gustav back in 2008. But now they are praying for something bigger than that."

"Look Rodrigue I don't know anything about your history, but surely ..."

"Bill, it is a lot more complicated than that. Don't get me wrong; I think it is great what you are doing here and in this school and the Ghetto Biennale and everything. But even you being here is linked in with this whole thing. It is what they would want. Do you understand?"

I don't know if I did understand or even wanted to. Rodrigue was a sharp, intelligent, and good-looking man, plus he had buckets of charisma.

And he let us know that he is on first-name terms with René Préval, the president of the country.

"So why do you not go into politics?"

"Bill, there is a very simple answer to that – I would either end up being killed or more likely end up being as corrupt as them."

The conversation drifted on to other subjects like women and how many children we had and how his current woman was expecting their first in mid January. Louko turned up and he drove us all back up to the Oloffson.

The rest of the week, or at least during the daylight hours available, was taken up with staging another large scale score to be performed by 100 Haitian members of The17 down in the streets off the Grand Rue. And there was the task of doing the graffiti – IMAGINE WAKING UP TOMORROW & ALL MUSIC HAD DISAPPEARED – but in *Kreyòl*.

But as the light began to fade on each day we, along with the other Western artists, retreated to the safety of the Oloffson. And there we would be on the veranda drinking our Rum and Sours, ordering our Steak Diane or American Club Sandwich, or "Why not try a local delicacy?" We complained about the service and the accoutrements and everything else that we complain about in restaurants that are somehow not to our liking. All the while beyond the armed guards at the gate, there was another world. A world where there was never enough to eat, no health care, no running water fit to drink, rampant corruption, no nothing but rotting rubbish and darkness. The hotel had its own generator; the city below only had a couple of hours power a day if they were lucky.

And I started to question why I, or any of us were here. And Rodrigue's words kept going round my head. That stuff about poverty being their only industry. Maybe I was part of that too. Maybe I was only here because of its poverty. If Haiti were not so far down the poverty league table it would not have had the desired inverted glamour for me to want to spend however much it has cost to get here and stay in this hotel.

It is so easy to blame our colonial pasts. Were we not doing the same thing? There was an argument to say that us lot were only here because it might look good on the C.V., or for what we thought it might say about ourselves, because we had gone to the poorest country in the Western hemisphere to make art. It might not be cheap labor we were exploiting or mineral wealth we were raping from the ground but we were here to take. The type of taking we were doing was in some sort of conceptual or intellectual way; it is what I am doing right now as I write these words and you are reading them.

So there we sat on the veranda of the Oloffson like the Mick Jaggers and Graham Greenes and John Gielguds and Jackie Kennedys before us. The pampered and the spoilt. Drinking our cocktails and over-priced imported beers, forming cliques and having squabbles and I was above none of this. But I did do some calculations – airfares and hotel bills must have come to well over £60,000 for the 40 of us that were taking part in the Ghetto Biennale. And it doesn't take much hindsight to realize that the £60,000 could have been put to far better use.

And a reader might be thinking: "£60,000? What about a certain one million quid that went up in smoke Mr. Drummond?" Yeah, Yeah, I know and what do you expect me to say? Leah Gordon had me up on that one while I was there. I had been quibbling about the fact that I did not want the money burning mentioned while I was there working down on the Grand Rue, that if the locals had knowledge of that, then everything I was trying to do there with The17 would be judged in the context of that particular action. She told me, in so many words, that the only reason that I was able to do so much of what I do, is because of that one action and that if I am not man enough to deal with the consequences of it, I should go and get a proper job. So that was telling me.

As for the Haitian artists, there is no way that I could relate to what they did. Their work was mainly sculpture made out of the scrap and rubbish that they could find in the streets, stuff that no longer had much practical use. So it ticked a lot of boxes on the recycling front, not that they were bothered if it ticked boxes, they were just doing what they did, using whatever was available to them. There was a lot of welding involved in their sculptures; I always like welding. The imagery that they used was drawn from Voodoo. Voodoo, or Vodou as they spell it in Haiti, is one of their official national religions. But I got nothing from this sculpture of theirs. I could not stop myself from thinking that they were using the Vodou imagery not because these sculptures were going to be used in Vodou ceremonies, but because Vodou is the one thing that the outside world might know about Haiti. We have all heard of Vodou and zombies, and Haiti is the home of them. Kilts and haggis equal Scotland – Vodou and zombies equal Haiti, it is their one unique selling point, to use that cliché. I wanted to say how much I was into it, but I would have been lying, I would have felt that I was patronizing them.

Then there is another problem I was having with it. Every time I look at or experience a work of art, I cannot help myself asking the question: "What is this art for?" This is something that I have done since I was an art student back in the early 1970s. And the loudest of the answers that came back to me in my head was – "This art is to sell to wealthy Americans."

This was all compounded by conversations that I was having with Louko, the artist cum driver for the Biennale. I have a habit of asking artists the question – "So why are you an artist?" I asked Louko the question and he told me how he used to be a carpenter, which is how I used to earn my living in the 1970s, so it felt like we had something in common. Me, Louko, and Jesus. And he told me he used to watch all these Americans come and visit Eugene and they would buy his sculptures.

"And Eugene had respect from everybody. And I thought I would like to be like Eugene and I thought I could do what Eugene did, because I knew how to make things. And I saw the sort of things that the Americans liked to buy – the Vodou with human skulls and big cocks made from all the things that we could find that nobody in Port-au-Prince needed anymore. So I started to make sculptures and Eugene thought they were good. And one day an American came and paid $100 for something that I had made. I had never had that much money in my life. And I said to Eugene, 'How much do you want for selling it for me?' And Eugene said 'You keep it all Louko and let us go and have a beer to celebrate.' And that is when I stopped being a carpenter and started to be an artist all the time. And then the Haitian National Gallery bought one of my big sculptures and it stands in the garden outside the museum."

Of all the artists that I have asked the same question in the U.K. I have never had an answer like that. I guess Louko was not considering himself being radical in some way by saying this, just stating the obvious. The next question that I asked him was:

"What ambitions do you have as an artist?"

"I want to have an exhibition in New York in a big white gallery and I want to know that my sculptures are in the homes of rich Americans. And I want an American or English woman."

"Why do you want that?"

"Because they like to have a black artist. Because we are strong and make good sex. And they can get me out of Haiti and they will look after me." He says this with a twinkle in his eye.

Suddenly everything was making a sense of sorts. We Western artists were in Haiti for all sorts of intellectual reasons making our conceptual art lite. The last thing any of us would ever demean ourselves by doing is making art in the hope that some rich American would want to buy it. We are here for the Brownie points and the vanity and whatever else it is. And maybe for the black artist that does good sex. Whereas the Haitian artists are in this for something else altogether. They are hoping that we in some way are the gatekeepers to this world where people will buy their art for thousands and they can live like superstars. I realize that in writing this I am open to all sorts of criticisms, almost bordering on racism. But this was the conversation. What the man was saying.

Maybe I should stop writing now before I say anything that I am going to regret. And get back to finding out what is going on in Haiti right now and leave all this other stuff to another time.

*   *   *

On the Friday morning (January 15) I learnt Louko had been killed in the earthquake. He had been sitting in a bar with a glass of beer in his hand when the earthquake hit and the roof collapsed on him; he was killed instantly.

23

Took my heart to a Vodou priest,
I said, "What can you do Papa?
It's all screwed up...."

Leah Gordon

The first time I arrived in Haiti the spirits' brutal hoof struck my heart and wore it to the bone. In England I am an atheist, but in Haiti, agnostic veering on the possessed. Charles Simic writes in *Dime-store Alchemy* that "All art is a magic operation, or, if you prefer, a prayer for a new image." On each of my visits to Haiti to date, the prayer has been answered.

I am going to start this essay, which reflects on what it is it about Haiti that has intrigued me all these years, with a quotation from Michel-Rolph Trouillot's essay "The Odd and the Ordinary." For me there is no better quotation to begin to express my relationship with Haiti. Which is not to say that I completely agree with Trouillot's sentiments; rather, I have a vague sense of obstinate, but guilty, misunderstanding and disagreement. "Haitian Studies cannot proceed without making a theoretical leap," says Trouillot. "We need to drop the fiction that Haiti is unique – if by unique one means that it escapes analysis and comparison. Haiti is not that weird. It is the fiction of Haitian exceptionalism that is weird."

And this is my confession: it is the "fiction of Haitian exceptionalism" to which I am drawn. The possibilities that these fictions offer my imagination. It is the "fiction of Haitian exceptionalism" that I bathe and luxuriate in. It is a plethora of fictions of Haitian exceptionalism that brings me a lion's share of my life's personal joy. I would pout like a spoilt child denied its favorite toy if that were taken away. But then the bottom drops away, and I remember a lot of bad things, and feel kind of tacky having the privilege to paddle in the many fictions of Haitian exceptionalism with so much pleasure. This is a country of dirt and disorder, unquiet and – at times – dangerous politics, and paltry governmental agricultural, educational, or medical support. For that reason it is a painful and complicated task to articulate how, and nigh impossible to say why, Haiti has inspired me, and continues to, but I'll give it a "four bottles of Peroni and a stream of consciousness" kind of go!

I first visited Haiti in 1991 and I have been questioning what keeps taking me back there ever since. I went after hearing a BBC holiday program presenter wax lyrically about the marvelous family holidays to be found in the Dominican Republic, only to end her piece warning viewers not to accidently stray into the other side of the island, as that was another country, Haiti. This, she continued, was a country of dictatorships, military coups, black magic, Vodou, and death. It was a bitter British winter day and I had a job driving a van for the Communist Party – "all that and hot weather," I thought and within a month I was sitting by myself on a flight from Miami to Port-au-Prince nervously wondering if "I'd done the right thing?" Before I'd left I'd bought the obligatory copy *of The Comedians* and when I landed I did the only thing one could do in the situation – I asked the taxi driver to take me to the Oloffson Hotel.

It is primarily history that binds me to Haiti. I used to say Haiti seemed to be on a fault line of history. But I think it's best that I avoid that metaphor. But maybe history as lava, bubbling and spitting through cracks and craters, or as a volcanic steam, hissing and spouting through blowholes and geysers. Now there's a thing. And I can sense it under every step I take in Haiti.

And it's not just a case of the uniqueness of Haitian history. For me what is important is how Haiti reveals its history. I have visited other Caribbean islands where it feels that history has been mopped up, rather like blood after an airport massacre, and then re-presented as idyllic views on restaurant place mats or murals on hotel walls. But those cities and nations feel history-less. Lands with weaker breaths of life or culture, beside the glut of bars and hotels for tourists, businesses that are utterly fearful of any wrong-footed historical connotations. By comparison, Haitian people are continually transmitting, telling, retelling and reinterpreting Haitian history. School fees are excessive for the majority of the Haitian people, and education standards poor, but you will be hard pushed to find a Haitian who doesn't know the vast and intimate details of their own history. But it is also the actual history too. I travel a lot for my work, and I always find it's strange that I find Africa oddly uninspiring and dull. Sometimes I'm haunted by the odd feeling that it's somehow inauthentic, whatever that means. As if really Africa is merely the suburbs but Haiti is the center of town. As if I love African culture only after it has passed through the warped and barbaric looking glass of slavery and forced immigration into the Americas. I am a post-colonial nightmare and seem to enjoy febrile religious experience and the exotic with an empty bag of excuses.

And then there's the visual aspect. I am a kind of scopophiliac, without the sex bit, and cannot tire of sucking Haiti in through my eyes. I know of no land that can give me more visual pleasure. A hideous contradiction for those that live there, I know. Which leads to the Vodou, the bastard offspring of Haiti's history and its visual imagination, crossed with performance arts and music. Possession appears to be the performative stage of Vodou art. I have seen incredible possession and very bad possession, from intense and ecstatic, to hammy and derivative. There is in Vodou ritual a poetic transgression at work that exists somewhere between theatre and trance. But what is more important is that all possession, good or bad, always has the capacity to command me and forbid any challenge. I collude with the drama wholeheartedly. I sometimes feel that this level of spectacle, so deeply entrenched in the religious life of the country, seeps out into politics and personal relationships. Politics seems so gestural and dramatic, life fraught with jealousy and subterfuge and of course there's always the ultimate tragic heroine fading before our eyes, the economy. In Haiti I can start to feel that all is theatre, all is spectacle, and everything is staged. Michael Taussig sums it up, for both the mortal and immortal world, in his work *The Magic of the State*. "Of course it's dramatic," he snarls. "Self consciously theatrical. How could a spirit otherwise exist? … it's because of their parlous reality that the spirits of the dead require deliberate artifice … that allows them to be real."

What else? I said earlier that I had an empty bag of excuses, but that was typical English self-deprecation. I would be crass to infer that my interest was purely a fetishization of the exotic. My attraction to Haiti is also a part of a trajectory. A culmination of my love of folk traditions and people's histories. From the feminist folk punk band I sang and wrote the lyrics for in the mid 1980s, to my enduring love of British folk traditions from the Burry Man to the Gloucestershire Cheese Rollers, from my photographs of fairground ghost trains and street-hawking children with Guy Fawkes, to my love of August Sander and Studs Terkel. I'm drawn to places where people keep hold of their own traditions, their own creativity and their own worth for their own class, without blanket consumerism and broadcast entertainment to dilute history. And what I feel we have lost in the U.K. I still find in Haiti – a nation tirelessly binding their history into sculptures, paintings, novels, poems, song, ritual, and costume. And it is these political instincts that keep me returning to work on projects like the Ghetto Biennale and Jacmel's Kanaval.

I've enjoyed Haiti and, I believe, it's enjoyed me. And as for the title of my essay, I wrote that line the first time I visited Haiti. Well I think after twenty years I can honestly say Haiti fixed that heart.

June 2010

24

Port-au-Prince, I Love You

Matthew J. Smith

Words don't come easily when trying to make sense of the catastrophe and numbing shock of the horror that has fallen on Haiti since January 12. The pain is very deep. Sadness, for many of us, seems infinite. Anger is not far from the surface. We have not been prepared for this. Haiti does not deserve this. Politics can't explain this. We cannot know the full extent of the massive human costs of this calamity and the grinding long-term effects on the people of Haiti. The magnitude of the losses suffered is overwhelming. We struggle to come to terms with the layers of consequences of this immense tragedy and mourn the hundreds of thousands lost, and the millions displaced and permanently traumatized.

It is our kin lost under the rubble. We have also lost something in the destruction of Port-au-Prince. A major site of Caribbean history has fallen. The severe wounds will slowly heal but the mark will forever remain. The city will one day be rebuilt. People will one day go back to school, church, and work in the city. But it won't be the same. We must never forget what it was and the influence of its evolution on the lifeline of Haiti and those of us close to the island.

The buildings that have now crumbled and dissolved into an ocean of concrete dust bore witness to one of the world's most dramatic cities of endurance, achievement, survival, and tragedy. Port-au-Prince has always known suffering and disaster. In 1770, the year it became the capital of the then French colony, Saint-Domingue, it was shaken to the ground by an extraordinary earthquake. The consequences of this calamity were so severe that it would be recorded by visitors to Haiti well into the nineteenth century. The city was rebuilt by the French and assumed its place in the following two decades as a major Caribbean port city. Picturesque gingerbread houses dotted the main streets near where piles of shattered stones lie today. At the port, French sailors, British merchants, slaves, free coloreds, and whites formed part of one of colonial America's most complex societies. Free coloreds wandered the markets in the street looking for food, while *petit blanc* Frenchmen passed by them reading newspapers from Paris. Near the wharf that is now cracked and in partial return to the sea, slaves loaded and unloaded European ships with sugar and coffee. Port-au-Prince was then the capital of the richest sugar colony in the world and thus one of the busiest centers of the Caribbean.

But it was not just sugar and coffee that went on and off those many ships; there were also stories of liberty, equality, fraternity, and revolution. In 1791, Saint-Domingue's chained blacks rose up and launched a long and brutal war against slavery and French colonialism. The Haitian Revolution shifted the earth under the feet of Port-au-Prince. Then, the aftershocks and tremors were felt not only in Haiti, but in every corner of the globe. Port-au-Prince, which was temporarily called Port Républicain during the years of revolt, was the nucleus of an unprecedented achievement in revolutionary freedom. In 1804, the revolutionaries succeeded in becoming the first independent black nation in the hemisphere. This was their Port-au-Prince; a fiercely defiant place where ex-slaves became its rulers and everyone who arrived on its shores, its citizens.

Victory came with a price. Various periods of isolation and non-recognition led to embargos, diplomatic neglect, a crushing 1825 French indemnity, and the decline in the lively trade of the prerevolutionary era. The nation-building project was hobbled. Port-au-Prince endured. Neither dictators nor the pervasive fires could demolish it. And they tried. Fires became an all too common feature of the city's history, consuming many of its wooden structures. Autocratic rulers from Emperor Faustin Soulouque in the 1850s to Lysius Salomon in the 1880s were ruthless in their attempts to shield the capital from provincial rivals. Many of its citizens left in exile, and most returned in hope. They brought with them Americans, Europeans, Arabs, and Caribbeans, attracted to freedom from oppression, racism, and colonialism. With each passing administration came the promise for the city to reclaim its role as a beacon for Haitian and black independence. Throughout the nineteenth century the city found enterprising ways to manage with precious little even as it began to crawl from the pier to the hillsides. At the same time, its inhabitants built together their own traditions of survival, improvised by will.

Outsiders mocked their efforts. On his brief visit to the capital in the 1880s, J. A. Froude called Port-au-Prince the "central ulcer" of Haiti, a model of Caribbean destitution that could hardly be called a capital. Even more, it was a blatant reminder of what the British Caribbean might become should its citizens push for self-government. The racism and disregard of autonomy inherent in European civilizing missions never allowed for a view of Port-au-Prince as anything else.

Yet the rest of the region saw it in different ways. If Port-au-Prince was the capital of the "Black Republic," it had great meaning for all territories touched by the Caribbean Sea. Once home to the Bahamian J. Robert Love who, after relocating to Kingston in the 1890s, would eventually become a pioneer in black Jamaican politics, Port-au-Prince contained the hopes, dreams, and fears of Caribbean people at the turn of the twentieth century. Jamaican writer J. Montaque Simpson, who temporarily lived in the Haitian capital in 1902, wrote that in spite of the dust and decay, Port-au-Prince was a vibrant, fast-developing urban center that accomplished far more than one might have expected. Simpson's purpose was clear: to redress the misperceptions of many Jamaicans about Haiti's capital and recast it as a shining example of Caribbean fortitude. This was made explicit in the early lines of the book:

> We in Jamaica often laugh heartily at what is stated, verbally or in print, of our own country when "seen as others see us," and give ridiculous state-ments a contemptuous sneer as the only recognition which they deserve. But I am sure Haitians must feel sad at the *mensonges en gross* [gross lies] which are so repeatedly said and written of them and their country. There-fore when one, *from his personal knowledge* is in a position to say a good word – *tout de bon* – it is but fair for him to do so, and the more exten-sively he can disseminate this acquired knowledge the more favourable to a maligned country and people.

Surveying the streets where today earthquake survivors search for food in the mounds of shattered concrete, Simpson was fascinated with the level of industry and promise he discovered at every turn. He found that in its cultural life and social interactions, where peasants in straw hats walked peacefully in the streets beside bourgeois businessmen in top hats, it was not unlike Kingston. In some ways, Port-au-Prince held more promise for Simpson. Another Jamaican, Rudolph Bonitto, who visited the capital a century ago, in a 1911 essay titled "Port-au-Prince today," was impressed with what he saw there, remarking that it was "not the Port-au-Prince I had heard and read about. Given a long era of peace, proper administration and judicious expenditure of money on improvements in the right direc-tion, Port-au-Prince can be made one of the finest cities in this part of the world."

On the crowded streets of the capital in these years, young boys jumped in the sea searching for coins tossed from ship-decks as Jamaican coachmen carried Martinican women around in horse-drawn buggies through mud-caked streets. In the air the mixed scents of garbage and fried pork mingled with the bitter taste of dust. The symphony of barking dogs, loudly spoken Kreyòl, French, and a little English and Spanish pierced through the sky. Skinny barefoot guards with ill-fitting clothes paced the sidewalks. At the Bord de Mer, Arab shopkeepers watched through wide-opened French jalousies as German ships docked carrying mail, ice, assorted goods, and people from New York, Kingston, Jacmel, and Havana. At the top of Rue Bonne-Foi, priests held daily services in the impressive new National Cathedral while outside uniformed school children walked around in search of *tablette* and *rapadou* (sweet candy) from the sellers on the side of the road. This was their Port-au-Prince; a teeming mix of integrated (not isolated) European, African, and unmistakably Caribbean culture.

But as the city grew, forces worked to wrest control from its owners. In the following decade Port-au-Prince resisted valiantly an interminable fight for its soul waged by aggressive foreign powers and avaricious and myopic rural generals. It was, after all, an epicenter of activity and a key node in the Caribbean nexus. The great powers, after the Cuban war for independence, accelerated their efforts for control of Haiti. Violence trumped vision and the United States invaded the country in 1915, occupying Port-au-Prince thereafter for almost two decades. The other port towns retracted and the capital, already beginning to receive its first waves of rural migrants, became the centre of Haiti under marine control. Curfews, de facto segregation, and martial law followed. Armed marines competed with market-women for space on the sidewalks of Grand Rue. This was their Port-au-Prince: an incomprehensible testing ground for militarized diplomacy.

The city resisted. Haitian culture remained stronger and more alive on the roads and *ruelles*, in the mountains, and in the cahiers of the city's poets and writers who refused to accept wholesale North American culture. It absorbed what it needed and spat out the rest. At the Lycée Pétion in downtown Port-au-Prince, which today has been hollowed out by the great quake, the brilliant intellectual Jean Price-Mars carved out a formula for Haitian survival: embrace and celebrate indigenous culture. His book, *So Spoke the Uncle* (1928) was said by a Haitian commentator to have "[shaken] Haiti to its very foundations," in its loud conclusion that Haitian identity was bound up in its folk culture. Its impact was immense. Across the hemisphere black consciousness movements pulled on the long web that connected them and found its strongest end in Port-au-Prince. The fire of a new generation was stoked. From their downtown balconies these young nationalist writers glanced out and breathed in their city as they penned passionate poems about the "new Haiti." Soon enough the people below would follow. In 1929 crowds of students and urban workers protested in the Champs-de-Mars against the U.S. occupation. On this sacred ground, not far from where the U.S. marines recently landed on the Palace lawn, bandleader Occide Jeanty defiantly performed his anthem *1804* in the face of their forefathers. Today a different sound punctures the skies above the Champs-de-Mars. These are the wails and choruses of praise that silence the hunger pangs of thousands of semi-ambulatory refugees that carpet its public space.

In 1934 the Americans left and Haiti began its "second birth." It is in Port-au-Prince, where today reporters from across the world scramble to capture high-definition images of its last gasps, that a different type of visitor rushed to catch a glimpse of its renaissance. By the 1940s Port-au-Prince was the centrifuge of a black literary world that welcomed a host of luminaries eager to see it with their own eyes: Langston Hughes, W. E. B. Dubois, Nicolás Guillén, Aimé Césaire, Katherine Dunham, and Zora Neale Hurston all visited and wrote of the importance of the place to the understanding of the Black Atlantic at a time when race consciousness was ascending. The now broken Centre d'Art was built during this period with the collaboration of the Haitian government and North American patrons, and provided a space for some of the greatest artists of Haiti to work, thrive, and have their pieces displayed and photographed for the entire world to see.

Troubadour bands played on the street corners of the Rue du Peuple for tourists who came in search of voodoo magic and found instead a densely colored tapestry of Vodou culture. In Bois Verna the lilting refrains of the parlor music that came from the porches of the elite couldn't drown out the clanging sounds of artisans sculpting fantastic pieces out of iron. Elsewhere, on Place Geffrard, the lively intellectual debates between black nationalists and Marxists on the future of Haitian governance filtered through the windows of the packed drawing rooms. And at the Bureau d'Ethnologie several streets over, Jacques Roumain, one of the city's greatest gifts to the world, sat quietly at his desk with a cigarette dangling between his lips as he wrote poems, novels, and articles that would later transform Caribbean literature. This was their Port-au-Prince: sophisticated, astute, engaged, and internationally revered.

Haitians never needed the affirmation of others to realize how special their capital was. In 1949–1950 President Dumarsais Estimé celebrated the two hundredth anniversary of Port-au-Prince with an extraordinary exposition that in scope stands as one of the most astounding cultural achievements of the Caribbean. New theatres and hotels were built, including the splendid Montana, which is now a heap of folded concrete. In Port-au-Prince, tourists from all over the world flocked to see Haitian arts and culture on stage and hear the songs of Marian Anderson and Haiti's own Billie Holiday, Lumane Casimir. Estimé's grand dream was to bring Port-au-Prince into the modern world. In these years, there was desperation and poverty. But, in equal measure the indestructible resourcefulness and legendary kindness shone through the wide-eyed smiles of the children that tourist magazines were so fond of photographing. Today, Estimé's mausoleum, the sight of the Exposition, is broken and cracked and photographers no longer search for smiles.

In Port-au-Prince's heyday in the 1940s and 1950s, U.S. jazz musicians performed swing in the nightclubs with Haitian bands such as Orchestre Saïeh. Later on that decade, Nemours Jean-Baptiste and Webert Sicot translated the country's swirls of pain and joy into a bright, smoking sound they labeled *kompa-direct*. Some Jamaicans would make annual pilgrimages there to glance in awe at the colorful Mardi Gras processions through the streets during Carnival time. Young traveling musicians from neighboring Kingston, including two of that city's legends, Ernest Ranglin and Don Drummond, cut their teeth in swanky Port-au-Prince clubs in the 1950s (years later, in 1972, a young Bob Marley would retrace these steps, roaming the streets of Port-au-Prince by himself on a brief trip to Haiti, an experience that some claim supplied him with the inspiration to write his anthem of resistance "Get Up, Stand Up").

Under the disintegrating concrete that today blocks the roads of Rue des Miracles and Rue de Centre remain the footprints of the thousands of laborers, unemployed workers, and various street people from Bel-Air, Croix-des-Bossales, La Saline, and the network of slums that ring the wharf who marched behind the charismatic labor leader Daniel Fignolé in the 1940s and 1950s. The articulate Fignolé, once called "the Moses of Port-au-Prince," believed in Haitian capacity to move from mere survival to success, despite the odds. The quest of Port-au-Prince's champions of nationalism was a reformed country where Haitians chose their own destiny. This was their Port-au-Prince: a pounding, exciting, progressive city that was in so many ways ahead of its neighbors.

For Fignolé and his followers the long march could only end inside the green gates of the National Palace. But this was not to be. The sight of khaki-clad soldiers in jeeps and Studebakers patrolling the city's corners became more frequent. Civil, color, and class wars were inevitable in the power struggle, and out of it came dictatorship. With little outside interference, François "Papa Doc" Duvalier, a native of the city, and his *Tontons*

Macoutes made the flag black and the streets of the capital red. They transformed the once open roads into virtual prisons, killing the body but not the soul of the city. It is indeed ironic that the one lasting mark of the Duvalier era that has remained and survived the earthquake is the splendid emancipation statue, the Unknown Maroon, Albert Mangonès's powerful portrait of freedom ironically laid during a time of psychological incarceration. His son, Jean-Claude "Baby Doc," continued this domination, scorning the city's inhabitants with ugly opulence. Jean-Claude deepened the voracity of the state. The gaping cavity of the Cathedral was once host to Jean-Claude's multimillion dollar wedding, a public coronation of his wife Michèle. This was their Port-au-Prince; a personal playground leveled by terror, exploitation, greed, and disregard.

The bruised spirit of the city remained uncrushed. Down Lalue, Rue Capois, and in front of Rex Theatre carnival bands marched, offering temporary release from the pains of repression. Ibo Combo, Bosso Combo, the legendary Tabou Combo, Scorpio, le Roi Coupe Cloue, Les Shleu-Shleu, Les Gypsies, D. P. Express, and Ti-Manno (Haiti's Bob Marley). Ti-Manno's words of unbowed patriotism in the face of natural disaster, written from afar after the devastating 1979 Hurricane David, take on new meaning today: "I will never die in a foreign country / Port-au-Prince, it's time for me to come back." This theme followed through to the "roots" music of Boukman Eksperyans, Boukan Ginen, and RAM in the 1980s and 1990s. The roots movements of the 1980s provided a life force for the resistance of the city's dwellers. Although it reached the ears of the growing Haitian diaspora, the music always carried greater force when it reverberated off the walls of Port-au-Prince. By then the city had sprawled wide and far, settling on the hillsides, which groaned under the weight of this new urban spread.

It was through the main arteries of the city – which tear-filled viewers thousands of miles away now watch live on television and the Internet as a dizzying number of search and rescue teams fight to pull lives from the rubble – that Haitians cried tears of joy when the Duvalier dictatorship crashed in February 1986. The city transformed yet again. The Duvaliers were gone, Macoutes on the way out, and a young, incredibly popular priest on the way in. Through elections, overthrow, return, and military re-occupation in the 1990s, to street violence and kidnapping in the 2000s, Port-au-Prince kept its steady pulse.

In Port-au-Prince, hope and despair held hands while darting through the tombstones in Portail-Léogane, and danced *tet kole* to the konpa, zouk, and reggae pumping out of the bloated tap-taps as they whizzed by

Avenue Jean-Jacques Dessalines. The top of these rainbow-colored buses bore the inscriptions of faith that kept the city moving. A tap-tap theology: "Christ Can," "God is King," "Thank You Lord." Schoolboys on their way to St. Louis de Gonzague passed the hungry-eyed *timoun lari* (street children) just surfacing from the tin-shack maze of Cité Soleil. Across the street a woman fanned flies from the *banan peze* (green plantains), *diri kole* (rice and peas), and *cola courounne* (soda) she was selling. A battalion of men walked down the clogged streets in punishing heat while singing advertisements for soap, batteries, water, and umbrellas: "Para Para pliiiiii!!!! Para Para pliiiii!!!" This was their Port-au-Prince: tense, thick, and tenacious.

And standing careful watch over it all was the magnificent National Palace, the Citadel of the twentieth century; an audacious testament to Haitian resilience in the face of cruel and unfair adversity. Its white crown gleamed in the midst of deprivation, pulling all passersby into its force field, daring them to look away. Built nearly a century ago with American assistance after the explosion of the first palace, it was the home of the designated saviors and sinners of the country. To see it was to stand at the crossroads of the city's past and present.

The past has never felt further away than it does today. The crushed center crown of the crumbling Palace is now bowed in quiet sadness at the unthinkable fate of the city and its dwellers. The pulse has now stopped. Time remains trapped in the ruins. The earth opened up and took with it the capital that for two hundred and sixty years held the dreams and nightmares of so many: Port-au-Prince, Port-Républicain, la capitale, "the Republic," Potoprens, Lavil.

The starving survivors sit wounded in frustration as they wait for relief and the earth continues to move intermittently beneath them. Those who have tired of waiting are now leaving en masse to Cap Haïtien, Jérémie, and many locations between them. For those who remain, the sky and the walls made of bed-sheets are their only home. They are all victims of a peculiar disaster where twenty-first-century technology saves lives, and primitive surgeries take limbs away.

This is their Port-au-Prince: a broken shell that can no longer protect them. The children of history now live a dystopian nightmare choking on the smell of death around them. They have set up camps, which continue to mushroom on football fields, open lawns, and any available public space; refugees on their own soil. The men and women who fought, bled, wrote, sang, and surrendered their lives to make their country and its capital a better place are somewhere weeping for Port-au-Prince.

How can we come to terms with this heavy loss? How can we even begin to understand what it means for the millions of courageous people who are now abandoned and wander around Port-au-Prince in stunned silence at its devastation, or the others for whom the swollen city, once a refuge from the hardships of the countryside, has now become their tomb?

In times of incredible hurt, music is often our most comfortable retreat. The right songs can serve as a balm or reflection of what our shell-shocked minds struggle to convey. Of the dozens of songs that pass through the mind at a time like this, one keeps echoing for me. An upbeat Haitian dance song of the 1970s simply titled *Port-au-Prince*, by the group *Les Ambassadeurs*. In music it suggests that in spite of everything hope remains constant. In its lyrics it captures the feelings of all who have lived, loved, and witnessed the battered and proud heritage of Haiti's capital:

Port-au-Prince, I love you.

It is at your feet I want to spend my life.

If I have to leave you temporarily don't consider it a divorce ...

One day I will return to your feet.

Even if life takes me very far away, you will always be right in front of my eyes.

January 2010

Contributors

MARLÈNE RIGAUD APOLLON was born in Haiti in 1945 and emigrated to the United States in 1964. She is the author of essays on Haitian culture, two biographies, books for children, and four poetry collections, including *Cris de Colère, Chants d'espoir* (1992) and *I want to Dance* (1996), on the Haitian and Haitian immigrant experience. She recently translated and re-edited *La Mystique de la Citadelle* (2009), first published by her historian grandfather, Louis Mercier, in 1945.

BEVERLY BELL first went to Haiti as a teenager. Since then she has dedicated most of her life to working for democracy, women's rights, and economic justice in that country. She founded or co-founded six organizations and networks to support the Haitian people, including Washington Office on Haiti and the Lambi Fund of Haiti. She worked for presidents Jean-Bertrand Aristide and René Préval, and is author of the PEN-New Mexico award-winning *Walking on Fire: Haitian Women's Stories of Survival and Resistance* (Cornell University Press, 2001). Today she runs Other Worlds and is associate fellow at the Institute for Policy Studies. She resides in her hometown of New Orleans.

MADISON SMARTT BELL is the author of 12 novels and two collections of short stories. His eighth novel, *All Souls' Rising*, was a finalist for the 1995 National Book Award and the 1996 PEN/Faulkner Award and winner of the 1996 Anisfield/Wolf Award for the best book of the year dealing with matters of race. Born and raised in Tennessee, he has lived in New York and London and now lives in Baltimore, Maryland. Since 1984 he has taught at Goucher College, along with his wife, the poet Elizabeth Squires.

PATRICK BELLEGARDE-SMITH works in the areas of African and Neo-African religions and African diasporic social thought and philosophy. He holds a PhD in international relations, comparative politics, and history. He has taught in all these areas in black studies and women's studies over the last three decades at the University of Wisconsin-Milwaukee.

LEGRACE BENSON holds a PhD from Cornell University and is currently associate editor of the *Journal of Haitian Studies* and a member of the Board of the Haitian Studies Association. Her numerous articles have appeared in scholarly journals and she has contributed chapters to several books on Haitian and Caribbean topics. Her book, *How the Sun Illuminates Under Cover of Darkness,* a study of Haitian art and artists in religious, historical, and environmental context, is to appear in late 2010.

JEAN CASIMIR is a professor at the Université d'Etat d'Haïti and former ambassador to the United States, and author most recently of *Haïti et ses élites: L'interminable dialogue de sourds* (Presses de l'Université d'Etat d'Haïti, 2009). A selection of his writings is available at: http://www.jhfc.duke.edu/wko/dossiers/1.3/contents.php.

MARYSE CONDÉ was born in Guadeloupe. At sixteen she went to France to pursue her studies and there discovered the works of Aimé Césaire, Negritude, and her African origin. She subsequently lived for twelve years in Africa, and returned to France where she obtained her doctorate in comparative literature at the Sorbonne. Her literary work reflects her life's itinerary. She has taught at many universities, including Columbia, where she founded the Center for French and Francophone Studies. She is now a Columbia professor emeritus and remains very active as a lecturer in the U.S. and Europe. She has won numerous awards and prizes for her novels and has been distinguished several times by the French government. Her latest novel, *En attendant la montée des eaux* (September 2010), is largely devoted to the Haitian crisis

Born in Trinidad, J. MICHAEL DASH is professor of French at New York University. He has published a monograph on Edouard Glissant and a number of books on Haiti including *Literature and Ideology in Haiti* (1981), *Haiti and the United States* (1988), and *Culture and Customs of Haiti* (2001).

LESLIE G. DESMANGLES is the Charles A. Dana Research Professor of Religion and International Studies at Trinity College in Hartford, Connecticut. A native of Haiti, he holds a doctorate in Anthropology of Religion from Temple University in Philadelphia. Among other published works, he is the author of the award-winning book, *The Faces of the Gods: Vodou and Roman Catholicism in Haiti*, and served as an associate editor of the *Encyclopedia of African and African American Religions*.

Scottish artist BILL DRUMMOND (1953) has used various media in his practice including actions, music, and words. His actions, too numerous to list, some more infamous than others; his music from the multi-million-selling KLF to the choral music of The17; the words have accumulated into numerous books. His work of the last ten years is documented at www.penkiln-burn.com.

LAURENT DUBOIS is professor of history and romance studies at Duke University, and author of *Avengers of the New World: The Story of the Haitian Revolution* (Harvard, 2004) and *Soccer Empire: The World Cup and the Future of France* (University of California Press, 2010).

JOHN D. GARRIGUS is an associate professor of history at the University of Texas at Arlington. He is the author of *Before Haiti: Race and Citizenship in Saint-Domingue* (2006) and co-editor, with Laurent Dubois, of *Slave Revolution in the Caribbean, 1789–1804: A Brief History with Documents* (2006).

LEAH GORDON is from the U.K. and has worked as a photographer, filmmaker, and curator. She visited Haiti for the first time in 1991, and has continued to have a relationship with the country to this day. As a reportage photographer Gordon covered the coup in the early 1990s and then began to make work inspired more by the culture and religion than the politics. She made a film for Channel 4 TV about the pig eradication program in Haiti called "A Pig's Tale" in 1998. In 2006 she commissioned the Grand Rue Sculptors from Haiti to make "Freedom Sculpture," a permanent exhibit for the International Museum of Slavery in Liverpool. In 2008 she completed a film about the artists called "Atis-Rezistans: the Sculptors of Grand Rue." Continuing her relationship with the Grand Rue artists, Gordon organized and co-curated the Ghetto Biennale in Port-au-Prince in December 2009. She has also been involved in a range of film, photographic, and curatorial projects including documenting experiences of homophobia in London, cross-dressing in Vodou, links between the Slave Trade and the River Thames, and carnival practice in Jacmel, Haiti. Her photography book *Kanaval: Vodou, Politics and Revolution on the Streets of Haiti* was published by Soul Jazz publishing in June 2010.

JASON HERBECK is associate professor of French at Boise State University (Idaho). His teaching and research focuses primarily on evolving narrative forms in twentieth- and twenty-first-century French and Caribbean literatures, and how these forms relate to socio-cultural, philosophical, and historical constructions of identity.

RÉGINE MICHELLE JEAN-CHARLES is an assistant professor of African and African Diaspora studies and Romance languages and literatures at Boston

College. She is also a board member, performer, and lecturer for A Long Walk Home, Inc., an organization that uses the arts for healing, education, and awareness about violence against women and girls.

DEBORAH JENSON is professor of French at Duke University, where she developed a Creole studies course sequence and is co-director with Laurent Dubois of the Franklin Humanities Institute "Haiti Lab." She has published widely on Haiti and has a forthcoming book, *Beyond the Slave Narrative: Politics, Sex, and Manuscripts in the Haitian Revolution*, with Liverpool University Press.

YANICK LAHENS was born in Port-au-Prince in 1953. She has published two novels, four short story collections, and numerous essays on themes relating to Haitian culture, history, and politics. After teaching literature for several years at L'Ecole Normale Supérieure she now writes and coordinates educational projects "avec des jeunes."

MICHEL LE BRIS was born in Brittany in 1944. A writer and philosopher, he has published more than 40 books, including essays, novels, and travel writing. His last novel, *La Beauté du monde*, was a finalist for the Goncourt prize in 2008. A close friend of Jean-Paul Sartre, he directed with him *La Cause du Peuple*, and the collection *La France Sauvage* (Gallimard). He was also co-founder of the daily newpaper *Libération*. A specialist on R. L. Stevenson and German romanticism, he has edited as publisher about 400 books. To promote his concept of "littérature-monde," Le Bris created in 1990 the Etonnants Voyageurs literary festival, with extentions in Missoula (USA), Dublin (Ireland), Sarajevo (Bosnia), Bamako (Mali), Haifa (Israel), and Port-au-Prince (Haiti). He is the initiator of the manifesto "Pour une littérature-monde en français," signed by 44 major francophone writers, including J. M. G. Le Clezio and published by *Le Monde* in March 2007. He was in Port-au-Prince in January 2010 to organize the second Haitian editions of Etonnants Voyageurs.

ELIZABETH MCALISTER is associate professor in the Religion department and also teaches in African American studies and American studies at Wesleyan University. Her research focuses on Afro-Caribbean religions, Caribbean music, and race theory, with a focus on Haiti. McAlister is author of *Rara! Vodou, Power and Performance in Haiti and Its Diaspora* (2002) and co-editor of *Race, Nation, and Religion in the Americas* (2004). McAlister has produced three compilations of Afro-Haitian religious music: *Rhythms of Rapture* (Smithsonian Folkways), *Angels in the Mirror* (Ellipsis Arts), and *Rara*, the CD that accompanies her first book. Her current research focuses on relationships and spatial and sonic imaginings shared by American and Haitian evangelicals. She is currently a member of the Social Science Research Council working group on Spirituality, Political Engagement, and Public Life.

NADÈVE MÉNARD is professor of literature at École Normale Supérieure of the Université d'État d'Haïti in Port-au-Prince. She has published articles in *International Journal of Francophone Studies, Cahier des Anneaux de la Mémoire*, and *Conjonction*. Forthcoming from Karthala is an edited volume of essays and interviews titled *Ecrits d'Haïti: perspectives sur la littérature haïtienne contemporaine (1986–2006)*.

MARTIN MUNRO is professor of French at Florida State University. His latest publications are *Different Drummers: Rhythm and Race in the New World* and *Edwidge Danticat: A Reader's Guide*.

RAOUL PECK was born in Haiti in 1953. He has lived and studied in the Democratic Republic of the Congo, the United States, France, and Germany. Considered Haiti's best-known filmmaker, his major works include *Haitian Corner* (1988), *L'Homme sur les quais* (1993), *Lumumba* (2000), *Sometimes in April* (2004), and *Moloch Tropical* (2009). He served as Minister of Culture of the Republic of Haiti between 1996 and 1997. In 2001, he was honoured with the prestigious Human Rights Watch Irene Diamond Award for his body of work on human rights. He is currently the chairman of the École Nationale Supérieure des Métiers de l'Image et du Son (La Fémis), France's national film school.

MATTHEW J. SMITH is a senior lecturer in history at the University of the West Indies, Mona in Jamaica. He is the author of *Red and Black in Haiti: Radicalism, Conflict, and Political Change, 1934–1957* (UNC Press, 2009) and several articles on nineteenth- and twentieth-century Haitian political and social history.

THOMAS C. SPEAR is professor of French at CUNY. Editor of *La Culture française vue d'ici et d'ailleurs* (2002) and *Une journée haïtienne* (2007), he writes especially on forms of autobiography, and is the creator and editor of *Île en île*, a database featuring authors from francophone islands.

EVELYNE TROUILLOT was born in 1954 in Port-au-Prince, where she still lives. A playwright, poet, essayist, novelist, and educator, she has published four novels: *Rosalie l'infâme* (2003), *L'Œil-Totem* (2006), *Le Mirador aux étoiles* (2007), and *La Mémoire aux abois* (2010).

LAURA WAGNER is a PhD candidate in anthropology at University of North Carolina, Chapel Hill. At the time of the January 12, 2010 earthquake, she was living in Port-au-Prince doing dissertation research on human rights and people who work in others' homes. In April 2010, she went back to Haiti.